Quicken 2007 on Demand

Gina Carrillo

Que Publishing
800 East 96th Street
Indianapolis, IN 46240 USA

Quicken® 2007 On Demand

International Standard Book Number: 0-7897-3638-1

Printed in the United States of America

First Printing: October 2006

09   08   07   06   4   3   2   1

Trademarks

Warning and Disclaimer

Bulk Sales

Que Publishing offers excellent discounts on this book when ordered in quantity for bulk purchases or special sales. For more information, please contact

U.S. Corporate and Government Sales

1-800-382-3419

corpsales@pearsontechgroup.com

For sales outside of the United States, please contact

International Sales

international@pearsoned.com

Associate Publisher
Greg Wiegand

Acquisitions Editor
Michelle Newcomb

Development Editor
Laura Norman

Managing Editor
Patrick Kanouse

Project Editor
Seth Kerney

Indexer
Ken Johnson

Technical Editor
Mark Reddin

Publishing Coordinator
Cindy Teeters

Designer
Anne Jones

Page Layout
Amy Hassos

Acknowledgments

Dedication

Para mi nena. Tú éres mi corazón y mi vida eterna.

Acknowledgments

It takes a village to raise a child and it takes a team to produce these books. I have been fortunate enough to continue working with some of the same team members on this book as I did on the previous version of Quicken. Thanks once again to Michelle for working closely with me on this book and trying to keep things on track. These projects never seem to go as smoothly as we'd like and I am grateful to have you to back me up when I need the support. Thank you to Laura and Mark for being my second and third sets of eyes. Your attention to detail is greatly appreciated. There are numerous others that play a part in ensuring this book looks the way it should, all Is are dotted and Ts are crossed, the book is indexed, and ready for production. Thank you for all you do.

Thanks to my family and close friends for your continual support and love. You mean the world to me. Gabriela, thank you for understanding when most of my extra time was devoted to this book. You're the best daughter a mother could ask for.

About The Author

Gina Carrillo is a technical writer, an instructional designer, an instructor, an author, an editor, and a mother. She has worked in the technical communications and distance-learning industry for 13 years. She works full time developing Help systems, CBTs, training manuals, and user guides for software systems. The software systems Gina has worked with encompass a vast array of technological realms. These systems include many financial systems, ranging from consumer financial systems, such as Quicken and Microsoft Money, to corporate systems, such as PeopleSoft, and government financial systems.

With a special interest in both education and technical communication, in 2000, Gina helped develop a certificate program for technical communicators at the University of South Florida, where she taught RoboHelp and technical editing for two years. In addition to her writing, editing, instructional design, and teaching endeavors, she also writes and edits for Que Publishing and Sams Publishing. Gina has written the books Show Me Quicken 2006, Easy Microsoft Money 2004, and Easy Web Pages, 2nd Edition, and she was the technical editor for the books Sams Teach Yourself Microsoft FrontPage 2000 in 10 Minutes, Sams Teach Yourself to Create Web Pages in 24 Hours, and Easy Microsoft FrontPage 2000.

We Want To Hear From You!

As the reader of this book, you are our most important critic and commentator. We value your opinion and want to know what we're doing right, what we could do better, what areas you'd like to see us publish in, and any other words of wisdom you're willing to pass our way.

As an associate publisher for Que Publishing, I welcome your comments. You can email or write me directly to let me know what you did or didn't like about this book—as well as what we can do to make our books better.

Please note that I cannot help you with technical problems related to the topic of this book. We do have a User Services group, however, where I will forward specific technical questions related to the book.

When you write, please be sure to include this book's title and author as well as your name, email address, and phone number. I will carefully review your comments and share them with the author and editors who worked on the book.

Email: feedback@quepublishing.com

Mail: Greg Wiegand
Associate Publisher
Que Publishing
800 East 96th Street
Indianapolis, IN 46240 USA

For more information about this book or another Que Publishing title, visit our website at www.quepublishing.com. Type the ISBN (excluding hyphens) or the title of a book in the Search field to find the page you're looking for.

This Book Is Safari Enabled

Contents

Introduction

Welcome to *Quicken 2007 On Demand*, a visual quick reference guide that shows you how you can take advantage of the nation's best-selling personal accounting program.

The Best Place to Start

The best place to start is with a question. What do you want to know? What's not working the way you expect it to work? What Quicken features do you think should provide you with more value? What kind of information are you trying to get from your Quicken program? Ask the question and then go to the table of contents or the index to find the area of the book that contains the answer.

Chances are, you'll begin by finding the answer to your question, and then you'll start paging through the book, discovering new features and learning tips for making your Quicken experience more worthwhile and efficient.

How This Book Works

Each task is presented on one page or two facing pages, with step-by-step instructions in the left column and screen illustrations on the right. This arrangement lets you focus on a single task without having to turn the page.

Step-by-Step Instructions

This book provides concise step-by-step instructions that show you how to accomplish a task. Each set of instructions includes illustrations that directly correspond to the easy-to-follow steps. Also included in the text are timesavers, checklists, and sidebars to help you work more efficiently or to provide you with more in-depth information. A "Did You Know?" feature provides tips and techniques to help you work smarter, and a "See Also" feature directs you to other parts of the book containing related information about the task.

Managing All Your Scheduled Transactions

To create new, make changes to, or delete scheduled transactions, you use the Scheduled Transaction List window. All your transactions are included in the Scheduled Transaction List window. You can access this window from the Scheduled Bills & Deposits section of the Cash Flow Center, from any account register, or from the Tools menu.

Easy-to-follow introductions focus on a single concept.

Manage All Your Scheduled Transactions

1. If you don't already have the Cash Flow Center open, on the account bar, click **Cash Flow Center** and then scroll down to the Scheduled Bills & Deposits section.

   TIMESAVER As an alternate way of opening the Bills & Deposits window, you can select **Scheduled Transaction List** from the Tools menu or use the short cut key, *Ctrl + J*.

2. Click **Show Full List**.

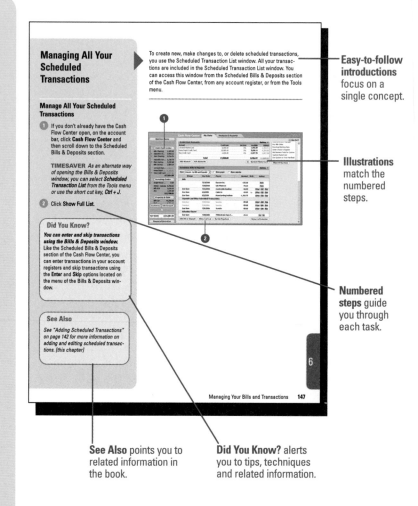

Illustrations match the numbered steps.

Numbered steps guide you through each task.

Did You Know?

You can enter and skip transactions using the Bills & Deposits window. Like the Scheduled Bills & Deposits section of the Cash Flow Center, you can enter transactions in your account registers and skip transactions using the **Enter** and **Skip** options located on the menu of the Bills & Deposits window.

See Also

See "Adding Scheduled Transactions" on page 142 for more information on adding and editing scheduled transactions. [this chapter]

6

Managing Your Bills and Transactions   147

See Also points you to related information in the book.

Did You Know? alerts you to tips, techniques and related information.

Organization of the Book

Quicken 2007 On Demand is arranged in chapters that correspond with various features of the program. Although every chapter might not apply to your financial situation, there's ample information about the Quicken program throughout the book, along with cross-references to other areas of the book, so after you find the answer to one question, you will likely be led to related information.

By chapter, these are the topics covered in this book:

◆ **Chapter 1, "Setting Up Quicken"**—This chapter provides step-by-step instructions on installing Quicken 2007 or upgrading to version 2007 from a previous version. In addition, you will find tips on what information you need on hand before installing or upgrading the software, how to set up your personal information, and your banking, paycheck, and bill information. If you have a financial file that you want to import from another financial management software, there is information how to pull that information into Quicken as well.

◆ **Chapter 2, "Learning Quicken Basics"**—This chapter provides an overview of basic Quicken functionality; for example, customizing the toolbar to include the buttons that you want to use, and creating, backing up, restoring, and importing Quicken files. You'll also learn how to use reminders for your bills and transactions, password-protect your financial files, set up remote access to your accounts, and set your Internet connection.

◆ **Chapter 3, "Using Quicken Home Page Features"**—Starting at home base, you'll learn to use the different features that the Quicken Home page offers; for example, the account bar, activity centers, online updates, and more. All of these features help save you time in moving around the program and finding the information you need quickly.

◆ **Chapter 4, "Managing Your Accounts"**—Using this chapter, you will learn how to create new accounts, edit your existing accounts, and delete accounts.

◆ **Chapter 5, "Getting the Big Picture a Snapshot at a Time"**—In this chapter, you will learn how to analyze and track your financial information for all your accounts using the account centers. You will analyze your cash flow, investment and retirement performance, and your property and debt. In addition, you will learn how to set up reminders when you need to take action on your transactions.

◆ **Chapter 6, "Managing Your Bills and Transactions"**—This chapter shows you how to keep all of your bills and transactions for all of your accounts up-to-date. You will learn how to track your bills, download transactions into your account registers, enter transactions manually into your account registers, balance your accounts, and manage all your transactions using alerts. In addition, you will learn how to attach documents to and flag transactions for follow-up, perform searches, and transfer funds.

◆ **Chapter 7, "Paying the Bills"**—In this chapter, you will learn how to set up and use Quicken's online bill payment service. In addition, you will learn how to order and print Quicken checks.

◆ **Chapter 8, "Managing Your Property and Debt"**—For this chapter, you will learn how to manage your debt by setting up and using a budget and creating a debt reduction plan. You will also learn how to take inventory of your home and personal property and keep track of your emergency records.

◆ **Chapter 9, "Planning for the Future"**—
Looking to the future, this chapter will help
you determine your financial needs for
retirement, plan for college, and figure out
how much you can afford to pay for a house.
You will also learn how to set savings goals
for yourself so that your financial situation is
worry free.

◆ **Chapter 10, "Analyzing Your Asset
Allocations and Portfolio"**—This chapter
provides instruction on using some of
Quicken's tools that help you with analyzing
your portfolio and asset allocation. You will be
able to determine if you have your assets
allocated appropriately, analyze potential
capital gains and losses, and learn to
rebalance your portfolio.

◆ **Chapter 11, "Working with Reports"**—
Reports, reports, and more reports. There are
endless possibilities for the reports that you
can create in Quicken. You will learn how to
pull out of Quicken the information you need
to analyze your finances from just about any
angle. You also learn the basics of using
reports; for example, how to view, customize,
export, and save.

◆ **Chapter 12, "Managing Your Tax
Information"**—There are some features in
Quicken that can help you out at tax time.
This chapter shows you what those features
are, how to find deductions, estimate
withholdings, and find reliable tax resources.

Setting Up Quicken

Introduction

Before you can begin using the 2007 version of Quicken, you must install it. This chapter provides detailed information on installing, registering, and setting up Quicken with all your financial and account information. If you are new to Quicken, you'll use the Quicken Express Setup to add all your financial information, including your personal information, such as your name, and your financial information, such as your checking account, credit cards, bills, and expenses.

If you have used Quicken before and are upgrading to the 2007 version, your information will automatically be converted to the new version after you install the upgrade.

The easiest way to get your financial information into Quicken is by downloading it. However, this requires that you have online access to your account(s) already, have an Internet connection, and have a valid login ID and password for your accounts. If you have all these things, you are set. If not, that's okay; you can still enter the information. However, whether you're downloading the account information or entering it yourself, you need to gather your statements to ensure that you are providing Quicken with the latest information, such as your balances, interest rates, payment due dates, and so on. Quicken uses all this information to help manage your accounts, remind you when payments are due, and make projections for your taxes or savings goals. It's like having an accountant at your fingertips, except all these services come at a much lower cost.

To ensure that you have everything you need to install and set up Quicken, review the "Quicken Setup Checklist" and "Backing Up Quicken Files" sections before you get started with Quicken Express Setup. Having all the information you need before you start will help save you time so that you can get started using Quicken right away.

1

What You'll Do

Install Quicken

Register Quicken

Use Quicken Express Setup

Enter Your Personal Information

Add Your Checking Accounts

Add Your Paychecks and Income

Add Your Bills and Expenses

Review and Complete the Setup

Quicken Setup Checklist

Before you install and start using Quicken, there are a few things you should gather to make the setup process as efficient and quick as possible. Review the following checklist and collect all the most recent information that is applicable to you:

- ◆ Bank statements for all your checking and savings accounts
- ◆ Credit card statements
- ◆ Investment and retirement statements
- ◆ Mortgage statement or rental agreement
- ◆ Loan statements (car loans, personal loans, student loans, and so on) and other liabilities information
- ◆ Information on any assets you own (antiques, art, jewelry, family heirlooms, and so on), including their value
- ◆ Paycheck stubs for you and/or your spouse, if applicable
- ◆ Statements for all your bills (utilities, insurance, and other nondebt expenses)
- ◆ Login IDs and passwords for all accounts (bank, credit card, utilities, and so on) that you access online

Backing Up Quicken Files

If you already use Quicken and you are upgrading from an older version, as a precautionary measure, make a backup of your existing Quicken file(s). To ensure that your existing files are not overwritten, save the backup file(s) to a separate location where all your current Quicken software files are located or, better yet, to a CD or diskette.

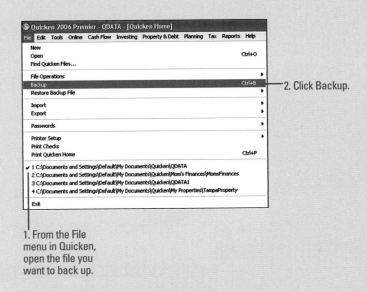

2. Click Backup.

1. From the File menu in Quicken, open the file you want to back up.

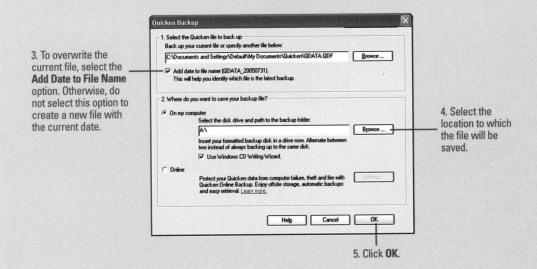

3. To overwrite the current file, select the **Add Date to File Name** option. Otherwise, do not select this option to create a new file with the current date.

4. Select the location to which the file will be saved.

5. Click **OK**.

Installing Quicken

Before you install Quicken, ensure that you have all your account information gathered, as indicated in the "Quicken Setup Checklist," and you have your software ready to install. Depending on whether you downloaded the software or have a CD, your installation may look slightly different from what is shown here.

Perform a New Installation

1 Click **Install Quicken**.

See Also

Refer to "Backing Up Files" on page 33 for more information on backing up Quicken files.

2 Click **Next** to begin installing Quicken.

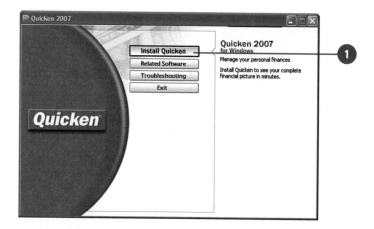

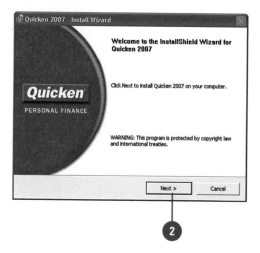

3 Read the license agreement, select **I Agree to the Terms of the License Agreement and Acknowledge Receipt of the Quicken Privacy Statement**, and click **Next**.

4 It is recommended that you accept the installation location for the Quicken files. However, to change it, click **Change** and locate the folder you want to use. Then click **Next** to proceed.

5 To go back and change any of the installation settings, click **Back**; otherwise, click **Install**. The Installation Wizard begins installing Quicken 2007 and automatically opens the Check for Quicken Updates dialog box.

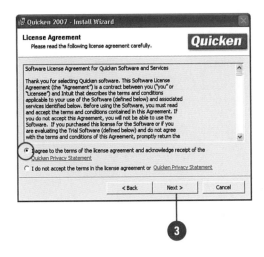

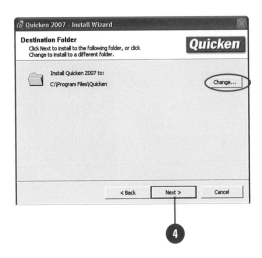

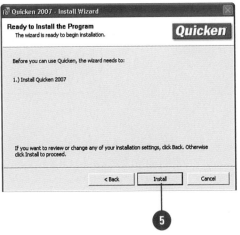

⑥ Click **Get Update** to check for software updates or click **Next** to complete the installation.

⑦ Ensure that the **Launch Quicken 2007** option is selected and click **Done**. Quicken opens and displays the Get Started with Quicken 2007 window.

Did You Know?

Get the latest updates to Quicken 2007. You can check for any updates to your Quicken 2006 software by selecting **Get Update** (be sure that you are connected to the Internet) in step 7. This ensures that you have the latest files and that your software runs as efficiently as possible. When Quicken is finished searching for and installing the updates, go to step 8.

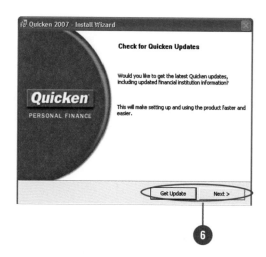

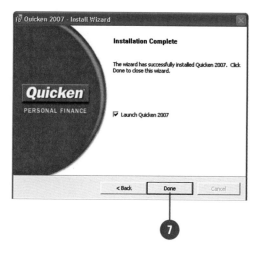

For Your Information

If you do not select the Launch Quicken 2007 option shown in step 7, Quicken does not open after you click **Done**.

8 If you are brand new to Quicken, select the **I Am New to Quicken** option; otherwise, select **I Am Already a Quicken User**. Then click **Next**.

9 Select an option indicating where you would like to keep your Quicken files and click **Next**. If you do not change the location of the Quicken files, the Express Setup opens.

See Also

Refer to "Using the Express Setup" on page 16 for information on setting up your financial information using Express Setup.

10 If you are changing the location of your Quicken files, click **Save In** and select the location you want to use.

11 If you are changing the name of your Quicken file, type it in the **File Name** field. Do not change the .QDF extension.

12 Click **OK**. The Express Setup opens.

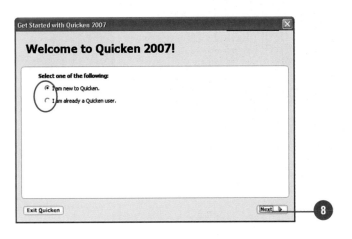

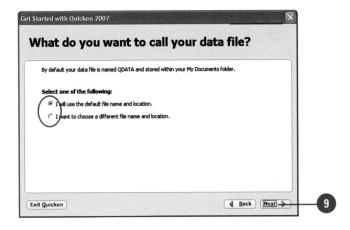

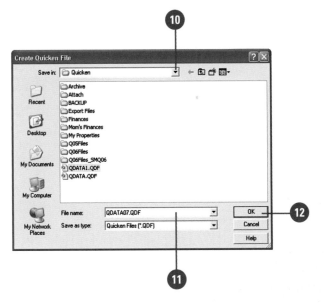

Perform an Upgrade Installation

1 Click **Next** to begin installing Quicken.

> ### Did You Know?
>
> **No need to uninstall the previous version.** Quicken now automatically uninstalls the previous version before it installs the 2007 version so that you don't have to.

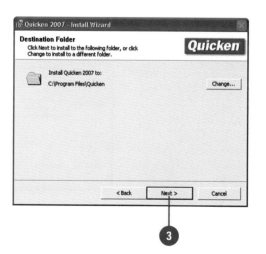

2 Read the license agreement, select **I Agree to the Terms of the License Agreement and Acknowledge Receipt of the Quicken Privacy Statement**, and click **Next**.

3 It is recommended that you accept the installation location for the Quicken files. However, to change it, click **Change** and locate the folder you want to use. Then click **Next** to proceed.

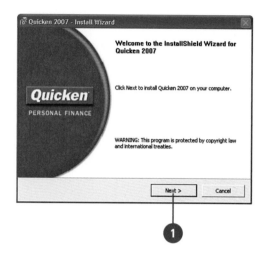

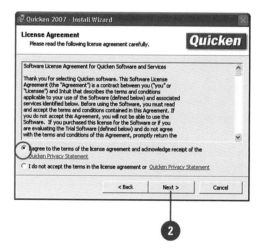

4. To go back and change any of the installation settings, click **Back**; otherwise, click **Install**. The Install Wizard begins installing Quicken 2007 and automatically opens the Check for Quicken Updates dialog box.

5. Click **Get Update** to check for software updates or click **Next** to complete the installation.

6. Ensure that the **Launch Quicken 2007** option is selected and click **Done**.

Did You Know?

Get the latest updates to Quicken 2007. You can check for any updates to your Quicken 2006 software by selecting **Get Updates** (be sure that you are connected to the Internet) in step 5. This ensures that you have the latest files and that your software runs as efficiently as possible. When Quicken is finished searching for and installing the updates, go to step 7.

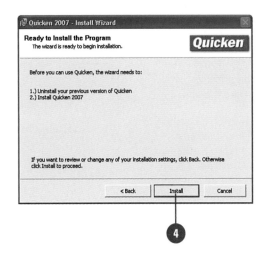

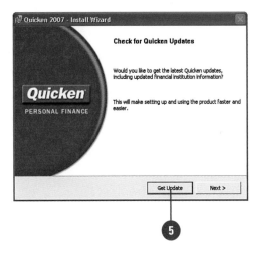

7 When the installation is complete, the Convert Your Data File window opens to convert all your information from the previous version of Quicken into this one. Click **OK**.

TIMESAVER *When Quicken converts your information from a previous version of Quicken, it is bringing over all of your accounts, payees, and so on. When the upgrade and conversion are complete, the Quicken Home Page opens with all of your information, just as it was in the previous version of Quicken. You won't miss a beat and can start using the new version right away.*

8 Click **Next** to review and set up your information to use in Quicken 2007.

9 If you are interested in using Quicken Bill Pay, an online bill payment service, to pay your bills, review your eligible accounts and select the **Yes, I'm Interested in Paying Bills Online** option if you would like to participate. Then click **Next**.

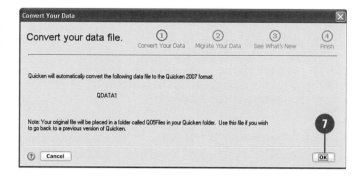

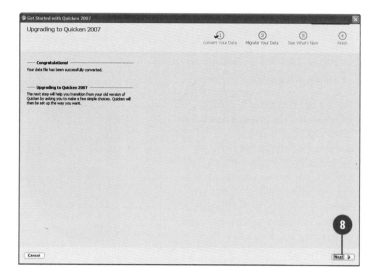

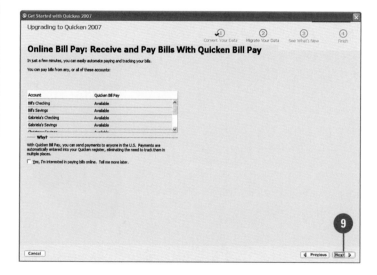

10 Click a link to review the new and enhanced features for Quicken 2007. Then click **Next**.

11 Click **Done**.

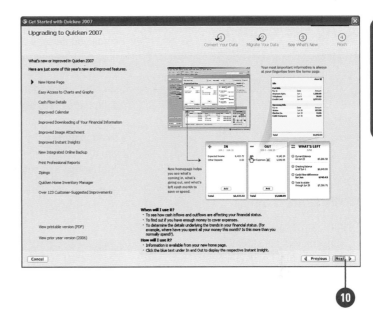

10

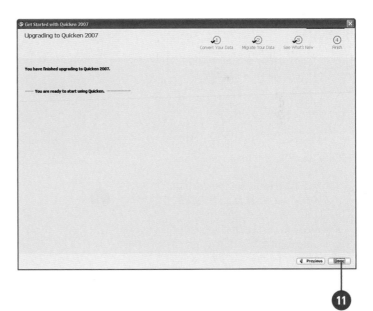

11

Using the Express Setup

If you haven't used Quicken before, you'll find that the Express Setup steps you through the process of entering all your financial information, such as your bank accounts, credit cards, mortgage, bills, and so on. As you move through the setup, Quicken asks you to enter specific information about yourself and your accounts. If you have online access to some of your accounts, you are given the option to download the account information directly into Quicken. There is still some manual entry involved, but it is less than typing it in yourself. If you don't have online access to your accounts, you can enter the information and set it up for online access later, if it's available.

Use the Express Setup

1 Click **Skip Setup** to start using Quicken without setting up your accounts and financial information. You can return to the setup later, if needed to set up your accounts, or you can add them using other features.

> ### See Also
> *Refer to "Adding New Accounts" on page 88 for information on setting up new accounts.*

2 Click **Next Step** to begin the setup.

TIMESAVER *To save some time in figuring out what to enter, grab all those statements, paychecks, and so on to ensure that you enter accurate information during the setup process. Refer to the "Quicken Setup Checklist" on page 6 previously in this chapter for a list of items you will most likely need during the setup.*

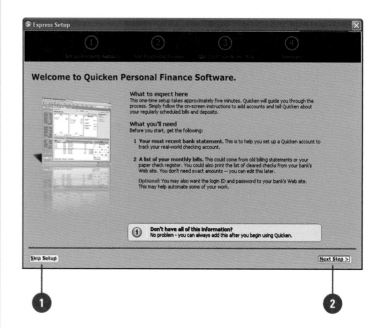

Entering Your Personal Information

The first section in the Express Setup is the Personal Information section. Quicken asks for some basic information, such as your name, and it asks some questions that help Quicken determine what information it needs to obtain in order to create the accounts that fit your needs.

Enter Your Personal Information

1 Type your name. If you have a spouse or significant other for whom you are also entering information, select **I Am Married** and type your spouse's name.

2 Select any of the other options that apply to you.

3 Click **Next Step** to proceed.

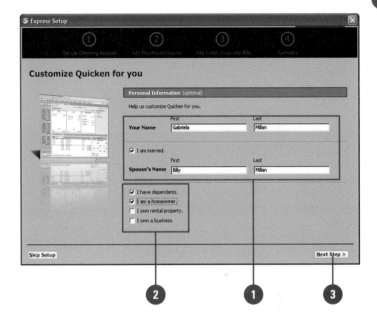

Adding Your Checking Account

The first account to set up is your checking account, which is considered a cash flow account in Quicken. Gather your bank statement for your primary checking account and use it to enter the latest information about this account in Quicken. If you have online access to your bank account, retrieve your login ID and password so that you can download the information into Quicken during the setup.

Set Up a Checking Account

1 Type the name of the financial institution where your checking account is held and then click **Next Step**.

> **TIMESAVER** Click in the text box beneath **This Account Is Held at the Following Institution** and start typing the name of your bank. The drop-down menu lists the bank names closest to what you type. Select the name of your financial institution. If it is not listed, finish typing the name. Then click **Next**. If Quicken finds a bank with multiple locations, you may be prompted to specify the location of the bank.

2 Select **Yes** if you can download the account information directly from your financial institution. Select **No** to enter the account information yourself.

3 If you can download your account information, type your login ID in **User Name** and your account password in **Password** and **Reenter Password**.

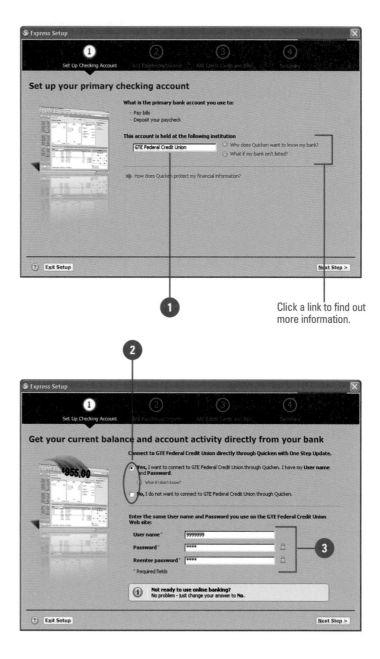

Click a link to find out more information.

4 If you are entering the information manually, in **Name Your Account**, type the name you want to give this account and complete the rest of the information.

Did You Know?

The account name is used in Quicken. The name you give your account is used only within Quicken, to help you identify it and differentiate it from your other accounts.

5 If you are downloading your account information, ensure that you are connected to the Internet and click **Next Step**.

Quicken connects to your financial institution and locates your account(s). If you manually entered the information, go to the next task, "Adding Your Paychecks and Income."

6 Select the account(s) you want to download into Quicken by selecting the box in the **Add** column.

7 If needed, change the names of the account(s) by clicking in the text boxes and typing the name(s) you want to use in Quicken. Then click **Next Step**.

See Also

Refer to "Adding New Accounts" on page 88 for information on adding additional checking or savings accounts.

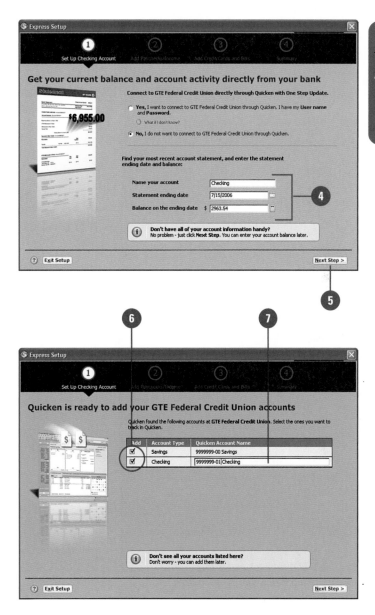

Did You Know?

You must have a login ID and password to download your bank account information. In order to download your bank account information, you must already have a login ID and password from your financial institution. If you don't, click **No** in step 2 and enter your account information manually. You can call your financial institution to set up access, if it is offered, and change your account to online later.

Adding Your Paychecks and Income

You can track your income by entering your paycheck(s) information for you and anyone else you want to track for your household. Quicken uses this information to manage your income and expenses, track taxes you pay, and help you plan for the future. Before proceeding, you should get your paycheck stubs to assist you in entering income information.

Add Your Paychecks and Income

1. From the Add Paychecks/Income section of Express Setup, click in the text box in the **Company Name** column and type the name of your employer or source of income.

2. Select a category; for example, Salary.

3. Type your net income for an individual paycheck.

4. Select the frequency of payment.

5. Type or select the date of your next payment.

6. Select the account into which the paycheck is deposited.

7. To add additional paychecks or income, click **Add Row** and repeat steps 1–6.

8. Click **Next Step** to add bills and expenses.

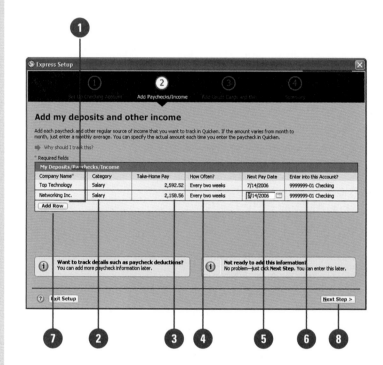

Adding Your Bills and Expenses

Now comes the fun part: adding all your bills and expenses. Gather all your credit card and billing statements for your utilities, magazine and newspaper subscriptions, association dues, and any other bills you pay regularly. The Add Regular Bills and Expenses section of the Express Setup allows you to add all this information. However, if you don't have all the information you need to set up your bills, don't worry. You will have plenty of opportunities to add them later.

Add Your Bills and Expenses

1. To add credit card accounts, from the My Credit Cards table of Express Setup, click in the text box in the **Name** column and type the name of the credit card company.

2. In **Average Payment**, type the amount you typically pay each month.

3. In **Next Due Date**, type the date the payment is due.

4. In **Enter into this Account**, select the account from which payments are made.

5. To add another credit card, click **Add Row** and repeat steps 1–4.

6. To add bills, from the My Bill Reminders table, enter the information the same way you added the credit cards.

7. When you are finished adding all your credit cards and bills, click **Next Step**.

Click to view information on tracking your bills and expenses.

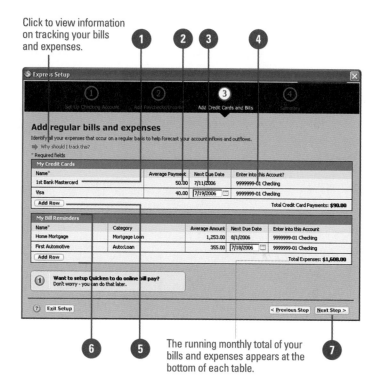

The running monthly total of your bills and expenses appears at the bottom of each table.

Did You Know?

You can pay your bills by using Quicken Bill Pay. Quicken offers an online bill payment service that you can use to pay all your bills automatically. There is a fee associated with the service, but you may find the service worth the price. If you are interested in having all your bills in one place and paying them with a click of a button, or if you already use an online bill payment service and are looking for a new one, click **Quicken Bill Pay** to learn more. Be aware that for you to be able to pay your bills online, the company has to offer online access to your accounts.

Assigning Categories to Your Bills Is Important

When you add bills, you are asked to select a category to use to track your payments. You can use categories to track how much you spend on individual expenses, such as clothing, deposits, and other financial information. Quicken uses this information to produce reports and in budgets to help you analyze and manage your finances.

1. If you don't find the category you want to use, type the name you want to use to create a new category. A message appears, asking if you want to create a new category.

2. Click **Yes**.

3. Type the name, description, and group you want to assign to the category.

4. Select the type of category. If you want to use an existing category, but assign the bill to a subcategory, select it from the **Subcategory Of** drop-down menu.

5. If the category is associated with a tax line item, select it from the drop-down menu. If the category can be used for your taxes, select the **Tax-Related** option and select appropriate line item option.

6. Click **OK**.

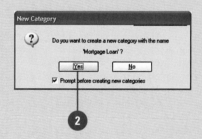

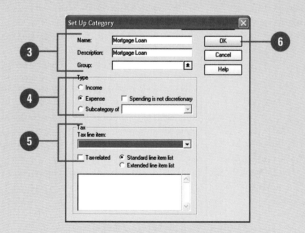

Reviewing and Completing the Setup

Review and Complete the Setup

1 From the **Summary** section of the setup, review all your information.

2 To change information about any of the accounts—for example, the name of an account—click in the appropriate text box and change the information.

3 To remove an account, click **Delete** next to the item you want to remove. A message appears, asking if you want to delete the item.

4 Click **Yes** to remove it or click **No** to keep it.

5 To add a new account, click **Add Row** and enter the account information.

6 When you are finished reviewing and making changes, click **Next Step**

7 Click **Finish**.

You should now have your checking, income, credit card, bills, and expenses information entered in Express Setup. If not, you have the opportunity to review it all, make changes, if necessary, and get started using Quicken.

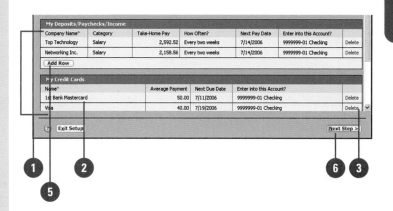

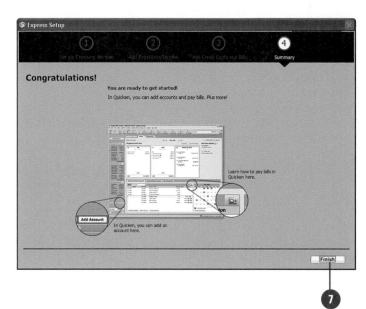

Did You Know?

This is not your last chance to make changes to all of your setup information. You can always add, change, or delete information in Quicken either from the Quicken Home Page or from the accounts. In addition, you can click **Setup** on the toolbar and go back into the Express Setup.

Registering Quicken

After you install Quicken, you should automatically be prompted to register it. If you have already used a previous version of Quicken, your information is transferred to the new version. You must register Quicken before you can use any of the online features, such as online banking; downloading transactions for your investments, credit cards, and so on; or Quicken.com features. As you use this version of Quicken, over time, you may also be prompted to install the free updates.

Register Quicken

1 Ensure that you are connected to the Internet and click **Register Now**. Quicken connects to the registration site.

Did You Know?

You can register Quicken at a later time. If you are not able to register Quicken at the time you are prompted to do so, click **Register Later** on the Product Registration window (shown in step 1). You can complete the registration when you are prompted again; for example, when you try to use an online feature. Or you can access and complete the registration by selecting **Register Quicken** from the Help menu. If you have already registered Quicken, this menu option does not appear.

2 Complete the required registration information. Required fields are indicated by a red dot next to the field title.

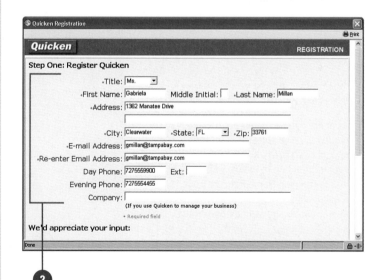

Click to register Quicken at a later time and start using Quicken right away.

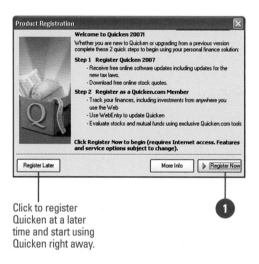

3 Complete the optional questions and click **Register**.

4 If you already have a login ID and password for Quicken.com, type your member ID and password and click **Sign In**.

5 If you don't have a Quicken ID and password, review the Create an Account section, click **Continue** and follow the directions to obtain a Quicken ID and password.

Did You Know?

Quicken.com allows remote access to your accounts. Quicken.com is a secure Quicken site where you can access basic account information, such as your balances. You can obtain a login ID and password to utilize this feature by referring to the Create an Account section shown in step 5. After you're set up, you can access your account information from anywhere, as long as you have an Internet connection. Refer to "Setting up Remote Access to Your Accounts" on page 53 for more information.

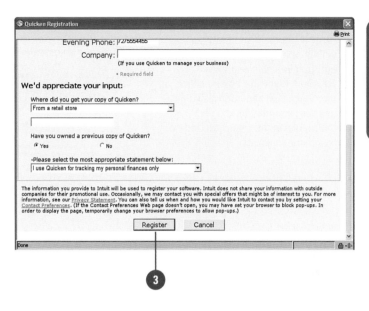

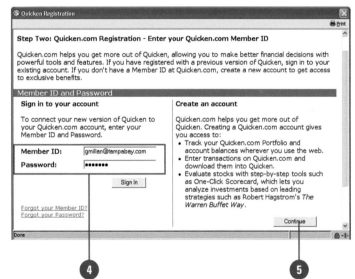

6 Review the tools and features you will be able to use with Quicken and Quicken.com and click **Finished**. If you set up any online accounts, Quicken updates your account information and displays the results in the One Step Update Summary window.

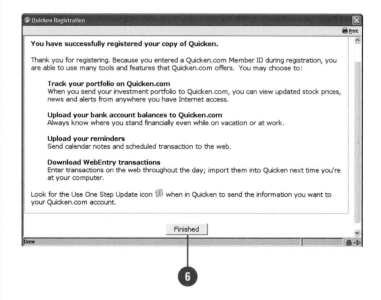

Learning Quicken Basics

Introduction

There are basic Quicken options and features that you should become familiar with that will cut down on the amount of information you have to manually enter into Quicken and make using it more efficient. For example, there are options that allow you to tell Quicken how you want for it to present some information. You can also import financial information from a previous version of Quicken or from other financial software. In addition, you can ensure that Quicken serves your needs quickly by customizing the toolbar. Setting preferences is another way to use Quicken the way you want to use it so that you can easily find what you're looking for.

There are other features that allow you to take advantage of online access to your accounts. If you have an Internet connection and have accounts that provide online access to your statements and transactions, you can download the information right into Quicken. Downloading your account information ensures that the information is accurate, timely, easier to maintain and manage, and saves you the time it would have taken to manually enter it. In addition, the Quicken.com feature allows you to access your account information remotely.

What You'll Do

Customize the Toolbar

Create New Quicken Files

Back Up Files

Import and Export Files

Set Up Passwords

Set Quicken Preferences

Set Up an Internet Connection

Set Up Remote Internet Access to Your Accounts

Customizing the Toolbar

The *toolbar* is your portal to quickly moving to specific areas of Quicken. To make accessing specific information even more convenient, you can customize the buttons on the toolbar to show only the buttons you want to use and the order in which you want them to appear. Handpicking and organizing the buttons on the toolbar ensures that the areas most important to you are only a click away.

Add and Remove Buttons

1 From the toolbar, click **Edit**, **Customize Toolbar**. The buttons that are currently on the toolbar are listed in the Current Toolbar Order column in the order in which they appear on the toolbar; those that are not on your toolbar are listed in the Add to Toolbar column.

2 To add a button to the toolbar, from the **Add to Toolbar** column, select a button title. You can add more than one button at a time by holding down the **Ctrl** key and clicking each title you want to add. The titles you select are boldfaced.

3 When you have selected all items you want to add to the toolbar, click **Add**.

4 To remove a button from the toolbar, from the **Current Toolbar Order** column, select the button title and click **Remove**.

5 To view all available toolbar buttons, select **Show All Toolbar Choices**.

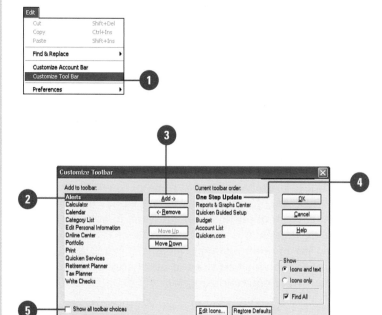

See Also

See Chapter 3, "Using Quicken Home Page Features," on page 57 for more information on the home page.

Change the Order and Appearance of Buttons

1. To move a button to the left on the toolbar, select the button that you want to move and click **Move Up**. Each time you click Move Up, the button moves left one position. Click Move Up as many times as necessary to move it where you want it.

2. To move a button to the right on the toolbar, select the button you want to move and click **Move Down**. Click Move Down as many times as necessary to move the button where you want it.

3. To view only the button icon (and not the text), select **Icons Only**; otherwise, select **Icons and Text** to view both.

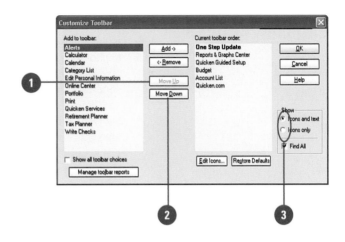

Rename Buttons and Assign Shortcuts

1. To rename a button title, select the button title and click **Edit** Icons.

2. In the **Label** box, type the new name for the button, keeping in mind the amount of space on the toolbar for lengthy names.

3. If you want to assign a shortcut to the button, in the **Shortcut** box, type the shortcut you want to use. For example, if you type **A** for the Accounts List button (renamed "My Accounts"), you can open the My Accounts window by pressing **Alt+Shift+A**.

4. Click **OK**.

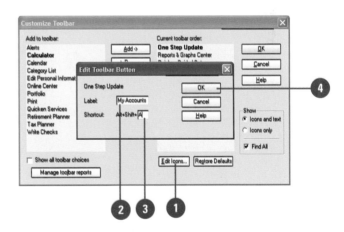

Did You Know?

Changing a button title does not change where the button takes you. For example, if you change the name of the Accounts List button to My Accounts, when you click that button on the toolbar, the window titled Account List always opens, no matter what you've titled the button.

Creating New Quicken Files

It is recommended that you create separate Quicken files if you intend to track expenses, assets, taxes, or other financial information for a business, for volunteer work, or for someone else. You can also keep separate Quicken files to keep your financial information separate from that of your spouse; however, it is not entirely necessary. If you share some of your bills and finances with your spouse but want to keep only certain accounts separate, you can hide the accounts, such as certain bills you don't want included in joint financial areas. We will talk more about hiding accounts in Chapter 3. For now, let's walk through creating a new Quicken file.

Create a New Quicken File

1 Click **File**, **New**.

2 Select **New Quicken File** and click **OK**.

   TIMESAVER *You can quickly open files you have recently worked with. To open a file that you recently worked on, click the **File** menu and select a filename from the bottom of the menu. Files are numbered in the order in which they were last opened.*

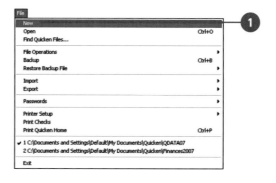

3. To change where to save the file, click the **Save In** drop-down menu and select the new location.

4. To create a new folder, click the **Create New Folder** button and type the name of the new folder.

5. Click in the **File Name** text box and type the name of the new file. You do not have to type the **.qdf** extension. Quicken automatically adds it for you.

6. Click **OK**.

Continued, next page

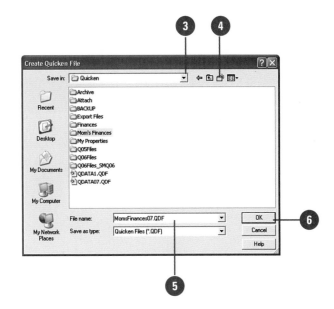

Did You Know?

You can name and store Quicken files logically. It's a good idea to keep your Quicken files in separate folders and name them logically (for example, **Mom's Finances**). This will help you identify and manage your Quicken files more efficiently.

2

7 Set up your new file by using **Express Setup**, just as you did when you set up your first Quicken file in Chapter 1, "Setting Up Quicken."

8 If you do not want to go through Express Setup at this time, click **Skip Setup**. You can open the new file at another time to set it up.

See Also

See Chapter 1, "Setting Up Quicken," on page 5 for more information on using Quicken New User Setup.

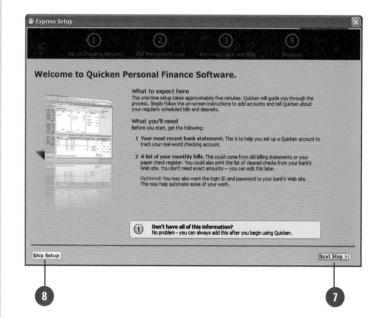

Backing Up Files

As you work in Quicken, adding accounts, transactions, securities, and so on, you are creating a lot of important and valuable information. So, what happens if your file is accidentally deleted or becomes corrupt, or if your computer goes down? Creating a backup of your Quicken files ensures that you have another copy in case you need to recover some or all of your financial information.

Back Up a File

1 Click **File, Backup**.

2 To back up the file you have open, don't change anything in the first section with the exception of the **Add Date to File Name** option. Select this option to help distinguish between backup files. However, if you do want to overwrite the existing backup, do not select the **Add Date to File Name** option.

3 Select the backup location for your file. To save it to your hard drive, a disk, or CD, click **Browse** and then select the location. Saving the file to a disk or CD is recommended because if you are not able to use your computer or the file is corrupt, you can recover your file from the disk or CD.

4 To save the file to an online location, such as Quicken Online Backup, select **Online**.

5 Click **OK**.

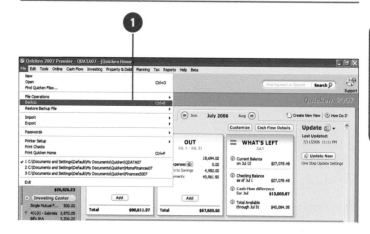

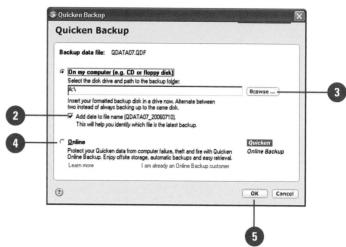

Did You Know?

You can store your backup files online. As part of Quicken Services, you can elect to use the Quicken data center to store your backup files by selecting the Online option shown in step 4. The data center uses two servers in two separate locations to ensure that your files are safe and retrievable. However, this service does come at a price. If you're interested in looking into this service, click the Learn More link under the description of the Online option.

Restoring Backups

Let's play devil's advocate for a minute. Let's say that you've been working hard getting all your financial information into Quicken and regularly keeping it up-to-date. Then your Quicken file becomes corrupt or you accidentally delete vital information from the file. What do you do? Well, if you created regular backups, you can restore the information by restoring the backup file. You can restore files from your computer, such as a CD, disk, or a location on your hard drive, or you can restore from an online source, such as Quicken Online Backup. The following example shows you how to restore a backup file from a CD:

1 Click **File**, **Restore Backup File**.

2 Select either **Browse My Computer** or **Browse Online Backup**.

3 Insert the CD into your CD drive.

4 From the **Restore Quicken File** dialog box, click **Look in**. Locate the CD drive and select the file you backed up.

5 Click **OK**. A message appears, telling you that the backup was restored.

6 Click **OK**.

7 Click **File**, **Open**, and open the file you just restored.

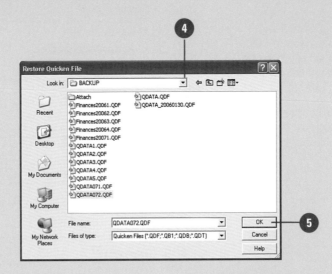

Importing and Exporting Files

If you have used another version of Quicken, have statements or other financial information in Quicken format, or have information from TurboTax that you would like to use, you can import the information from any of those files into Quicken. For example, some banks and creditors offer the option of saving and downloading your account information as Quicken files in QFX format, also known as *Web connect files*. By importing this information, you save time and ensure that the information is entered accurately.

On the flip side, if you need to export any information from Quicken into a file to save or send to someone (for example, your accountant), you have that option as well.

Import Files

1. Click **File**, **Import** and select the file type that you want to import. (TurboTax is the file format used for that software, Web Connect is a QFX format used by financial institutions, and QIF is a Quicken file.)

Continued, next page

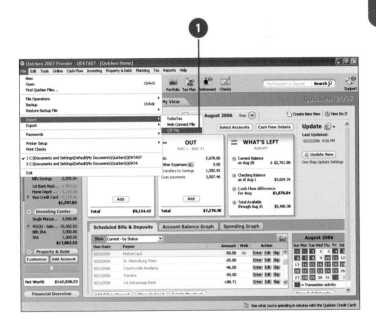

2 Click the **Look In** drop-down list and locate the file you want to import.

3 Click **Open**. Quicken imports the file and incorporates the information in the appropriate account. You might be prompted to activate the One Step Update if it is available for your financial institution.

See Also

See "Using Online Updates" on page 79 for information on using One Step Update.

4 To review and add the transactions to your account, open the appropriate account register by selecting the account from the Accounts List.

See Also

See "Downloading and Adding Transactions from Your Account Register" on page 162 for information on downloading transactions from your financial institution.

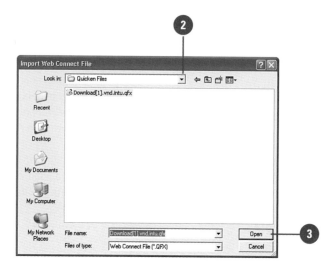

Did You Know?

You can no longer import QIF files for some accounts. The QIF (data import functionality) file format is not available anymore for checking, savings, credit cards, 401(K), and other types of brokerage accounts. According to Quicken, this is because the technology used for QIF files is old, wasn't originally intended for downloading purposes, and isn't as reliable as QFX (Quicken Financial Exchange), or Web connect files. QFX or Web connect files are available from some financial institutions, which you can download and then import into Quicken. These files can contain transactions and other account information that you can use to update your accounts in Quicken. Not all financial institutions offer QFX files. Check with your financial institution to find out if they offer download service for QFX files.

Export Files

1 Click **File, Export, QIF File**.

TIMESAVER *Even though QIF files are being phased out, you can still use them to transfer information from one Quicken account file to another. This saves you time when you're setting up a new account.*

2 Click **Browse** to select the location to which you want to save the Quicken file. You can export to any location on your hard drive, to a CD, or external drive.

3 If needed, you can change the name of the file. Be sure not to change the QIF extension.

4 From the drop-down menu, **Quicken Account to Export From**, select the account you want to export. To export information for all your accounts, select **All Accounts**.

5 From **Include Transactions in Dates**, select or type the dates of the transactions you want to export.

6 From the **Include in Export** section, select the information that you want to include in the exported file.

7 Click **OK**.

8 To transfer information to another file, open that file and import the QIF file.

See Also

See "Import Files" on page 35 for more information on importing files.

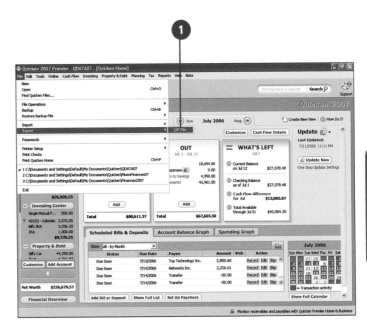

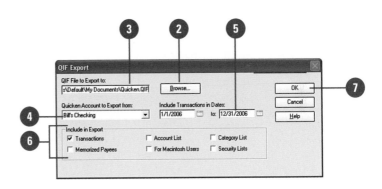

Password-Protecting Your Files

An easy way to provide a basic level of security for your financial information is to set up a password in Quicken. You can set up a password for every Quicken file you create. You can also protect transactions that occur before a specific date. After you set up a password, you are prompted to enter it each time you open the Quicken file or the transaction(s) to which you assign the password. Make sure you commit your passwords to memory or keep them in a safe place.

Assign a Password to a File

1. Open the Quicken file you want to password-protect and click **File**, **Passwords**, **File**.

2. In the **New Password** field, type your password. It is best to use at least six characters, including uppercase and lowercase letters, numbers, and special characters.

3. In the **Confirm Password** field, type the password again.

4. Click **OK**.

    IMPORTANT *It is good practice to change your password every three months or so. To change your password, click **File**, **Passwords**, **File**. Type the old password, the new password, and confirm the new password by typing it again. Then click **OK**.*

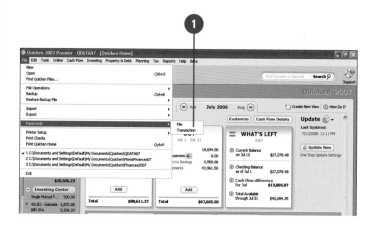

For Your Information

Passwords are case sensitive.

When you create your password, you can use both uppercase and lowercase letters. When you are prompted to enter your password, remember to type it using the proper case. For example, if you decide your password is going to be "MyPassword03," you would need to type it exactly the way you see it here. For example, "mypassword03" is not the same password as "MyPassword03."

Assign a Password to Transactions

① Click **File**, **Passwords**, **Transaction**.

> **IMPORTANT** *It is a good idea to protect transactions that you have reconciled or those you intend to archive to ensure that they cannot be changed.*

② In the **Password** field, type your password. It is best to use at least six characters, including uppercase letters, lowercase letters, numbers, and special characters.

③ In the **Confirm Password** field, type the password again.

④ In the **Required For Dates Through** field, type (or select from the calendar) the date through which you want all transactions to be password-protected. You can set this date as far in the future as you want.

⑤ Click **OK**.

Did You Know?

You can remove a password. To remove a password completely for either a file or a transaction, click **File**, **Passwords**, and select either **File** or **Transaction**. The Quicken File Password or Change Transaction Password dialog box opens (depending on whether you are removing a transaction or file password). In **Old Password**, type the existing password, leave both the **New Password** and **Confirm Password** text boxes blank, and click **OK**.

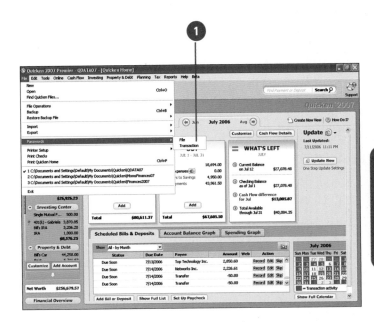

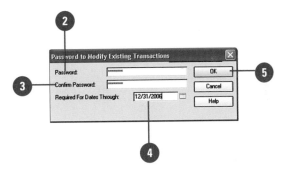

Setting Quicken Preferences

There are preferences or settings that you can change in Quicken to help control how you interact with Quicken and how you want it to work for you. For example, you can tell Quicken to track the fiscal year instead of the calendar year, or you can tell it to track foreign currency. In addition, you can specify what information you want to see when you open Quicken and set other preferences. Review the preferences and determine which settings you prefer. Then go for it.

Set Startup Preferences

① Click **Edit**, **Preferences**, **Quicken Program**.

② To change the page you see when you first open Quicken, from the **On Startup Open To** drop-down menu, select the center or account you prefer.

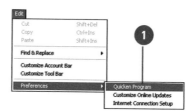

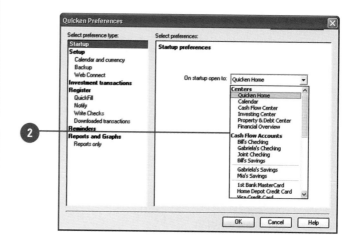

Set Quicken Preferences

1 Click the **Setup** item in the **Quicken Preferences** page, and you can change the location of the account bar (which contains the activity centers) by selecting **Left Side of the Screen** or **Right Side of the Screen**. Or to remove the account bar altogether, select **Never Display Account Bar**.

2 To use Quicken keyboard commands for cut, copy, and paste (Ctrl+X, Ctrl+C, and Ctrl+V in Windows), select **Quicken Standard** (see the For Your Information sidebar on this page). Or to use the Windows version of these commands, select **Windows Standard**.

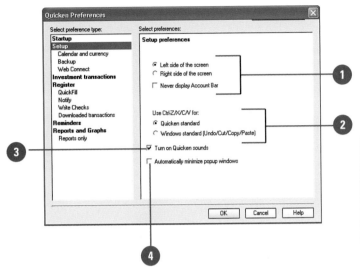

> ### See Also
>
> See "Keyboard Shortcuts" on page 84 for a complete list of Quicken keyboard shortcuts.

3 To hear Quicken sounds, select the **Turn On Quicken Sounds** option. Or to turn the sound off, click it again to remove the check mark.

4 To have Quicken minimize any pop-ups that open when you are using it, select **Automatically Minimize Popup Windows**.

Continued, next page ▶

For Your Information

If you elect to use Quicken standard keyboard commands in step 2, be aware the common keyboard commands for Windows are not the same in Quicken. For example, in order to use the Cut command while you're in Quicken world, the keyboard shortcut is **Shift+Del**. For Copy, it becomes **Crtl+Ins**, and for Paste, it's **Shift+Ins**. In addition, these commands work only in specific areas of Quicken; for example, account registers. If you are not sure of the commands available to you while you're in a specific area of the program, refer to the main menus. The available shortcuts appear on the appropriate menus in Quicken.

5 To set calendar and currency preferences, select **Calendar and Currency** from the **Select Preference Type** list.

6 Select **Calendar Year** to use the entire calendar year in Quicken. Or select **Fiscal Year** and specify when you want the fiscal year to begin from the **Starting Month** drop-down menu.

7 To track other currencies besides the American dollar, select **Multicurrency Support**.

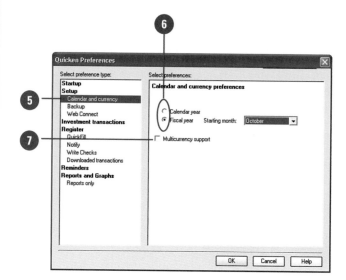

Did You Know?

You can track foreign currency in Quicken. If you elect to use foreign currency, Quicken assigns your preset or home currency to all your accounts and investments. In addition, it places a symbol next to the amounts in your registers, the Portfolio View window, and wherever else monetary amounts are listed. Quicken determines what your home currency is from the Windows Control Panel. To review what your home currency is, from your Windows Start menu, select **Control Panel** and then double-click **Regional and Language Options**.

8 To set preferences for backup files, select **Backup** from the **Select Preference Type** list.

9 Type how many times you want to be reminded to back up your files in **Remind After Running Quicken**. Then type the number of backup copies in the **Maximum Number of Backup Copies** field.

10 If you want Quicken to display a message to notify you before existing files are overwritten, select **Warn Before Overwriting Old Files**.

11 To set preferences for files you download, such as the QFX or Web connect files, select **Web Connect** from the **Select Preference Type** list.

12 To save the information that is downloaded in a separate file, select **Give Me the Option of Saving to a File Whenever I Download Web Connect Data**. This inhibits Quicken from automatically updating your online accounts.

13 To keep the web connection open after downloading and updating files, select **Keep Quicken Open After Web Connect Completes**.

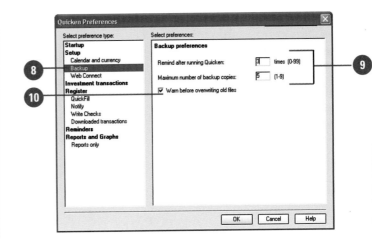

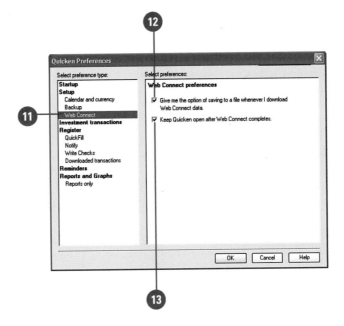

See Also

See "Downloading and Adding Transactions from Your Account Register" on page 162 for more information on downloading financial information and entering in your account registers.

Did You Know?

You can use Web Connect to download financial information from financial institution websites. *Web Connect* is a term some financial institutions use to refer to downloading your financial statements, transactions, and other financial information from their websites. The downloading process differs for each financial institution. However, most institutions offer download capability into Quicken. Contact your financial institution for details.

Set Investment Transaction Preferences

1. To set preferences for how you want to view investment transactions, select **Investment Transactions** from the **Select Preference Type** list.

2. In the **List Display** drop-down, select the number of lines you want to view and in **Sort Choice**, select how you want transactions sorted.

3. To view hidden transactions, select **Show Hidden Transactions**. To remove this option, click it again to remove the check mark.

4. To enable the Attach button, select **Show Attach Button**. This button allows you to attach files, such as images or online receipts, to transactions. It appears next to the Enter, Edit, and Delete buttons on the transactions listed in your account registers.

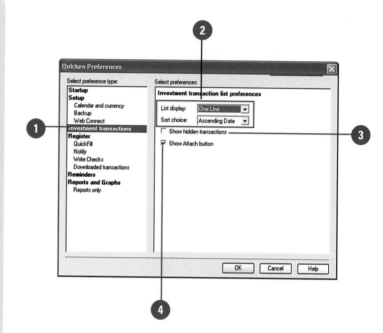

Set Register Preferences

1. To set preferences to specify how you want information to appear on your account registers, select **Register** from the **Select Preference Type** list.

2. To always list the date of your transactions in the first column of all your account registers, select the **Show Date in First Column** option.

3. To list the Memo column before the Category column, select the **Show Memo Before Category** option.

4. To be able to enter a transaction from the Split dialog box, select the **Automatically Enter Split Data** option.

5. To enable Quicken to suggest categories to assign to new transactions, select the **Use Automatic Categorization** option.

6. To allow Quicken to automatically insert two decimal points in figures you enter in the pop-up calculators, select the **Automatically Place Decimal Point** option.

7. To change the font, click the **Fonts** button and select the font and font size you want to use.

8. To change the colors used for your accounts in Quicken, click the **Colors** button and select the colors you want to use for each account.

9. To remove payee names that have not been used in a while, select the option **Remove Memorized Payees Not Used in Last**. Then type the number of months you want to apply.

10. To retain the filters you set up for your account registers, even after you close down Quicken, select the option **Keep Register Filters After Quicken Closes**.

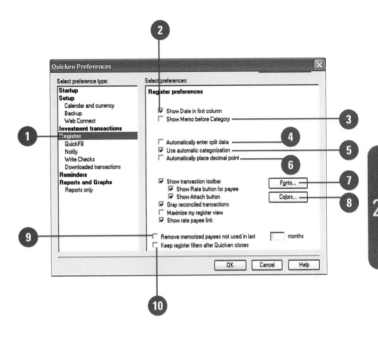

Did You Know?

Use different colors for your account registers. You can assign different colors to your account registers to color-code them for easy identification and visual appeal.

Set QuickFill Preferences

① To tell Quicken what you want it to do with the information you enter and whether to automatically update similar information, such as payee names, select **QuickFill** from the **Select Preference Type** list.

② Review and select the options you want to use for QuickFill.

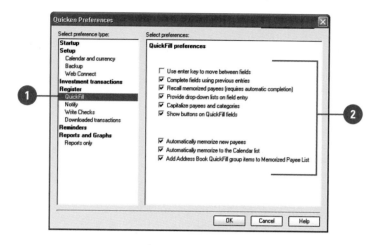

Did You Know?

QuickFill is a memory tool that you can use automatically complete entry of information. For example, when you enter a payee's name, Quicken takes note. Therefore, the next time you begin to enter the payee's name, Quicken automatically completes the payee's name for you. However, you always have the option of changing it or making a different selection from a list of memorized names. QuickFill works in the Address Book, the registers, the Write Checks window, and the Split Transaction window.

Set Notification Preferences

① To set preferences for what you want Quicken to warn you about when working with your account information, select **Notify**.

② Review and select the options you want to use. It is recommended that you keep all options that are currently selected. Click OK.

③ Click **OK**.

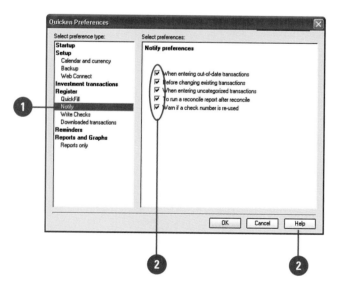

Set Check Preferences

① To set preferences for check-printing options, if you use Quicken checks, select **Write Checks** from the **Select Preference Type** list.

② Select **4-Digit Year** or **2-Digit Year** to have a four-digit or two-digit year appear on the printed checks.

③ Select any of the other options available for printed checks, and then click **OK**.

Set Downloaded Transactions Preferences

① To set preferences for how you want Quicken to handle renaming downloaded transactions, select **Downloaded Transactions** from the **Select Preference Type** list.

② To enable renaming rules, select the option **Apply Renaming Rules to Downloaded Transactions**.

③ Select how you want Quicken to handle renaming downloaded transactions. You can choose to have it occur automatically or to receive a message when a transaction is renamed.

④ To set up, view, or change renaming rules, click **Renaming Rules**.

See Also

See "Downloading and Adding Transactions from Your Account Register" on page 162 for more information on downloading financial information and renaming rules.

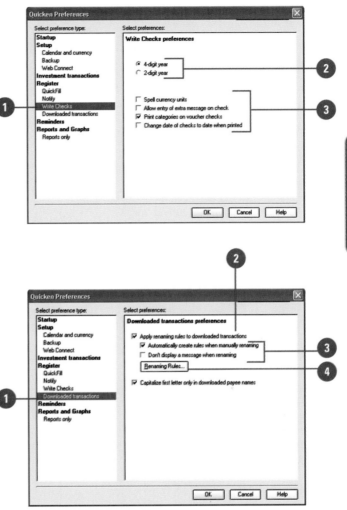

For Your Information

Using the renaming rule options is another timesaving tool that works similar to QuickFill. When you download transactions and change the payee's name or the memo information for a transaction, Quicken takes note. The next time you download a transaction from the same payee, Quicken automatically changes the payee's name and/or memo information before the transaction is recorded in your register. Quicken keeps renaming rules in the Renaming Rules for Downloaded Transactions window. You can update the rules as needed.

5. To add a new rule, click **New**.

6. Type the name you want to use for the payee.

7. Select whether to rename the payee or memo.

8. Select the criterion for renaming the payee or memo.

9. If you already know the payee name or memo information for a downloaded transaction, type the name or partial name, depending on the renaming criteria you chose in step 6.

10. Click **OK**.

11. To edit a rule, select it and click **Edit**.

12. To remove a rule, select it and click **Delete**.

13. Select whether you want the renaming rules to be off or on when transactions are downloaded and whether you want Quicken to automatically rename transactions (both options are recommended to be on).

14. When you are finished with the renaming rules, click **Done**.

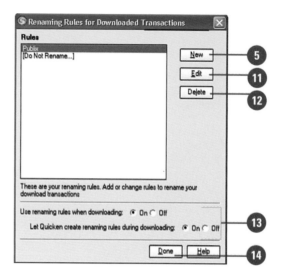

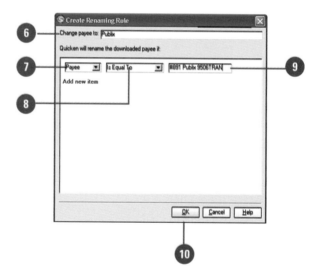

For Your Information

When transactions are downloaded, the payee name is often a series of numbers or a combination of numbers, letters, and symbols. Therefore, it is difficult to know what the payee name is until the transaction is downloaded. When you add the downloaded transaction to your register, you can edit the payee name at that time. Quicken adds this to the renaming rules and automatically changes the name the next time a transaction is downloaded for that payee.

Set Reminder Preferences

① To set preferences for when you want Quicken to display calendar notes, select **Reminders** in the **Select Preference Type** list

② Select the timeframe you want to use.

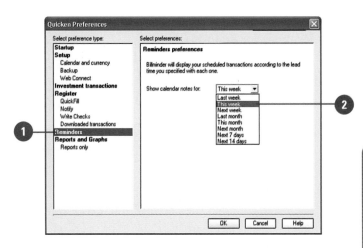

Set Reports and Graphs Preferences

① To set default date ranges for reports and graphs and customization preferences, select **Reports and Graphs** from the **Select Preference Type** list.

② To specify your own starting and ending dates, make the appropriate selections from the drop-down menus. Quicken uses these date ranges every time you create a report or graph.

③ To specify your own date ranges for comparison reports, make the appropriate selections from the drop-down menus. Quicken uses these date ranges whenever you create comparison reports.

④ Select whether to have Quicken create a new report/graph or change the existing report/graph when one is customized. Creating a new one retains the original report/graph and adds the customized report/graph as a new one. Customizing the report/graph overwrites the original version.

⑤ To customize reports before they are created, select **Customize Report/Graph Before Creating**. This allows you to customize report settings in the Customize window before you run the report/graph.

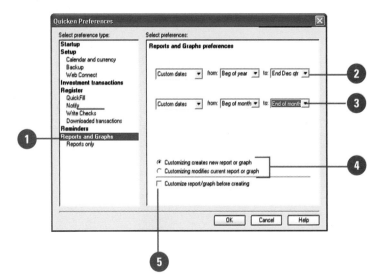

Set Preferences for Reports Only

1. To set preferences for only reports and not graphs, select **Reports Only** from the **Select Preference Type** list.

2. Select whether to show the account or category description, name, or both.

3. Select whether to use color, QuickZoom, and reminder options.

4. To set the decimal places for report figures, type the decimal points you want to use.

5. When you are finished setting up all your options, click **OK** to save your changes.

See Also

See "Working with Reports" on page 309 for more information about creating and customizing reports.

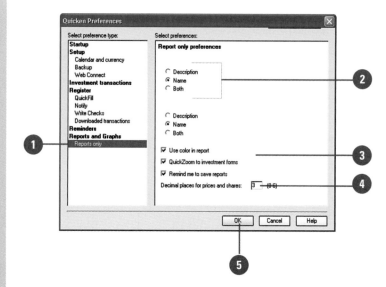

Setting Up Your Internet Connection

To use the online features in Quicken, such as downloading account information into Quicken or getting the latest stock quotes using One Step Update, you must have an Internet connection. If you do plan on using the online features, you can tell Quicken how you would like it to connect to the Internet.

Set Up an Internet Connection in Quicken

1 Click **Edit, Preferences, Internet Connection Setup**.

Continued, next page

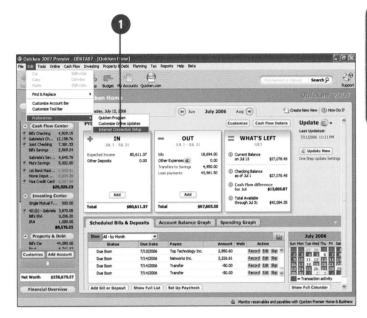

2 If you already have an Internet connection set up on your computer, select **Use My Computer's Internet Connection Settings to Establish a Connection When This Application Accesses the Internet**.

3 Click **Next**.

4 Review your connection information and click **Done**.

Did You Know?

You must register your copy of Quicken and have Internet service. Before you can use Quicken's online features, you must register your copy of the software and have Internet service set up on your computer. In addition, your creditor or bank must offer online services in order to set up and use online accounts.

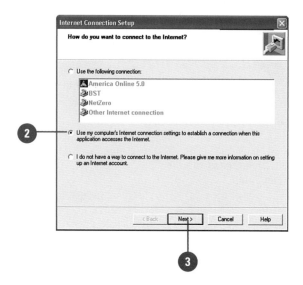

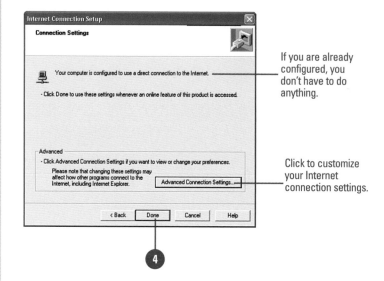

If you are already configured, you don't have to do anything.

Click to customize your Internet connection settings.

Setting Up Remote Internet Access to Your Accounts

Quicken offers a feature that allows you to access account and portfolio information (that is available for online access in Quicken) from anywhere that you have an Internet connection. For example, if you are on vacation, traveling for your job, or just away from your computer, you can tell Quicken to send your account information to Quicken.com. From that website, you can access your accounts, get updated portfolio share information, and so on. It's a way to manage your accounts and portfolio information when you are away from home.

Set Up Portfolio Accounts for Internet Access

1. Click **Edit, Preferences, Customize Online Updates**.

2. If you have portfolio accounts that you want to set up for remote access, click the **Portfolio** tab, and then click the accounts you want to set up.

    TIMESAVER *If you want all your accounts to be accessible from the Internet, you can quickly select them all by clicking **Mark All**. To quickly remove all accounts that are currently selected (check marks appear next the accounts that are selected for Internet access)—for example, when you are back home and don't need remote access any longer—click **Clear All**.*

3. Click the investment accounts that you want to access via the Internet. A check mark appears next to the accounts you select.

4. If you have investments on a watch list that you want to continue to track remotely, click the **Track My Watch List on Quicken.com** option.

> ### See Also
>
> *See "Tracking and Managing Investment Performance" on page 131 for more information about watch lists.*

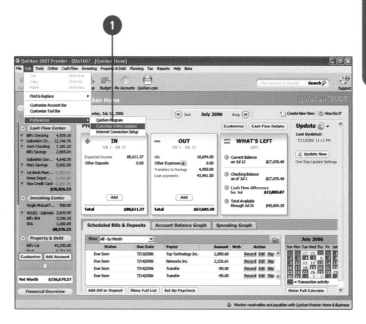

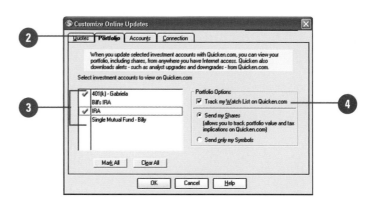

Continued, next page

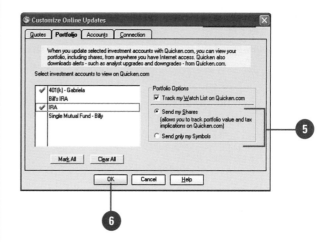

5 To view share (value and tax) information on Quicken.com, select **Send My Shares**. Or, to only see the symbols, select **Send Only My Symbols**.

6 Click **OK** to finish the setup or go to step 1 of the next task to set up or change remote access for your bank accounts.

Did You Know?

You can select the quotes you want to download. On the Quotes tab, you can select the quotes that you want to download to Quicken by clicking the security name. To add a new security, click **New Security**. To change an existing one, you select the security name and click **Edit Security**. In addition, you can look up security symbols by clicking the **Look Up** symbol.

Set Up Accounts for Internet Access

1 Click the **Accounts** tab.

2 Select the accounts that you want to access from Quicken.com.

See Also

See the previous task "Setting Up Remote Internet Access to Your Accounts" on page 53 for information on how to access the Accounts tab on the Customize Online Updates window.

3 If you already have accounts set up for remote access and you want to update the information on Quicken.com with the latest information from Quicken, select **Resend All Items to Quicken.com**.

4 Click **OK** or, to set Internet connection preferences, go to step 1 of the next task.

Did You Know?

You can view accounts on Quicken.com. Selecting accounts on the **Accounts** tab enables you to review account balances from anywhere, as long as you have Internet access and a login ID and password for Quicken.com.

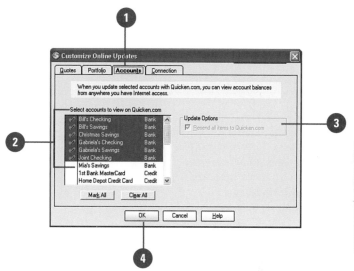

Did You Know?

The Resend All option is not available until after you update Quicken.com for the first time. After you update Quicken.com for the first time, the **Resend All Items to Quicken.com** option becomes available. For faster downloads using One Step Update, keep this check box cleared.

Set Connection Preferences

1 Click the **Connection** tab.

See Also

*See the "Set Up Portfolio Accounts for Internet Access" task on page 53 for information on how to access the **Connection** tab on the Customize Online Updates window.*

2 To participate in the usage study, select the **Quicken Usage Study** option. The usage study informs Intuit of how you use its software, information that's used to improve Quicken.

3 To send updated account information to Quicken.com each time you open Quicken, select **Run One Step Update When Starting Quicken.**

4 To be prompted to change your Quicken.com ID or password, select **Change My Quicken.Com Member ID and Password the Next Time I Run One Step Update**.

5 When you are finished making changes to the Customize Online Updates window, click **OK** to save all your changes.

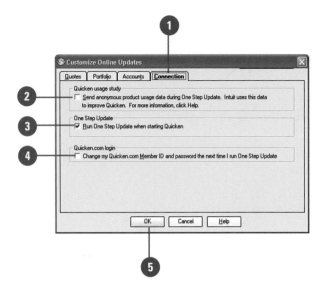

Using Quicken Home Page Features

Introduction

Whether you've been following along so far with installing and setting up Quicken or you've already been exploring other chapters and features, this chapter brings it all home—to the Quicken Home page, that is. The Quicken Home page is a central location for all your account information, where you can access, organize, and update account information; view a big picture of your financial health and well-being; and explore your net worth.

The account bar, which appears alongside the home page, provides quick access to all your accounts and is divided into activity centers that categorize your accounts in logical groups. You can use the centers to access each of your accounts.

In this chapter, you will learn how to record and manage your account transactions and how to automatically update account information using online updates. You'll also find helpful information on Quicken Tips and Quicken Services, which provide you with additional tools and advice to help you manage your finances. In addition, you'll be privy to some keyboard shortcuts that will have you tooling around Quicken like a pro in no time.

Using the Account Bar

See Also

See "Setting Quicken Preferences" on page 40 for more information on changing the position of the activity centers. See Chapters 4 through 6 for more information on using the different activity centers.

Navigate the Account Bar

1 If you're in another area of Quicken and want to return to the Home page, click **Quicken Home**.

2 To access your bank and credit card account information, click **Cash Flow Center**. You can also click an account name to go directly to the register for that account.

3 To access your investments, securities, or retirement account(s), click **Investing Center**.

4 To view property and debt accounts, such as your home, car, property loans, and so on, click **Property & Debt**.

5 Click the arrows at the bottom or top of the activity center to scroll down or up. The arrows appear lighter when there is information hiding and darker when there is no information hiding.

6 To change the width of the account bar, hover your mouse over the border between the account bar and the Home page until you see the double arrows. Then click, hold down your left mouse button, and drag to the right to expand it or drag to the left to reduce it.

The account bar contains the activity centers and is located on the left side of the home page (unless you changed the position or removed it in Chapter 2, "Learning Quicken Basics," when we covered setting Quicken preferences). The activity centers include the Cash Flow Center, which contains all your banking and credit card accounts; the Investing Center, which contains all your investment and retirement information; and the Property & Debt center, which contains account information for your property, assets, and liabilities. Each of these centers provides access to all your accounts, where you can review, change, and remove account information. The following task provides an overview of the activity centers and shows you how to quickly access your accounts and customize the account bar. We'll get into more of the specifics of using each activity center in Chapters 4, "Managing Your Accounts," through 6, "Managing Your Bills and Transactions."

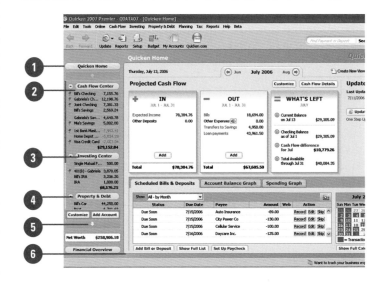

Did You Know?

You can also access account centers from the menus. All the account centers are accessible from the Cash Flow, Investing, and Property & Debt menus.

See Also

See "Setting Quicken Preferences" on page 40 for information on changing the position of the account bar.

Use the Activity Center

① Right-click in any area of the account bar to view a menu of actions you can perform. For example, you can hide the account bar completely, move it, or choose to view more or less information about each account.

② Create new accounts by clicking the **Add Account** button.

③ Your total net worth appears at the bottom of the account bar. To view a detailed breakdown of your net worth, click **Financial Overview**.

TIMESAVER *If there is a red flag next to one of your accounts, you can hover your mouse pointer (point, but don't click) over the account name to view the special message. Balances that appear in red and negative balances represent debt. Use the flags to help you keep up with your accounts. In the time it takes to take a quick glance at the activity bar, you'll know which accounts need your attention. This saves you the time and the effort of going into each account to review it.*

See Also

For more information on the Financial Overview center, see "Getting the Big Picture" on page 61.

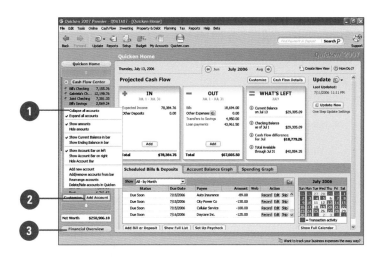

For Your Information

You can view a hidden account bar. If an account bar is hidden, a double-arrow (>>) appears in the upper-left corner of the Quicken window. Click it to view the hidden account bar.

3

Add or Remove Accounts on the Account Bar

① To change the accounts that appear and the order in which they appear on the account bar, click **Customize**.

② To remove an account from the account bar, select the appropriate box for that account in the **Hide in Navigation** column. A check indicates that the account does not appear in the account bar.

③ To add an account to the account bar, remove the check mark in the **Hide in Navigation** column check box.

④ Accounts automatically appear in alphabetic order. To move an account up or down on the list, select the account and click **Move Up** to move it up the list, or **Move Down** to move it down the list. Repeat the move until the account appears where you want it on the list.

⑤ To move an account to a different category—for example, to move a savings account to a spending account—select the account and click **Change Group**.

⑥ Select the new category for the account and click **OK**.

⑦ To return to the Quicken Home page, click **Close**.

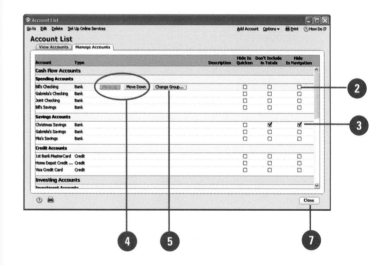

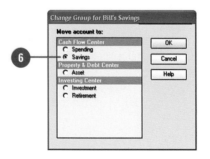

Getting the Big Picture

One nice feature of Quicken is the Financial Overview. It gives you a complete, big picture of your finances with the click of a button. It's a bird's-eye view of your overall net worth, based on your assets and liabilities for the month and for each month over the past year. Assets include savings or properties, and liabilities include your debt, such as credit card debt and loans. Your net worth is determined by subtracting your liabilities from your assets. You can see instantly where you stand and where you need to adjust your financial situation, if needed.

View Your Assets, Liabilities, and Net Worth

1 On the activity bar, click **Financial Overview**.

2 If you're not already there, click the **Net Worth** tab to view a graph view of your assets, liabilities, and net worth over the past year.

3 To view your assets, liabilities, or net worth for a specific month, hover your mouse pointer (point, but don't click) over a bar on the graph. A tooltip box pops up, showing you what your net worth was for that time period.

4 To see a full view of the graph, click **Show Full Graph**.

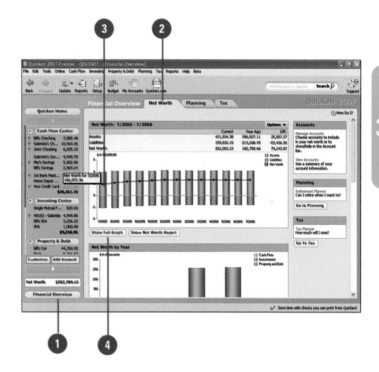

See Also

See Chapter 9, "Planning for the Future," on page 223, for more detailed information on using the Planning Center and creating plans. See Chapter 12, "Managing Your Tax Information," on page 325, for more information on using the Tax Center.

For Your Information

You can get a clue with the color key.

There is a color key in the upper-right corner to help you determine which colors on the graph represent assets, liabilities, and net worth.

View Net Worth Graph Details

1. From the Net Worth window, you can customize the graph by selecting a custom date from the **Date Range** drop-down or a different interval of time from the Interval drop-down.

See Also

See Chapter 11, "Working with Reports," on page 309, for more information on viewing, customizing, saving, and printing reports.

2. Click **Show Report** to see a detailed breakdown of your assets and liabilities, including their totals.

3. Click **Hide Graph** to view only the report showing the breakdown of your assets and liabilities. When you are finished reviewing the information, close the window.

Did You Know?

There are alternative ways of accessing the graph and report. There are multiple ways to access the full graph net worth view or the Net Worth report. You can use the Options menu located in the upper-right corner of the Net Worth tab on the Financial Overview to access the same information as shown in this and the preceding tasks. Clicking the **Show Net Worth Report** button (shown next to the **Show Full Graph** button in the previous task) also opens the Net Worth report. In addition, you can right-click the graph to access the full graph net worth view and report.

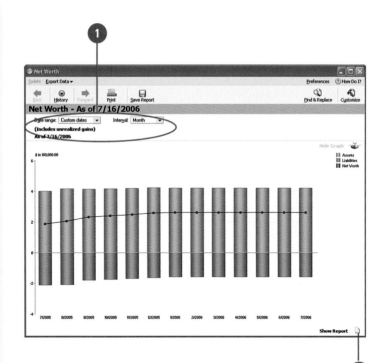

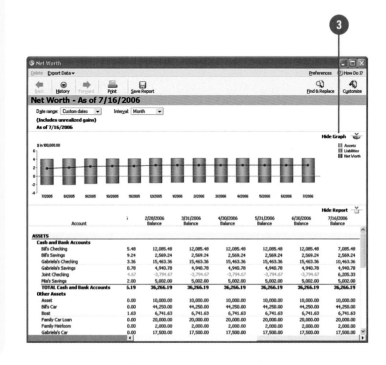

View Additional Net Worth Breakdowns

1 To view additional net worth information, scroll down to the **Net Worth** section to reveal additional details.

2 The **Net Worth by Year** section shows your cash flow, investment, or property and debt net worth for a specific year or year-to-date. Hover your mouse over the bars to see the net worth for each activity.

3 The **Net Worth Allocation** section shows what percentage of your net worth comes from your cash flow, investment, or property. Hover your mouse over the pie chart to see how the net worth percentages break down.

4 Scroll down farther to view the **Net Worth by Year Summary** section. It provides net worth by year and year-to-date for each of your cash flow, investment, and property accounts. Figures that appear in red are negative net worth.

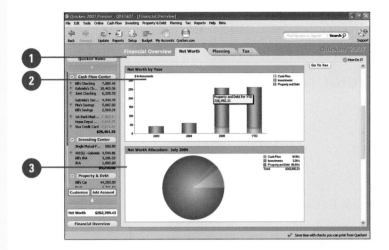

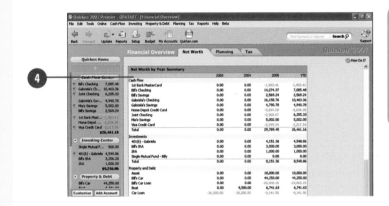

For Your Information

You can hide accounts in Quicken.

Hiding an account doesn't mean you'll need to open up a Swiss bank account with an alias. When you want Quicken to track the balance of an account, but you don't want that balance used for net worth or considered for a debt reduction plan, you can hide it. For example, if you have a savings goal, you can continue to save the set amount each month; Quicken tracks how much you are saving, but the account and the amount are hidden until you reach your goal. Another situation where you should hide an account is when an account is closed or has a zero balance. Instead of deleting it, you should hide it so that Quicken can still use it for reporting and forecasting, but the account won't clutter up your account lists. For more, see the task on the next page.

Selecting Accounts to Include in Your Net Worth

By default, Quicken uses all the accounts that you have set up to determine your net worth. You can add and remove the accounts you want Quicken to use when determining your net worth. Removing an account that you don't want to use for your net worth does not remove it from Quicken. You are simply telling Quicken that you don't want it to use the financials for that account when it calculates your net worth. By changing the accounts you want used for your net worth, you can make better financial decisions about your savings, investments, debt, and so on by seeing which accounts are working for you or against you.

Select Accounts to Include in Your Net Worth

1. On the Net Worth tab in the Financial Overview center, click the Manage Accounts link. The Account List window opens.

2. Select the boxes in the Hide in Quicken column for each account you want to hide from account lists and net worth totals. Or, to remove a hidden account, select the checked box for that account.

3. Select the boxes in the **Don't Include in Totals** column for each account you want to exclude from your net worth totals. Or, to include totals for an account, remove the check mark by clicking it.

4. When you are finished selecting or removing accounts for your net worth totals, click **Close**.

> ### Did You Know?
>
> **There are other ways to access the Account List window.** You can access the Account List window by clicking **My Accounts** on the toolbar or by clicking **Customize** on the account bar.

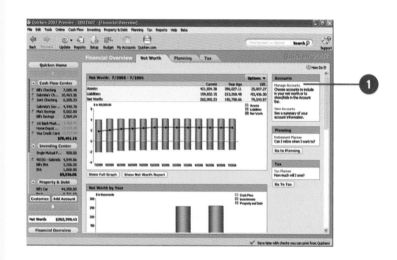

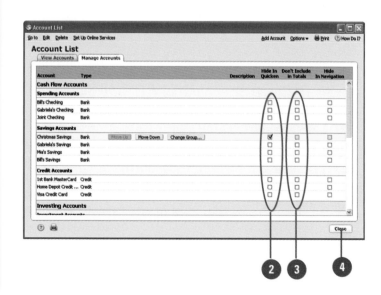

Using Projected Cash Flow

The first section on the Quicken Home page is Projected Cash Flow. It provides a forecast of your incoming and outgoing cash flow for the current month. Your projected cash flow is based on all the information you've entered into Quicken, including your scheduled transactions and historical trends, if applicable. You can view what your income and expenditures are and what's left after your expenditures have been subtracted from your income. In addition, you can add new income or expenditure transactions, access a comprehensive list of your income and expenditures, and view your cash flow for each day of the month. The Projected Cash Flow section allows you to have your finger on the pulse of your incoming and outgoing cash flow.

View Your Cash Flow

1. The **IN** section provides projections for all your income. Click **Expected Income** to view a list of your paid and scheduled income transactions by date.

2. Click **Close** when you are finished to return to the Projected Cash Flow page.

3. The **OUT** section provides projections for all your outgoing bills and expenses. Click **Bills** to view a list of your scheduled bills and transactions by date.

Continued, next page

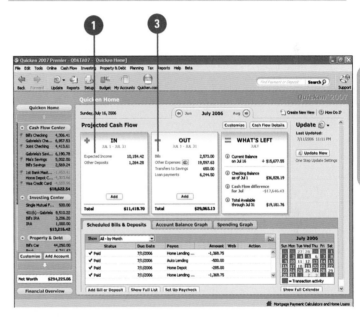

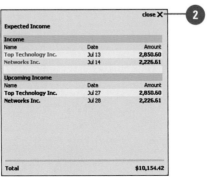

The **WHAT'S LEFT** section provides projected balances after your expenses and bills have been deducted from your income. Click **Cash Flow difference for [month]** to view a list of all your scheduled income and expenses by date.

From the Cash Flow Details window, you can access your account registers or print the list. Click **Close** when you are finished.

To add a new income or expense transaction, click **Add** and complete the Add Transaction window.

See Also

See "Adding New Bills" on page 149 for more information on adding account transactions.

To change the accounts in your cash flow or to exclude an account from your account totals, click **Customize** and make the appropriate changes.

See Also

See "Selecting Accounts to Include in Your Net Worth" on page 64 for more information on selecting or excluding the accounts used to determine your cash flow.

To view projections for a previous month, click the back arrow; to view future months, click the forward arrow.

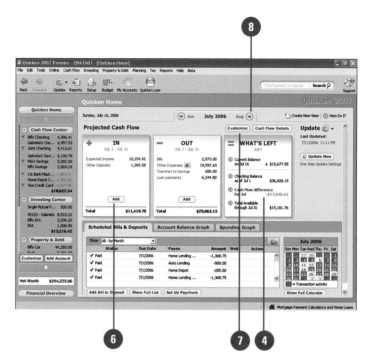

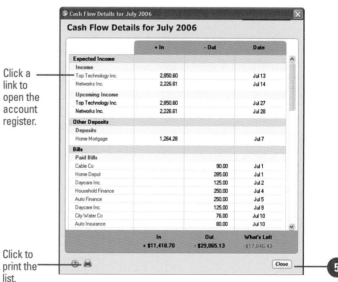

Click a link to open the account register.

Click to print the list.

For Your Information

You can click the **Cash Flow Details** button above the What's Left section to open the Cash Flow Details window, in addition to using the Cash Flow Difference link shown in step 4.

You Can Create Your Own Look for the Quicken Home Page

If the default Quicken Home page design doesn't work for you, change it. To do this, follow these steps:

1. From the Quicken Home page, click **Create New View**.

2. Type a name for the new view.

3. From the **Available Items** section, select the items you want to add to your view. You can select more than one item by holding down the **Ctrl** key and clicking each item you want to add.

4. Click **Add**. The items you select move to the Chosen Items section.

5. To remove an item, from the Chosen Items section, select it and click **Remove**.

6. To specify the order in which the items appear on the Quicken Home page, from the Chosen Items section, select an item and click **Move Up** to move it up one space or click **Move Down** to move it down one space. Repeat this step until the items appear the way you want.

7. When you are finished creating your new view, click **OK**. Quicken creates the new view and displays it on a new tab.

8. You can update your view by clicking the **Customize** drop-down menu on your new tab and selecting **Customize This View**.

9. To remove the view, select **Delete This View**.

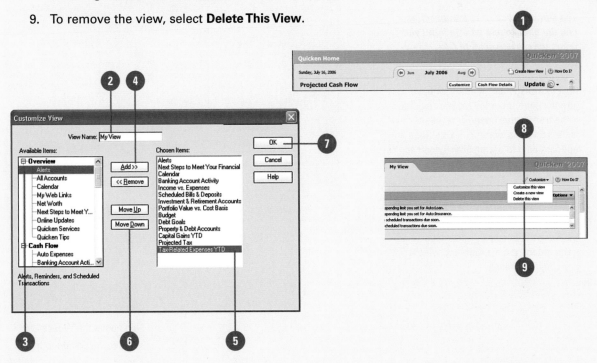

Using Scheduled Bills & Deposits

Record Transactions

1. Open the Quicken Home page and scroll down to the **Scheduled Bills & Deposits** tab.

2. If a Print button appears next to a transaction, it is because that transaction is paid using Quicken checks, which are printed on special checks that you print using your printer.

3. Click **Enter** to log a transaction in your register. The transaction information opens in the Record Transaction window.

Did You Know?

The status and color of a transaction and the check mark next to it tell you what actions you need to take. When you select the All–by Month option from the Show menu, the check marks next to transactions mean they have already been recorded in your register. If the transaction appears in red, it means that it is overdue. If Due Soon appears next to a transaction, look at the Due Date column to take note of when it is due. If Due Today appears in the Status column, the transaction is due on the current day. Use the Current–by Status to sort all your transactions to quickly see which transactions are overdue and which are coming up soon.

The Scheduled Bills & Deposits section of the Quicken Home page lists all transactions for the current month and those that have not been completed from previous months. Transactions include paychecks, bills, mortgage payments, utilities, banking, and every other account transaction you have entered in Quicken. You can use Scheduled Bills & Deposits to enter the transactions in your register—for example, when you make a payment for a bill or when a paycheck has been deposited into your bank account. In addition, you can add new transactions, change information for a single transaction, make changes to all transactions for an account, or delete a transaction. There are also some tools you can use to review your account checks and balances over a specific period of time by using graphs, or you can use the calendar to see exactly where your transactions fall within a month. Scheduled Bills & Deposits provides an efficient and quick way of keeping up with your incoming and outgoing account transactions.

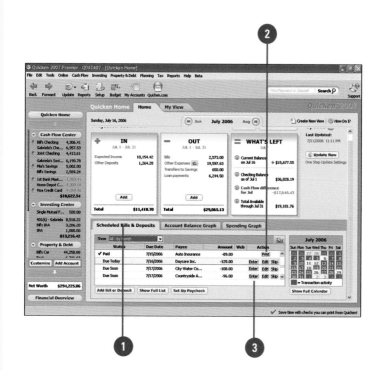

To make changes to this transaction—for example, an amount—clicking in any of the fields and type over the existing information.

You can also click the **Edit** and **Delete** buttons to change or remove information, respectively, as shown in this example.

To add information to a paycheck transaction, click one of the **Add** buttons. For example, in this instance we are updating a paycheck transaction by clicking **Add Pre-Tax Deduction** to add medical insurance information.

Change the name, if needed, select the category that you want to use to track this expense, type the amount, and click **OK**.

When you are finished making changes, or if you don't need to make any changes to the transaction, click **Enter** (as in this example). Or, if you are recording a payment, click **Record Payment**.

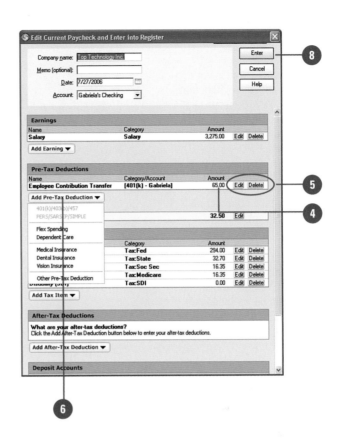

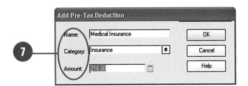

Did You Know?

Changes that you make when entering a transaction apply only to that transaction. When you enter a transaction and make changes to the transaction information, the change applies only to the current transaction. The change does not apply to future transactions for the account. If you want to make changes that apply to all transactions for an account, you must edit the transaction. See "Edit Transactions" on the next page.

Edit Transactions

1 To edit all future instances of a scheduled transaction, from the Scheduled Bills & Deposits section of the Quicken Home page, click **Edit** next to the transaction you want to update.

2 Make any changes needed, keeping in mind that these changes will take effect for all future transactions for this account.

3 To change when you want to be reminded the transaction is due, whether you want the transaction to appear as a bill in Scheduled Bills & Deposits, or to change the group to which it is assigned, click **Options**.

4 Click **OK** to save the changes.

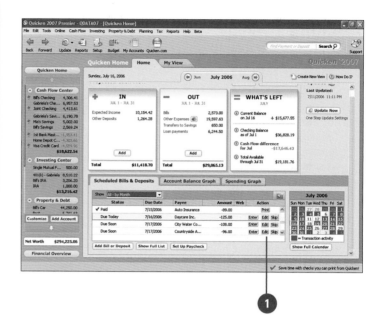

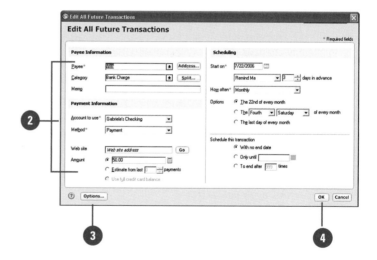

Tracking Transactions with Multiple Categories

If you want to track a transaction between different categories, you can add up to 30 categories. For example, if you want to track a payment you make to a credit card, for which part of the payment goes to the principal balance and part goes to satisfy interest, you could track this transaction under the Bank Charge and Interest categories.

1. You can split a scheduled transaction from either the Edit All Future Transactions window (accessed by using the **Edit** button from **Scheduled Bills & Deposits**) or the **Add Transaction** window (accessed from the Quicken Home page but not shown).

2. Click **Split** (not shown).

3. In the Split Transaction window, in the **Amount** box, type the amount you want to track for the first category.

4. Click the second line and from the **Category** drop-down menu, select the second category. Then type the amount for that category.

5. Create as many categories as you need (up to 30) and when you are finished, click **Adjust**. The figure in Transaction Total should equal the total amount of the transaction. If it is not, adjust your split amounts until the total equals the correct amount.

6. Click **OK** to complete the split. The Category field for this transaction now shows "Split" and is grayed out. You can change the split by repeating this task.

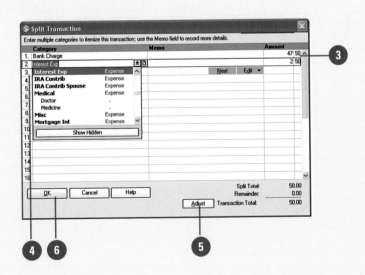

Skip Transactions

1. To skip the current transaction, for example, if you don't intend to apply a transaction for a particular time period (for example, for the current month), in Scheduled Bills & Deposits, click **Skip**.

2. Click **Yes** to skip the current transaction or **No** to cancel. If you click **Yes**, the transaction will show up in the Scheduled Bills & Deposits list the next time it is due.

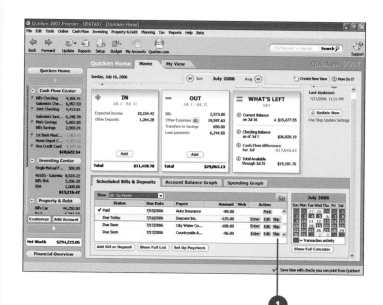

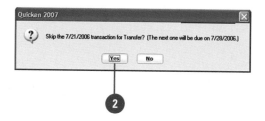

Did You Know?

Check marks show completed transactions. The check marks next to the transactions shown in step 1 indicate that those transactions have been entered in the appropriate registers.

Add a New Transaction

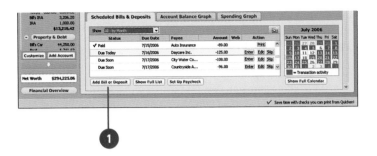

1 In Scheduled Bills & Deposits, click **Add Bill or Deposit**.

2 In **Payee**, type the name of the recipient (a person, company, creditor, or for money transfers, the name of the account) to which the transaction is being made, if applicable.

3 From **Category**, select the category you want to track for this transaction. If you don't see the category you want to use, type in a new one. (When you click OK in step 12, you are prompted to create the new category.)

4 To assign more than one catgory to a transaction (with the exception of transfers), click **Split**.

5 Click in **Memo** to type a note about the transaction, if desired.

6 From the **Account to Use** drop-down list, select the account from which payments are made.

7 From the **Method** drop-down list, select the type of transaction. This example uses Payment.

8 If a website is associated with this bill—for example, if you are making payments through a creditor's website—type the website address in the **Web Site** field.

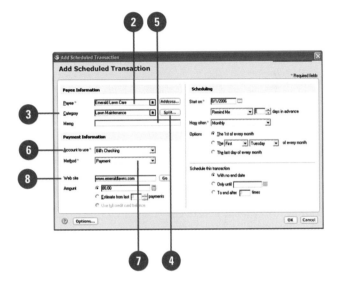

See Also

See "Working with Reports" on page 309 for more information on running reports. See "Tracking Transactions with Multiple Categories" in this chapter for information on assigning more than one category to a transaction.

Did You Know?

Assigning categories can help you track your spending. By assigning categories to all your transactions, you can see exactly where your money is going. Quicken tracks categories across all your accounts so that when you run a report, it can show you exactly how much you've spent for a specific category.

Continued, next page

9 In **Amount**, type the amount of the transaction. If you used split transactions, the amount will already be there, but will be grayed out so that you can't enter an amount. If the amount varies, type **0** or select the **Estimate** option and specify the number of payments to use as an average.

10 In the Scheduling section, select or enter the begin, end, and frequency information for the transaction. If this is a one-time transaction, from **How Often**, select **Only Once**.

11 In the Schedule this Transaction section, select an option to indicate when you want the transaction to stop. If the transaction does not have an end date or you are unsure when it will end, select **With No End Date**.

12 Click **OK**. The transaction is added to the Scheduled Bills & Deposits list.

13 If you entered a new category in step 3, you are prompted to enter a new category. Click **Yes** to set up the new category in the Set Up Category window or **No** to select a different category.

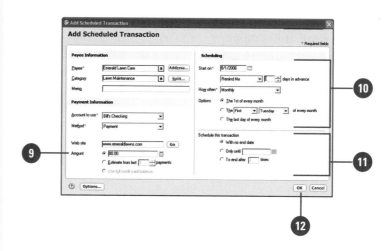

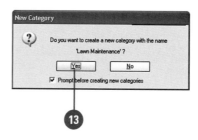

Did You Know?

You can pay your online bills directly from Quicken. When you enter a website address in the Web Site field in the Add Scheduled Transaction window, Quicken places a Go link next to that transaction in the Scheduled Bills & Deposits section of the Quicken Home page and in the Cash Flow Center. You can click **Go** and open the site to pay your bill without leaving Quicken.

Did You Know?

You can add the payee address to use later. To add the address for a payee, click the **Address** button next to the Payee drop-down menu and complete the Address window. Be sure to select the **QuickFill List** option so that the payee is available throughout Quicken. By selecting this option, when you are working in other areas of Quicken and you need to use this payee—for example, when using Quicken checks—Quicken can automatically complete the payee address information for you and print the information on Quicken checks. In addition, if you have the Premier Home and Business version of Quicken, you can use the address for printing mailing labels, envelopes, and business forms.

Create an Alternative View of the Transactions

1. To change the transactions you see, select an option from the **Show** drop-down menu.

2. To see a bar graph view of your finances, click the **Account Balance Graph** tab. Hover your mouse over a bar on the graph to view your balance for that time period.

3. To view a different account, select it from the **Show** drop-down list.

Continued, next page

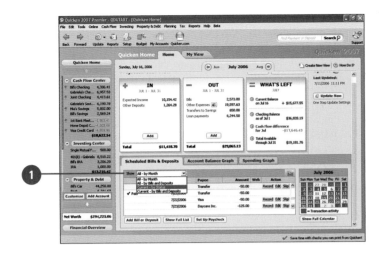

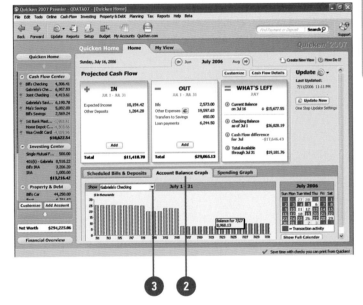

④ To view spending for your accounts broken down by category and payee, click **Spending Graph**.

⑤ To get a closer look at a specific category or payee, hover your mouse over a slice of the pie graph.

⑥ To view the Expenses report for either your account categories or payees, click the **Show Full Graph** button.

⑦ To add or remove accounts, or change the categories that are included in the spending, click **Customize**.

⑧ From the **Accounts** tab, select or clear the accounts you want included in the spending totals and from the **Categories** tab, select or clear the categories you want to use.

⑨ Click **OK** when you are finished.

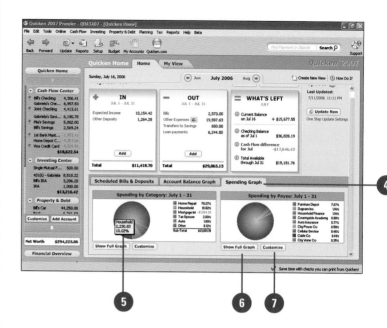

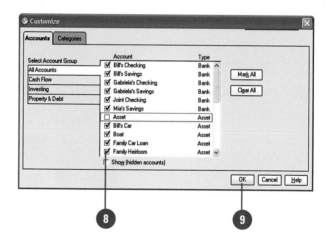

Use the Calendar to View Monthly Transactions

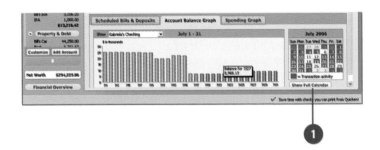

1 To view calendars with the dates of all your transactions, from either the Scheduled Bills & Deposits or Account Balance Graph tabs, click **Show Full Calendar**.

2 Click **More** on any day of the calendar to view the transactions for that day in detail.

3 Perform actions to manage your transactions, such as creating a new transaction, recording, or editing the transaction.

4 Click **Close** when you are finished.

5 To add a note to a day on the calendar, right-click the day and select **Note**. You can also click **Add Note** on the menu.

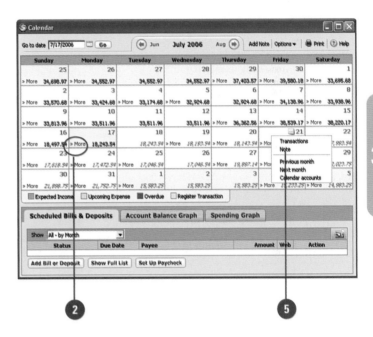

Did You Know?

Use the calendar to manage your transactions and bills. Print the calendar to keep as a reminder or reference when paying your bills by clicking **Print** on the Calendar window menu.

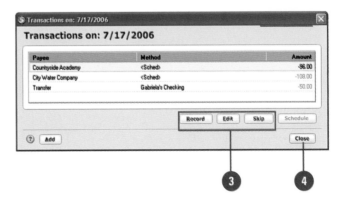

Type your note and click **OK**. The note shows up on the calendar as a small sticky note, which you can click to open, edit, or delete.

To view a different month, select it from the **Go to Date** field and click **Go**. You can also click the back and forward arrows.

You can perform the same functions from the calendar as you can from the Quicken Home page.

When you are finished using the calendar and ready to return to the Quicken Home page, close the calendar.

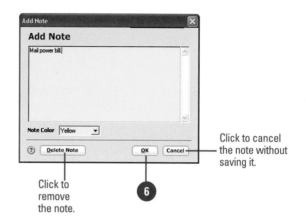

Click to cancel the note without saving it.

Click to remove the note.

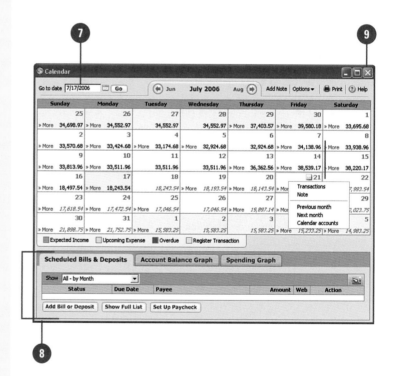

Using Online Updates

There is a little feature on the Quicken Home page that shouldn't be overlooked. You can use it to make your life easier when it comes to managing your financial goals and maintaining all your accounts. It is the Update feature, which you can use to tell Quicken the accounts for which you want to download cleared transactions or quotes, when you want to download them, and how often. You can also select account information that you want to upload to Quicken.com via the Internet. You use the One Step Update to do all of this. In addition, using the Update feature, you can also manage your passwords and schedule your online account updates.

Set Up Online Updates

① Click **Update** and select **One Step Update**.

② Select a specific account you want to update or select **All Accounts** to update all of your accounts in Quicken. If you have not set up any of your accounts for online updates, you are prompted to do so. Also, if you have not already registered Quicken, are prompted to do so.

IMPORTANT *Only the accounts that you have set up for online access are listed for you to choose from. Remember that your copy of Quicken must be registered before you can use this feature. If your bank or creditor offers online access to your account information, you should have a login ID and password. You will need this information to set up One Step Update.*

> ## See Also
>
> *See "Registering Quicken" on page 24 for more information on registering your copy of Quicken.*

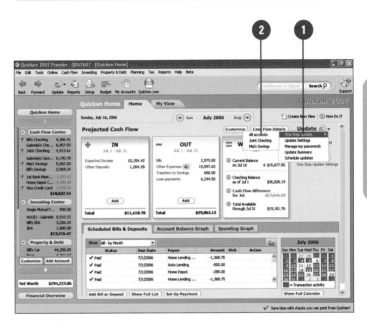

To set up or change updating investment and stock quotes, select the **Download Quotes, Asset Classes, Headlines, and Alerts** option.

If an account has already been set up for online updates, select the accounts you want to use or clear the accounts you no longer want to download.

If an account has not been set up yet but online update is available, click **Activate for One Step Update**.

To upload information to Quicken.com, select the **Quicken.com** option and then select **Select Quicken.Com Data to Download**.

To select the information you want to download and/or update, click **Schedule Updates**.

Continued, next page ▶

See Also

See "Setting Up Remote Internet Access to Your Accounts" on page 53 for more information on using Quicken.com.

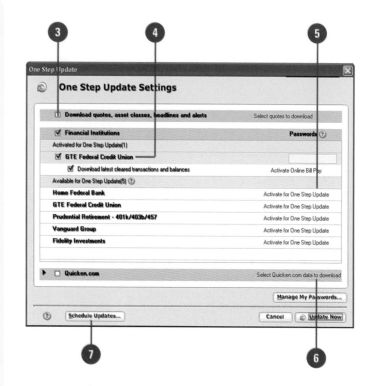

8 Select the information for which you want to schedule times to download.

9 Select the days on which you want the update to run and then from the **At** drop-down list, select the run time. Updates run within 15 minutes of the time you select.

10 Select when you would like to be prompted to enter your password.

11 To set up a PIN Vault password, click **Password Vault**. A PIN Vault password is required in order to use scheduled updates.

TIMESAVER *Take advantage of the online updates. Using the online updates to download your account transactions and investment quotes enables you to always keep your accounts up-to-date with the latest information. When you download your transactions, Quicken automatically places the transactions on the Downloaded Transactions tabs in each of the appropriate account registers. From there, all you have to do is add the transactions to your register. This saves you time and ensures that your balances and transaction information are accurate. This saves you even more time and frustration when it comes time to balance your accounts.*

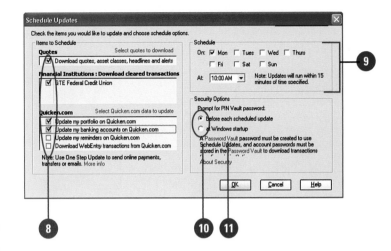

3

Set Up Your Passwords in the Password Vault

① Review the Password Vault information and click **Next**.

② Select the financial institution for which you want to enter the account password and click **Next**.

③ Click **Add Password Vault** to set up a password to protect the Password Vault (not shown).

④ In **Password**, type your PIN Vault password. In **Re-enter**, type it again, and then click **Add**.

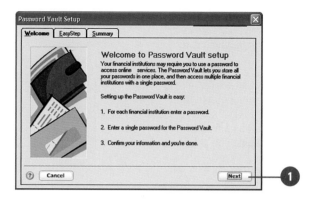

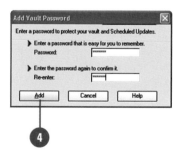

Did You Know?

You can use the Password Vault to keep track of all your account passwords. So that you don't have to remember your account passwords for all your online accounts, use the Password Vault. Once you enter all of your account passwords into the Password Vault, you can then set up one password that will allow you to access all of your online accounts through Quicken. Do your research to make sure that your accounts are safe. Ensure that your financial institutions offer secure connections, you have a good Internet service provider that offers secure and private Internet access, secure your computer with a personal firewall and virus protection software, and password-protect your Quicken file. Also, regularly change your passwords (every three months or so) as an extra security measure.

Continued, next page

5 To change your Password Vault password, click **Change Vault Password**.

6 To add a new password, click **Add Password**.

7 To change your password, click **Change Password**.

8 To remove a password, select it and click **Delete Password**.

9 To print the list of passwords, click **Print**.

10 When you are finished with your passwords, click **Done**.

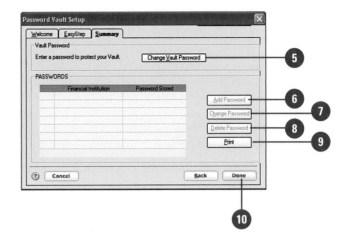

Keyboard Shortcuts

There are alternative ways you can move around in Quicken, other than using the menus or links found on Quicken windows. You can use certain keyboard key combinations, as shown in Table 3.1, to quickly get where you want to go. Keyboard commands are broken down into logical categories. Some shortcut commands require two or more keys. To use these shortcuts, you press and hold the first key and then press and hold the second. For example, to open the Quicken Home page from anywhere in the program, you hold down the Alt key and then press the Home key.

If you elected in Quicken Preferences to use Quicken standard keyboard commands, be aware the common keyboard commands for Windows change when you're in Quicken. For example, to use the Windows **Cut** command while you're in Quicken world, the keyboard shortcut is **Shift+Del**; for **Copy**, it becomes **Crtl+Ins**; and for **Paste**, it's **Shift+Ins**. In addition, these commands only work in specific areas of Quicken—for example, account registers. If you are not sure of the commands available to you while you're in a specific area of the program, refer to the main menus. The available shortcuts appear on the appropriate menus in Quicken.

Table 3.1   Quicken Keyboard Shortcuts

Quicken Features	
Command	**Shortcut**
Go to the Quicken Home page	Alt+Home
Go to the register	Ctrl+R
Write checks	Ctrl+W
Go to the calendar	Ctrl+K
View loans	Ctrl+H
Go to the Account list	Ctrl+A
Go to the Category list	Ctrl+C
Go to the Class list	Ctrl+L
Go to the Scheduled Transaction list	Ctrl+J
Go to the Memorized Payee list	Ctrl+T
Print	Ctrl+P
Select an item in a list	Type the first letter of the item

Check Features

Command	Shortcut
Decrease date or check number	- (minus key)
Increase date or check number	+ (plus key)
Copy data from the field above the currently ' selected field in the Split Transaction window	(single quote key)
Copy the payee name when the address field is selected in the Write Checks window	' (single quote key)
Copy a field in the register	Ctrl+Ins
Cut a field in the register	Shift+Del
Paste a field in the register	Shift+Ins
Delete a transaction or split line	Ctrl+D
Find a transaction	Ctrl+F
Go to a new transaction	Ctrl+N
Insert a transaction	Ctrl+I
Memorize a transaction	Ctrl+M
QuickFill, automatic recall	Type payee name
QuickFill, automatic completion	Tab
Record a transaction	Enter or Ctrl+Enter
Open the Split Transaction window	Ctrl+S
Go to Transfer	Ctrl+X
Void a transaction	Ctrl+V

Investment Features

Command	Shortcut
Go to Portfolio view	Ctrl+U
Decrease or increase a security price by $1/16$	- (minus key) or + (plus key)
Select a security	Ctrl+Y

Help

Command	Shortcut
Open the Help contents	F1

3

Review and Complete Online Updates

1 Review your scheduled updates selections and make any necessary changes.

2 Click **OK** to complete the scheduled updates.

3 Click **OK**. At the scheduled time, Quicken displays the Password dialog box, prompts you to type your Password Vault password, and downloads/uploads the latest transactions. When the transmission is complete, a summary window opens showing the accounts were successfully downloaded.

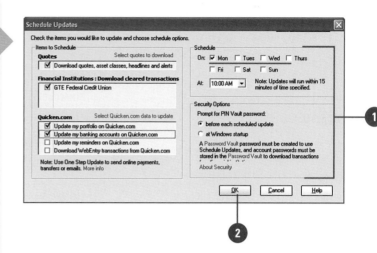

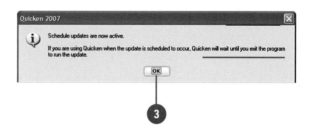

Did You Know?

Quicken cannot update accounts while it is open. You cannot have Quicken open when it downloads account information. Instead, you are prompted to enter your Password Vault password and the information is downloaded at the designated time. You should see an icon in your Windows taskbar that lets you know Quicken is downloading. If you are in Quicken at the time an update is scheduled to run, Quicken waits until you are out of the program to download the transactions and upload any online payments.

Managing Your Accounts

Introduction

To get the most out of Quicken features and to ensure that the reports, graphs, and other analysis tools provide you with an accurate portrayal of your financial situation, you should keep all your account information current in Quicken. This means from time-to-time you'll have to add new accounts, edit existing account information, and possibly remove accounts.

There are several locations from which you can manage your accounts in Quicken. You can add and edit accounts from the individual account centers; for example, the Spending & Savings account center. You can also use the Quicken Home page and the Quicken Express Setup.

Although you can manage your accounts from just about anywhere in Quicken, the most convenient area to manage all your accounts is the Account List window. All your accounts to date are listed in this window. From the Account List window, you can add, edit, delete, and set up online services for each of your accounts. In addition, there are several other tasks you can perform using this window. This chapter shows you how to add the most common account types, edit your accounts, and delete your accounts.

What You'll Do

Add New Spending and Savings Accounts

Add New Credit Card Accounts

Add New Investment Accounts

Add New Property and Debt Accounts

Edit Accounts

Delete Accounts

Manage Loan Accounts

Adding New Accounts

Adding accounts is very similar for all account types. The following tasks step through the setup process for each of the following account types: spending and savings, credit card, investment, and property and debt. Depending on the types of accounts you have, online accessibility, and other differences, such as currency, the steps to add accounts may differ from what you see here.

Add New Spending or Savings Accounts

① Open the Account List window by clicking **My Accounts** on the toolbar.

TIMESAVER *You can also access the Account List window by clicking the **Tools** menu and selecting **Account List**.*

② Click **Add Account**.

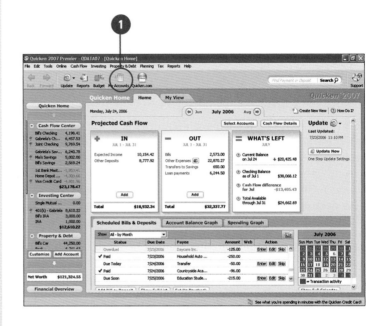

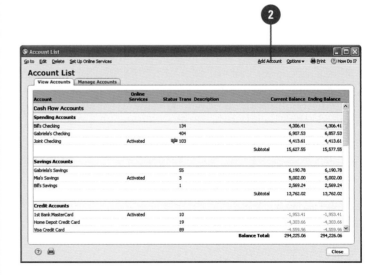

③ Type or select the name of the financial institution where the account is held and click **Next**.

④ Select **Yes** if you can download the account information directly from your financial institution (shown in this example) or select **No** to enter the account information yourself. Then click **Next**.

See Also

See "Add New Investment Retirement or Accounts" on page 95 in this chapter to learn how to add accounts manually.

Did You Know?

You cannot use online features to add accounts Quicken does not recognize. If Quicken does not recognize the name you entered in step 3, you are prompted to select the name of your financial institution. If the name is not listed, click **None of These** and then click **Next**. You will have to enter the rest of the account information manually, rather than download the information, as shown in this task.

Continued, next page ▶

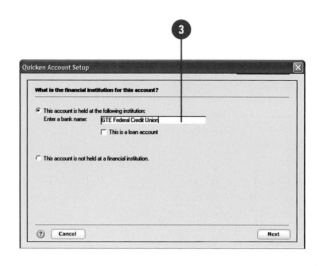

③

Quicken Account Setup

What is the financial institution for this account?

⊙ This account is held at the following institution:
Enter a bank name: GTE Federal Credit Union

☐ This is a loan account

○ This account is not held at a financial institution.

⑦ Cancel   Next

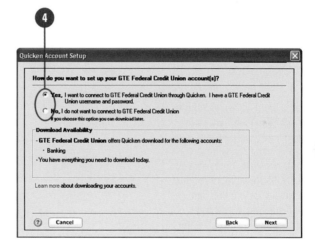

④

Quicken Account Setup

How do you want to set up your GTE Federal Credit Union account(s)?

⊙ **Yes**, I want to connect to GTE Federal Credit Union through Quicken. I have a GTE Federal Credit Union username and password.

○ **No**, I do not want to connect to GTE Federal Credit Union. If you choose this option you can download later.

Download Availability
- GTE Federal Credit Union offers Quicken download for the following accounts:
  · Banking
- You have everything you need to download today.

Learn more about downloading your accounts.

⑦ Cancel   Back   Next

4

5 Make sure that you are connected to the Internet, type your login ID (this is usually your account number), your password, and in the Confirm field, type your password again. Then click **Next**. Quicken connects to your financial institution and locates your account(s).

6 To use an existing account name, select it from the Quicken Account Name drop-down list; otherwise, select **Add a New Account in Quicken** to create a new name.

7 Type the name of the new Quicken account and click **OK**. This is the name that will be used within Quicken only.

Did You Know?

You must have a login ID and password to download your bank account information. To download your bank account information, you must already have a login ID and password. If you don't, you can click the link (if provided) to request an ID and password, or you can call your financial institution. If you don't have online access now, you can enter your bank information manually, and when you get your login ID and password, you can start downloading your account information from then on.

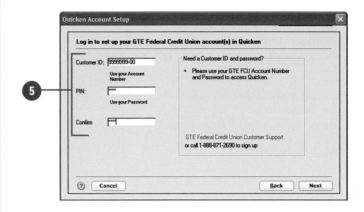

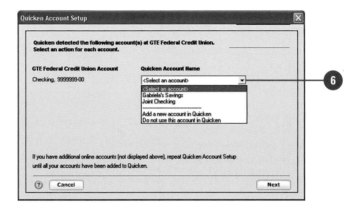

8 Click **Done**. Quicken creates the account and connects to your financial institution to download your transactions.

9 On the One Step Update Summary, click **Close**.

10 Repeat steps 2–9 for each spending or savings account you want to add.

See Also

See "Downloading and Adding Transactions from Your Account Register" on page 162 for information on how to add the transactions that were downloaded to your account register.

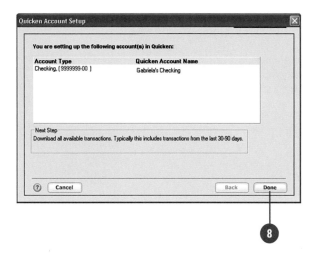

8

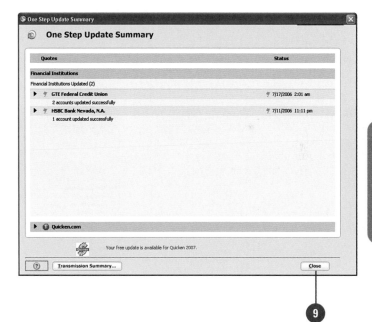

9

Add New Credit Card Accounts

① Open the Account List window by clicking **My Accounts** on the toolbar. You can also click the Tools menu and select Account List.

② Click **Add Account**.

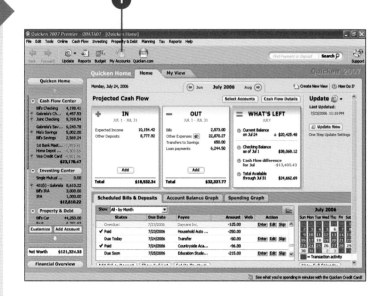

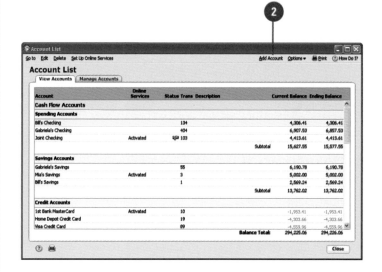

3 Type or select the name of the financial institution where the credit card account is held and click **Next**.

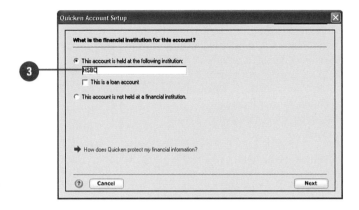

Did You Know?

You cannot use online features to add accounts Quicken does not recognize. If Quicken does not recognize the name you entered in step 3, you are prompted to select the name of your financial institution. If the name is not listed, click **None of These** and then click **Next**. You will have to enter the rest of the account information manually, rather than download the information, as shown in this task.

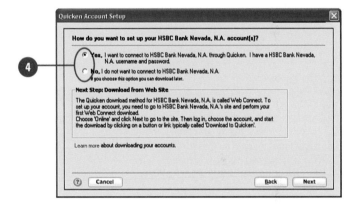

4 Select **Yes** if you can download the account information directly from your financial institution. Or select **No** to enter the account information yourself. Then click **Next.**

Did You Know?

You can set up an account manually and update it later online. If you don't have online access to this credit card account or if you want to set up the account first and download your account transactions later, click No in step 4 and follow the setup prompts. When the account is created, you can go into the account register or use the Account List window to set up online access for the account.

Continued, next page

4

5 Make sure that you are connected to the Internet, type your login ID password, and in Reenter Password, type your password again. Then click **Next**. Quicken connects to your financial institution and locates your account(s).

6 Complete the account set up as show in steps 6–9 of the previous task, "Add New Spending or Savings Accounts."

7 Repeat steps 2–6 for each credit card account you want to add.

Did You Know?

You must have a login ID and password to download your bank account information. In order to download your credit card account information, you must already have a login ID and password. If you don't, you can click the **Sign Up Now** button to request the ID and password, or you can call your financial institution. If you don't have online access now, you can enter your statement and credit limit information manually. When you get your login ID and password, you can start downloading your account information from then on. In addition, you may be able to download your account information from your financial institution's website using Web connect files, and then import the information into Quicken. For more information about importing files, see Chapter 2.

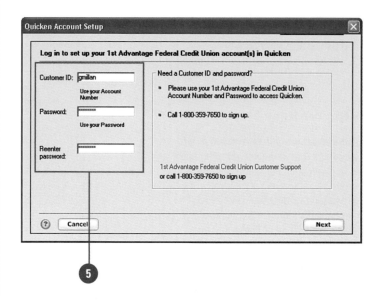

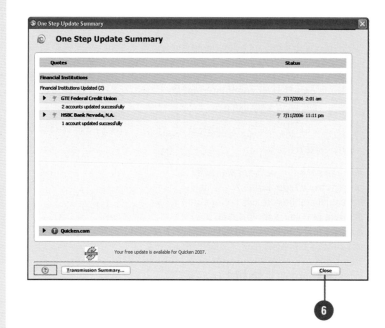

Add New Investment or Retirement Accounts

1 Open the Account List window by clicking **My Accounts** on the toolbar. You can also click the Tools menu and select Account List.

2 Click **Add Account**.

Continued, next page

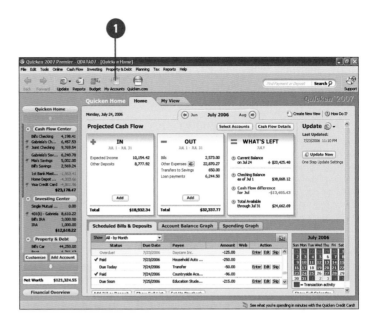

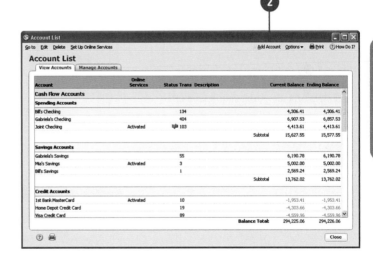

3
Type or select the name of the financial institution where the investment or retirement account is held and then click **Next**.

4
Select **Yes** to download the account information directly from your financial institution. Select **No** (as shown in this example) to enter the account manually. Then click **Next**.

5
Select the type of investment you are adding and click **Next**. This example shows a 401(k).

Did You Know?

You can set up an account to have online access. If you have online access to an account, select Yes in step 4 and follow the setup prompts. When the account is created, you can get automatic updates each time you use One Step Update or download from the Investing Center. Then the account pretty much takes care of itself. In addition, you may be able to download your account information from your financial institution's website using Web connect files, and then import the information into Quicken. For more information about importing files, see Chapter 2.

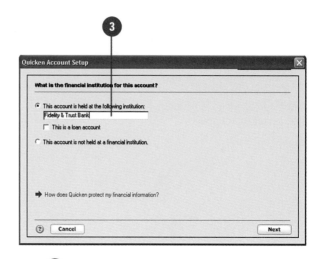

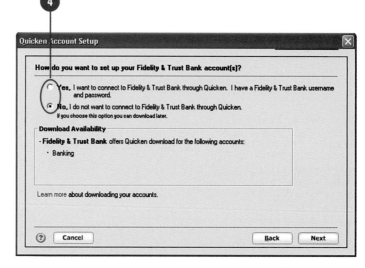

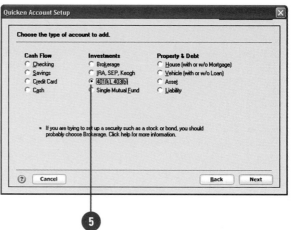

6 Type the name you want to use in Quicken for this account and click **Next**.

7 Type the statement end date or the date your account information was posted on the investment company's website and your employer's name. Then select whose account this is and whether your statement lists the shares of the securities you own. Then click **Next**.

8 Select whether you have any loans against your retirement or investment account. If you do, type the number of loans you have and click **Next**.

Continued, next page ▶

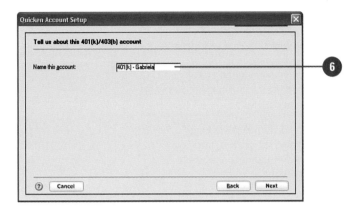

6

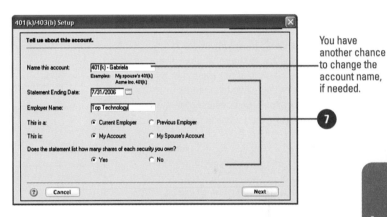

You have another chance to change the account name, if needed.

7

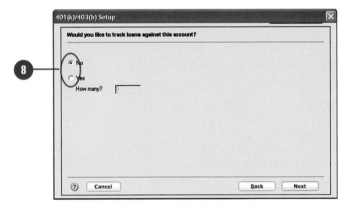

8

For Your Information

If you do have loans associated with your account, you are prompted to enter this information before proceeding.

9 Type the ticker symbols and security names. If you don't know the ticker symbol, click **Ticker Symbol Lookup** to locate, copy, and then paste the symbol in the Ticker box. Then click **Next**.

10 Type the number of shares and market value for each security type and click **Next**. Quicken provides a summary of the account information you just entered.

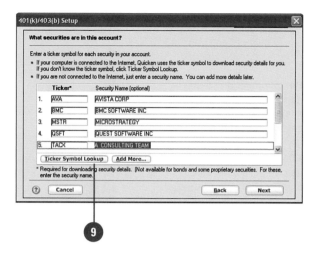

9

Did You Know?

You can enter approximate share and market value amounts. If you aren't sure of the number of shares and/or market value for each of the securities you own, enter approximate amounts. You can always edit the account information later using the Investing Center.

11 Click **Back** to change any of the information or click **Done** if you are finished.

12 Repeat steps 2–11 for each investment or retirement account that you want to add.

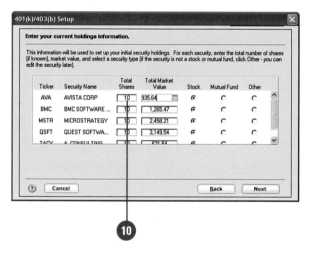

10

Did You Know?

Locate ticker symbols. To locate ticker symbols, click the **Ticker Symbol Lookup** button shown in step 9. On the Quicken Symbol Lookup page, click in the box under step 2 and type the partial or full symbol letters and click **Search**. A list of possible matches appear. Scroll through the list and when you find the symbol you want, highlight it with your mouse and copy it. Then switch back to Quicken and, in the Ticker box, paste the symbol. Repeat this process for each ticker symbol and security name you want to add.

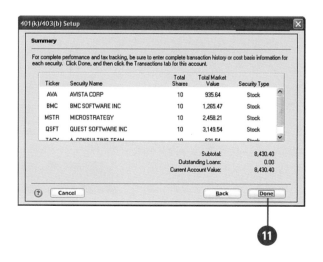

11

Add New Property or Debt Accounts

1. Open the Account List window by clicking **My Accounts** on the toolbar. You can also click the Tools menu and select Account List.

> ### See Also
>
> See "Add an Auto Loan" on page 108 for information on adding a new auto loan using the Property & Debt Center.

2. Click **Add Account**.

Continued, next page

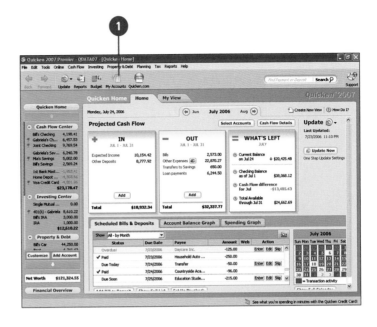

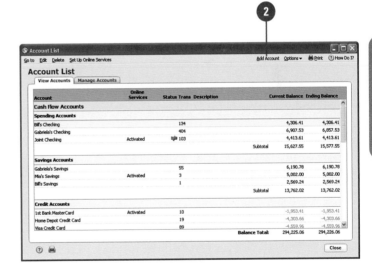

4

3 Type the name of the financial institution where the account is held, if applicable. If the account is not held at a financial institute, select the option **This Account Is Not Held at a Financial Institution**.

4 If Quicken finds the name of your financial institution, the name is listed; otherwise, the closest matches are listed. Select the appropriate name from the list or select **None of These** to enter the information using the name you entered. Then click **Next**.

5 Select the type of property or debt account you want to add and click **Next**. The setup options you see depend on which type you select. For the purposes of this example, a home is added.

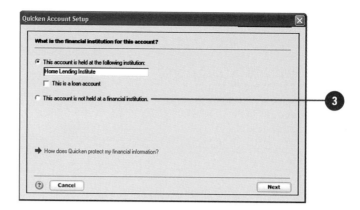

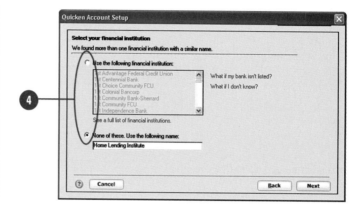

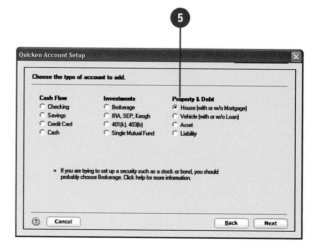

6 Type a name for the account. This name will be used in Quicken only.

7 Type the date you purchased or acquired the property or asset, the price you paid for it, and the approximate value. You can edit this account later and update the amount when you have an exact value, if needed.

8 If there is a loan associated with the asset or liability and it is not already in Quicken, select the first option. If there is already a loan in Quicken associated with it, select the second option, and then select the account from the drop-down list. If the asset or liability is already paid for, select the third option. Then click **Next**.

Continued, next page

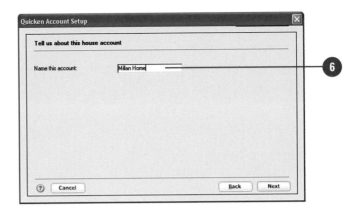

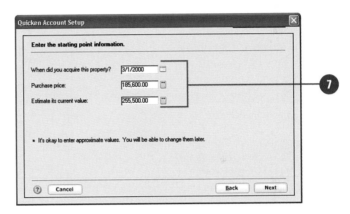

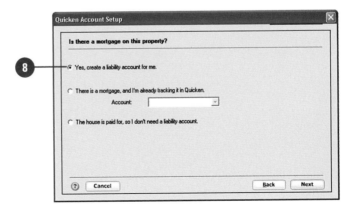

4

9. Complete the loan and payment period information and click **Next**.

10. Complete the balloon, balance, and payment information and click **Done**.

11. Verify your payment information and enter your transaction information so that Quicken can create a scheduled transaction for the account loan payments. If you want for the transactions to show as a bill, select **Show As a Bill**.

12. Click **OK**. The account register for the new account opens, where you can add, edit, and delete account transactions, and perform other functions.

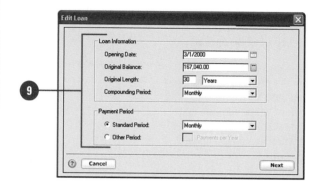

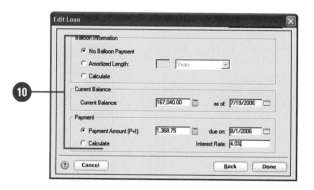

See Also

See "Managing Your Bills and Transactions" on page 143 for information on creating new, updating, or deleting account transactions.

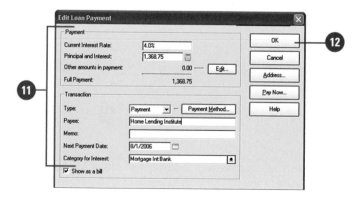

Editing Accounts

As you work with your accounts, you most likely will need to update account information, such as the interest rate, minimum or maximum balances, the account name, or the online services information. Because the editing process is similar for all accounts, the following task steps through the process for one account type using the Account List window. Therefore, the steps to edit account details may differ from what you see here depending on the type of account you are editing.

Edit Accounts

1 Open the Account List window by clicking **My Accounts** on the toolbar. You can also click the Tools menu and select Account List.

2 Scroll to the section of the window where the account you want to edit is listed. For example, to update a checking account, scroll to the Spending Accounts section and select the account you want to update

3 Click **Edit**.

Continued, next page

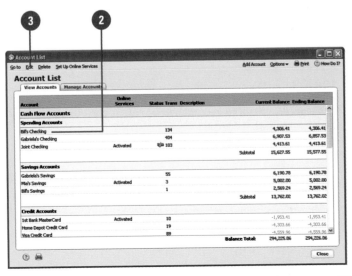

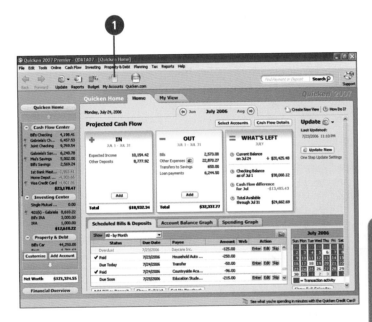

4

Managing Your Accounts   **103**

④ On the Account Details window, type, select, or change the account information.

⑤ To update online information for the account, click the **Online Services** tab.

⑥ If the account is already set up and you want to deactivate it, click **Remove from One Step Update** (not shown).

⑦ If the online services are available, but not activated and you want to activate it, click **Activate One Step Update** and complete the setup.

See Also

See "Using Online Updates" on page 79 for more information on setting up accounts for online access.

⑧ To review or change the tax schedules associated with this account, click **Tax Schedule Info**.

⑨ Select new tax schedules, if needed, and click **OK**.

⑩ When you are finished making changes, click **OK**.

Did You Know?

You cannot deactivate an account with active transactions. If there are transactions waiting to be entered into the account register, a message appears telling you so. Enter all transactions before deactivating the online account.

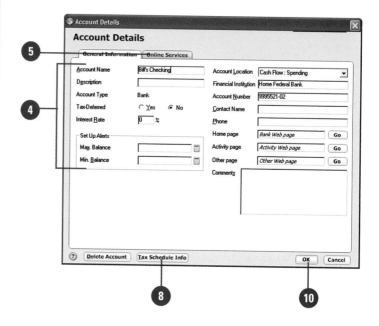

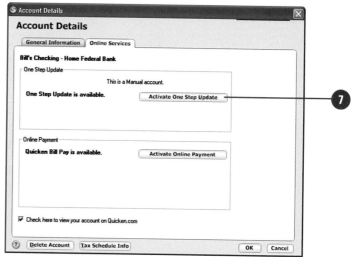

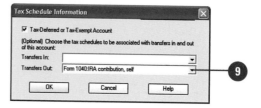

Performing Additional Functions in the Account List Window

You can use the menu bar on the Account List window to access other areas of Quicken, such as the following:

- You can open an account register by selecting the account and clicking **Go To**.
- You can set up an account for online access by selecting the account and clicking **Set Up Online Services**.
- You can print the account list by clicking **Print**.
- You can select print options or change the list view by using the **Options** menu.
- You can click **How Do I?** to access Quicken's Help system.

Did You Know?

It is beneficial to track tax-deferred accounts and tax schedules for accounts. Be sure to tell Quicken if an account can be tax deferred or is tax exempt. You should also tell Quicken about the tax schedules used for incoming and outgoing account funds. Quicken uses this information for tax reports, when estimating your taxes (for example, in the Tax Planner), and when you export tax-related information to TurboTax.

4

Deleting Accounts

See Also

See "Selecting Accounts to Include in Your Net Worth" on page 64 for information on hiding accounts in Quicken.

Delete Accounts

1 Open the Account List window by clicking **My Accounts** on the toolbar. You can also click the Tools menu and select Account List.

2 Select the account you want to remove.

3 Click **Delete**. A message appears, asking if you want to delete the account.

> **TIMESAVER** *You can delete an account by clicking the Delete button in the Account Details window or by using the Delete menu option in the Account List window.*

4 If you are sure that you want to delete the account, type **Yes** or click **Cancel** to keep the account.

5 If you choose to delete the account, click **OK**. A message appears, telling you that the account has been deleted.

6 Click **OK**.

> **IMPORTANT** *You cannot delete accounts that have active transactions. If there are transactions that are waiting to be entered into the account register, you must delete the transactions before you can remove the account.*

Like adding and editing accounts, you can remove accounts from Quicken using the Account List window. However, before you delete an account from Quicken, be sure you don't need the account—even if it's closed—for reporting, historical tracking, or forecasting. It is recommended that you hide an account instead. Deleting an account is permanent. The only way to restore it is if you have a backup of your Quicken file that you made before you deleted the account.

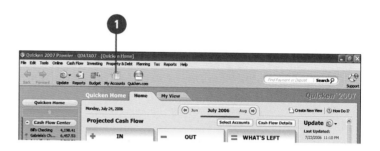

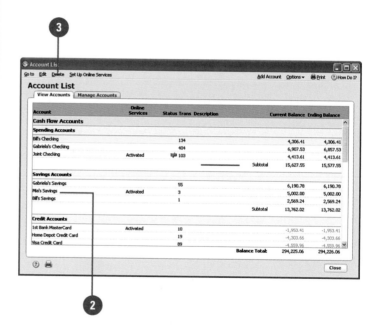

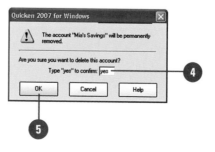

Managing Your Loan Accounts

After you set up your loan accounts, you can manage them all in one place – the Property & Debt Center. From there you can review all your loans in the Loan Accounts Summary section. You can review balances, interest rates, principal paid, and loan totals. In addition, you can access your loan account registers, add new loans, edit existing loans, and register payments.

Review Loan Accounts

1 On the account bar, click **Property & Debt** and scroll down to the **Loan Accounts Summary** section.

2 Each loan account you enter in Quicken is listed here. Click a link to open the account register for a loan.

3 In the **Int Rate** column, review the interest rate for each of your loans.

4 In the **Principal Pd** column, review the amount of principal you've paid thus far for each loan.

5 In the **Interest Pd** column, review the amount you've paid in interest for each of your loans n.

6 In the **Pmts Left** column, review the number of payments you have left to make for each of your loans.

7 In the **Balance** column, review the individual loan balances.

8 The **Total** row provides the sum of the principal paid, interest paid, and the balance for all your loans.

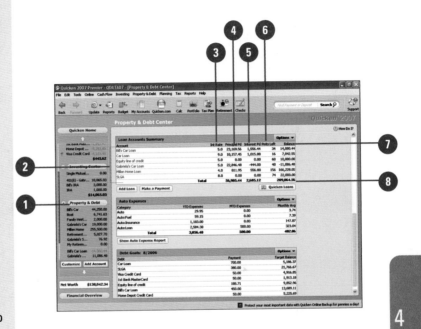

Add an Auto Loan

1. To add a new auto loan, from the Loan Accounts Summary section of the Property & Debt Center, click **Add Loan**.

2. Click **Next**.

3. Select the type of loan you have and click **Next**. This example uses the Borrow Money option.

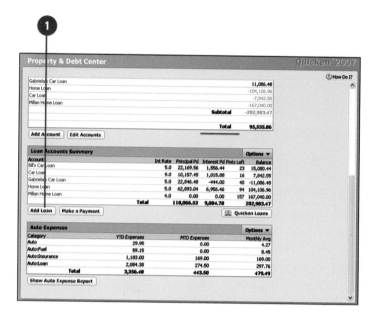

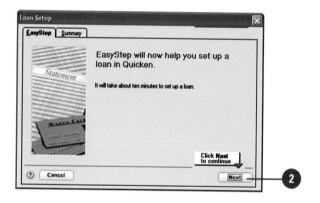

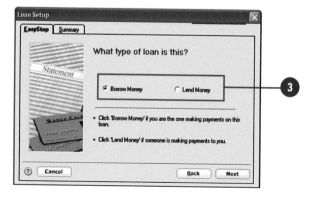

4 In the **New Account** field, type the name of the new loan account and click **Next**.

5 Select **Yes** if you have already made payments on the loan or **No** (shown in this example) if you haven't. Then click **Next**.

6 In the **Opening Date** field, type the date the loan was created and in the **Original Balance** field, type the amount of the beginning balance. Then click **Next**.

Did You Know?

If you are not sure of the beginning balance, enter an estimate in the Original Balance box. If needed, you can change the estimated amount later by editing the loan information. Refer to "Set Up Your Loan Payments" for information on editing loans.

Continued, next page

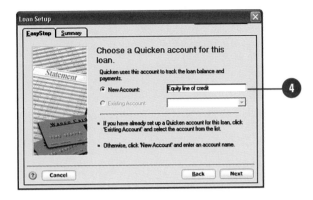

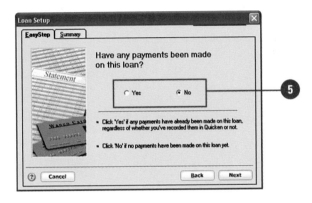

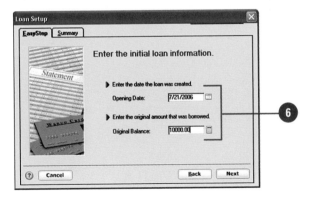

4

7. Select **Yes** if you will have a balloon payment at the end of your loan or **No** if you won't. Then click **Next**.

8. In the **Original Length** field, type the length of the loan, select the time period, and click **Next**.

9. Select **Standard Period** and select the frequency of payments or select **Other Period** and type the number of times per year you make the payments. Then click **Next**.

10. From the **Compounding Period** drop-down menu, select how often the loan interest is calculated and click **Next**.

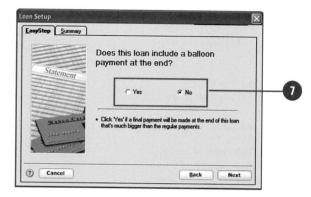

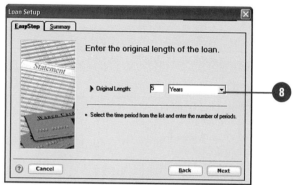

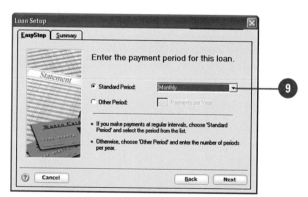

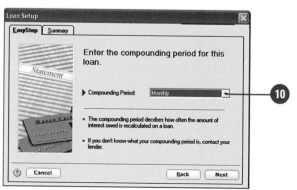

11 In the **Date of First Payment** field, type the date your next loan payment is due and click **Next**.

12 Select **Yes** if you know the amount of your next loan payment or **No** if you don't. Then click **Next**.

Continued, next page ▶

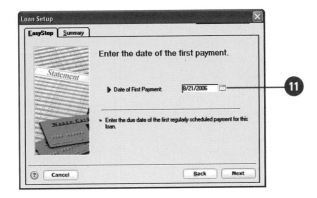

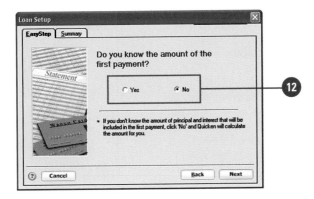

13 If you selected Yes in step 12, in the **Payment Amount** field, type your loan payment amount and click **Next**. (not shown)

14 In the **Interest Rate** field, type the interest rate and click **Next**.

15 Review all of your summary information by clicking **Next** until you've finished the summary, make changes if needed, and click **Done** when you are finished.

Based on the information you entered, if Quicken determines the principal balance is different from what you entered, a message appears asking if you want to change the balance. Click **Yes** to use Quicken's balance or **No** to use the balance you provided. If you did not enter the loan amount, Quicken determines your approximate loan amount and displays a message and the loan payment information.

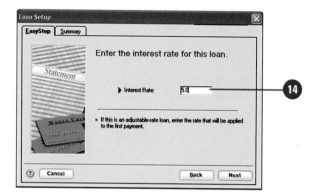

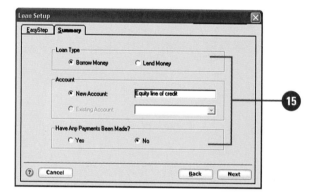

Set Up Your Loan Payments

1 When you are finished setting up your loan, you are automatically prompted to set up your loan payment. Review and change, if needed, the information in the **Payment** section.

2 From the **Type** drop-down menu, select how you want to make your payments and then click **Payment Method** to specify the payment details.

3 From the **Payment Type** section of the Select Payment Method dialog box, select the payment type.

4 From the **Register Entry** drop-down menu in the For Scheduled Transactions section, select how you want the transaction entered in your register.

5 From the **Account to Pay From** drop-down menu, select the account from which payments are made.

6 In the **Days in Advance** dialog, type the number of days in advance that you want the payment transaction to be entered in your register. Then click **OK**.

7 In the **Payee** field, type the name of your lender.

8 In the **Memo** field, type any additional information you want to log for this loan.

9 The Next Payment Date and Category for Interest information is completed for you, based on the information you entered about the loan. Change it, if needed, and then click **OK**.

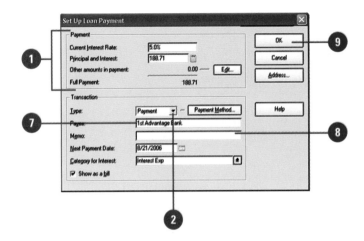

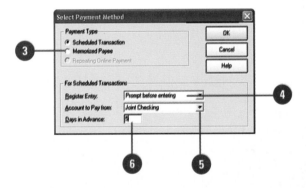

For Your Information

To assign more than one category to track your loan payments, interest paid, or other fees that may be rolled into your loan payment, click **Edit** next to Other Amounts in Payment. The Split Transaction window opens, where you can assign the categories you want to track.

See Also

See "Tracking Transactions with Multiple Categories" on page 71 for more information on assigning more than one category for your loan payments.

Create an Asset Account for a Loan

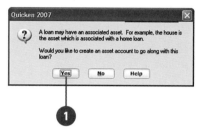

1. When you are finishing setting up loan payments, if a message appears, asking if you would like to create an asset for a loan, click **Yes** so that you can track the value of the property.

2. In the **Name This Account** field, type a name for the asset and click **Next**.

3. In the **As of Date** field, type the date the you would like to start tracking the asset. This doesn't have to be the same date that you acquired the object for which you have the loan.

4. In the **Value** field, type the value of the object. If you don't know it, estimate it now, and you can change it later. This amount is used as the opening balance for the new loan.

5. If the asset is eligible to be tax deferred or if you want to specify the tax schedule associated with incoming and outgoing funds for the account, click the **Tax** button and select the associated tax schedules.

6. Click **Done**. When you create the loan and asset accounts, they are added to your property and debt accounts, and you can manage them just as you do your other accounts.

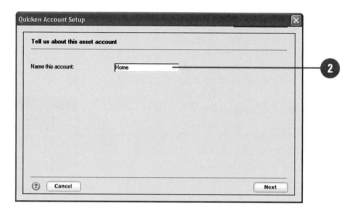

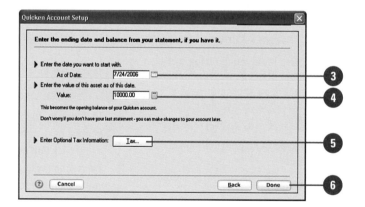

See Also

See "Editing and Deleting Transactions" on page 169 for more detailed information on making changes to transactions. See "Adding New Accounts" for more information on adding tax schedules.

Tracking a Refinanced Loan

If you are refinancing a loan, such as your mortgage, you should create the refinanced loan as a new loan and then in the register of the new loan, use the Split Transaction window to enter the payoff amount and fees for the old loan. This enables Quicken to track the payoff of the old loan and manage the new loan. Here's how you do it:

1. In the Loan Accounts Summary section of the Property & Debt Center, click **Add Loan**.

2. Click **Next** and set up the new loan, as shown in the task "Add a New Auto Loan," earlier in this chapter.

3. In the **Debt (Liabilities)** section of the Loan Accounts Summary section, click the link for the new loan to open its register.

4. Select the Opening Balance transaction and click **Split** under the Balance column.

5. In the Split Transaction window, click in the first row of the **Category** column and select **Transfer to/from** and the name of the old loan, for example, Transfer to/from Home Bank Mortgage.

6. Click **Amount**, type the payoff amount for the old loan, and click **Next**.

7. In the second row of the **Category** column, select the Interest Exp category or whichever category you selected to track the interest you paid for the old loan. Then in the **Amount** field, type the amount of mortgage interest you paid when you closed on the old loan and click **Next**.

8. In the third row of the **Category** column, select the Bank Charge category or whatever category you use for refinance fees and in Amount, type the amount you paid for the refinance fee. Then click **Next**.

9. If you are to get cash back from equity, in the fourth row of the **Category** column, select **Transfer to/from** + the name of the account to which the money is being sent (for example, your savings account).

10. In the **Amount** field, type the amount of equity and click **Next**.

11. Click **Adjust**. Quicken recalculates the total for you.

12. Click **OK** to close the Split Transaction window.

13. In the account register, click **Enter** to save your changes. The balance of your old loan should now have a zero balance.

Record Loan Payments

1. To record a loan payment, in the Loan Accounts Summary section of the Property & Debt Center, click **Make a Payment**.

2. Click the **Choose Loan** menu, select the loan you want to use, and then click **Make Payment**.

3. If this is a regularly scheduled payment, click **Regular**. If this is an additional payment, click **Extra**.

4. Verify that the loan information is correct. If you selected to make a regular payment, the amount is already filled in for you. If you selected to make an extra payment, the amount is empty so that you can type the amount you want to pay.

5. Click **OK**.

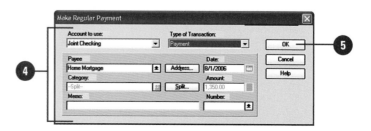

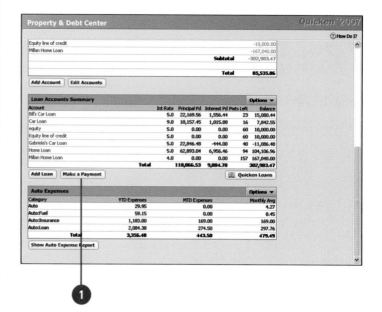

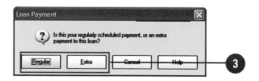

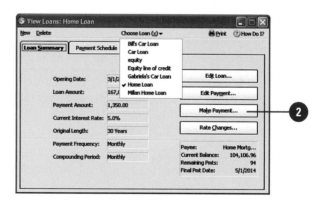

Getting the Big Picture a Snapshot at a Time

5

Introduction

All of your accounts are grouped into account types and housed in account centers: Cash Flow, Investing, and Property & Debt. The Cash Flow Center contains all your spending (checking), savings, and credit card accounts. In addition, your bills and scheduled transactions are housed in the Cash Flow Center. The Investing Center contains all your investment and retirement accounts. The last account center, the Property & Debt Center, contains all of your property accounts, such as your house, car, and other assets, as well as your liabilities, such as the loans that accompany your properties.

Quicken organizes all of your financial information into these centers to allow you to review, analyze, and manage your accounts. Account centers provide the big picture for all of your similar accounts. You can manage account information from each of the centers by monitoring balances, interest rates, setting up and editing alerts, adding and editing account information, and much more. In addition, you can access registers from the centers, access services specific to each center, and view reports and graphs. The account centers provide everything you need to analyze your financial information for all account types. This chapter shows you how to get the most out of the account centers.

Setting Up Alerts

Quicken uses alerts to remind you of any actions you need to take with your accounts (for example, paying a bill, transferring money to savings) and warnings (for example, when one of your balances reaches its limit or when your checking account is getting too low). Alerts can save you money by notifying you before you are charged over-the-limit fees or non-sufficient funds (NSF) fees. Alerts can also make money for you (for example, by watching your securities).

You have full control of the alerts you use and how often you are reminded. Alerts are listed on the Quicken Home Page and in each account center. For example, alerts for the Cash Flow Center appear in the Cash Flow Alerts section at the top of that center. You can view, change, and delete all alerts for all your accounts from the Alerts Center. You can also manage alerts from any of the account centers. With taxes, interest charges, fees of all sorts, and other financial leeches sucking the life out of your hard-earned money, you should protect yourself, take control, and set those alerts.

Set Up Alerts

1 To set up alerts, select **Tools, Set Up Alerts**.

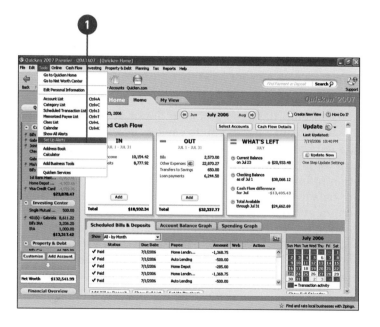

2 If it's not already open, click the **Setup** tab.

3 Select the type of alert you want to set up—for example, **Cash Flow**—and click the plus sign to expand the list. A check mark means the alert is active. A blank box means the alert is not active.

4 To set up an alert, click the box next to the name of the alert; for example, **Account Min. Balances**.

5 Complete the alert information. For example, to enter a minimum balance alert for a checking account, click in the **Min. Balance** column and type the minimum dollar amount allowed for that account.

6 Click in the **Remind Me At** column for that account and type the dollar amount you want Quicken to use for the alert. When your account reaches this amount, Quicken will display an alert to let you know that your account has reached this amount.

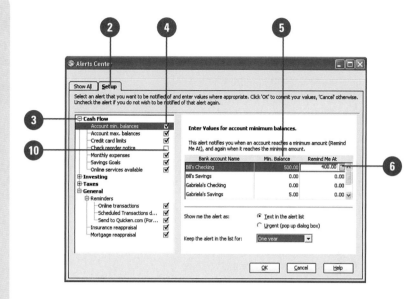

See Also

See "Managing Alerts" on page 144 for information on accessing and updating alerts from the activity centers.

Continued, next page ▶

Did You Know?

You can review and delete alerts. You can review all alerts by clicking the **Show All** tab. If you no longer need an alert, you can delete it by clicking the box next to the alert you want to remove and then clicking the **Delete** button at the bottom of the window. A message appears, asking if you want to delete the alert; click **OK**. Deleting an alert removes only one instance of the alert; it does not remove the alert altogether. If you no longer want to be reminded of an alert, you must disable it by performing step 10 in this task.

5

7. From the **Show Me the Alert As** section, select the type of alert you want: a text message that appears in the alert list in the appropriate account center or a pop-up type of message.

8. From the **Keep the Alert in the List For** menu, select the duration for which you would like Quicken to monitor and display the alert.

9. Repeat steps 3–4 and complete the related options for each alert you want to set up.

10. To disable an alert, clear the check from the box next to the alert name.

11. Review and change all alerts as needed, and then click **OK** when you are finished. The alerts you set up are now active. When you complete a task in an alert, it automatically goes away until it is triggered again.

IMPORTANT *Be sure to keep your account information and transactions up-to-date because alerts are only as current as the information in Quicken. In addition, review your alerts from time-to-time to ensure they are working for you.*

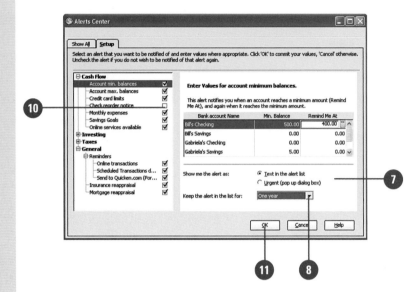

Reviewing and Analyzing Your Cash Flow

See Also

Refer to the preceding task, "Setting Up Alerts," for information on using the alerts.

Review Spending and Savings Accounts

1. On the account bar, click **Cash Flow Center**.

2. To view the account register and transactions for a specific spending or savings account, click the account name.

See Also

See Chapter 6, "Managing Your Bills and Transactions," on page 143 for information on using your account registers.

3. The minimum balance for each account is listed. If the account has a minimum balance and you have not set it, a zero appears. To change it, click the zero to open the Account Details window.

The Cash Flow Center is broken into the following sections: Cash Flow Alerts, Spending & Savings Accounts, Credit Card Accounts, and Scheduled Bills & Deposits. The Cash Flow Alerts section allows you to manage alerts specific to your Cash Flow accounts. Each of the other sections contains account and transaction information specific to that account type. In addition, you can access other areas of Quicken where you can manage each account in more detail.

The Spending & Savings Accounts section is divided between your expenditure accounts and your savings accounts, where you can manage all your expenditures, such as your checking and your savings accounts. The Credit Card Accounts section allows you to manage all your credit card account information. The Scheduled Bills & Deposits section lists your bills and scheduled transactions that are due.

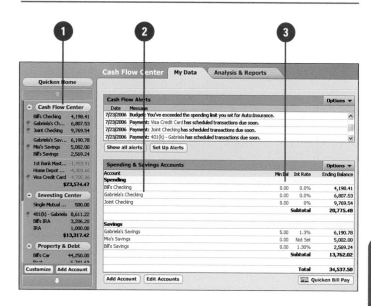

4 In the **Max Balance** or **Min Balance** fields, type the maximum and minimum account balances allowed, if applicable.

5 If you have not entered the interest rate, enter it in the **Interest Rate** box.

TIMESAVER *You can also click* **Not Set** *in the Spending & Savings Accounts section of the Cash Flow Center to open the Account Details window to update the interest rate.*

6 If the account is not assigned to the correct account type, select the appropriate account type from the **Account Location** drop-down list.

7 Enter any other account information, such as the account number or bank contact name and number, and click **OK**.

8 An ending balance is provided for each account, along with spending and savings subtotals, and a comprehensive total for all spending and savings accounts.

See Also

See "Setting Up Alerts" on page 118 for information on creating and editing alerts.

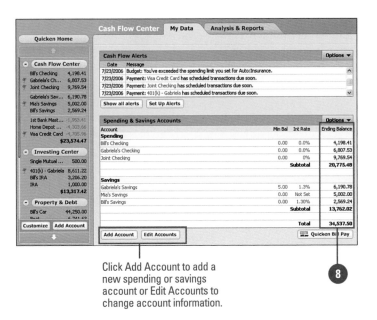

Click Add Account to add a new spending or savings account or Edit Accounts to change account information.

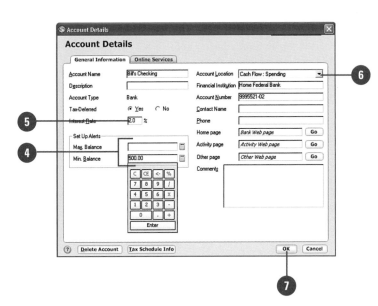

Review Credit Card Accounts

① If you don't already have the Cash Flow Center open, on the account bar, click Cash Flow Center and then scroll down to the Credit Card Accounts section.

② To view the account register and transactions for a specific credit card account, click the account name.

③ The credit limit is listed for each account. To change the credit limit, click the dollar amount to open the Credit Limit window.

④ Type the credit limit dollar amount and click **OK**.

⑤ The interest rate is provided for each account. If you have not entered the interest rate, click **Not Set**, or to change an existing rate, click the rate. The Interest Rate window opens.

⑥ Type the interest rate and click **OK**.

⑦ The available credit amount and current balance are listed for each account.

⑧ Totals are provided for your credit limit, available credit, and balance for all your credit cards.

⑨ Click **Add Account** to open the Quicken Account Setup window, where you can add a new credit card account.

⑩ Click **Edit Accounts** to open the Account List window, where you can edit all your credit card and other accounts.

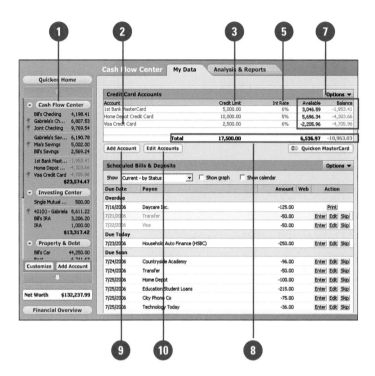

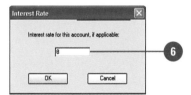

See Also

See "Adding New Accounts" on page 88 for more information on adding new credit card accounts.

5

Review Your Bills and Scheduled Transactions

1 If you don't already have the Cash Flow Center open, on the account bar, click Cash Flow Center and then scroll down to the Scheduled Bills & Deposits section.

2 All bills, deposits, and other transactions that are due or overdue are listed by the status, payee, and amount of the payment.

3 You can click **Enter** to record a transaction in the account register, click **Edit** to change transaction information, or click **Skip** to skip the current instance of a transaction.

4 To view the average amount spent for a transaction, hover your mouse over the transaction.

5 To view all transactions for a specific payee, click **Show Report** to open the Transaction report.

6 You can sort the list by clicking the **Show** drop-down list and selecting a different sort.

7 To view a bar graph view of your account balance over a month's time, select **Show Graph**.

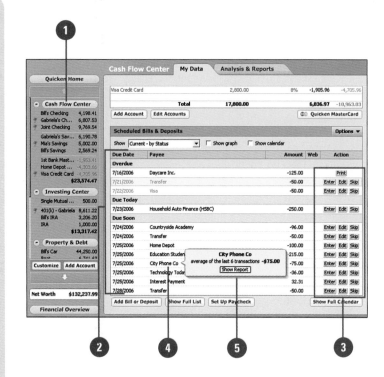

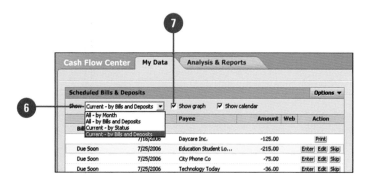

8 To view your account balance for a specific day, select the account from the **For Account** drop-down menu and then hover (point, don't click) your mouse over one of the bars. The bars represent a day of the month.

9 To change the month, click the back arrow to move back a month or click the forward arrow to move ahead a month.

10 To view the calendar month with the dates highlighted for the bills and transactions that are due, select **Show Calendar**.

11 To view the transactions that are due for a specific day, hover your mouse over that day on the calendar.

12 To get a more detailed look at the transactions that are due on the calendar, click one of the days or click the **Show Full Calendar** button.

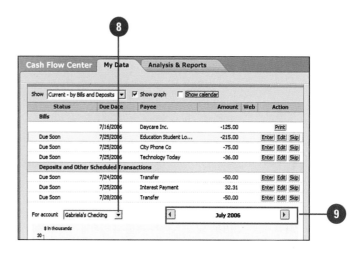

> ### See Also
>
> *See "Use the Calendar to View Monthly Transactions" on page 77 for more information on using the Calendar window.*

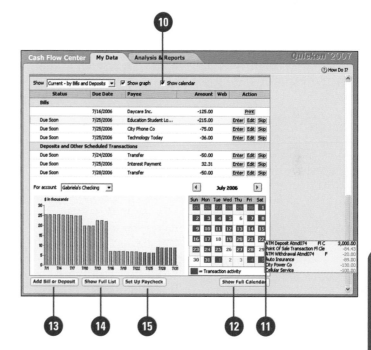

13 To add a new scheduled transaction for a deposit or bill, click **Add Bill or Deposit** and complete the Add Scheduled Transaction window.

14 To manage all your bills and deposits, click **Show Full List** to open the Bills & Deposits window.

15 To create a new paycheck or edit or delete an existing paycheck, click **Set Up Paycheck**.

> ### Did You Know?
>
> *You can view balances for more than one account.* To do this, select **Multiple Accounts** from the For Account drop-down menu shown in step 8. Then, from the Scheduled Transaction & Bill Accounts window, select the accounts you want to view on the graph and click **OK**.

5

Managing Your Cash Flow

From the Scheduled Bills & Deposits section of the Cash Flow Center, you can view transactions, add them to account registers, or skip the current transactions. In addition, you can access the Scheduled Transaction List window, where you can set up and manage all your scheduled transactions and add new paychecks.

Bills and transactions appear at the time that you specified when you set up the accounts. For example, if you indicated that you wanted to be reminded three days before a bill is due and it is due the 15th of every month, that bill appears on the Scheduled Bills & Deposits list on the 12th of every month. To help you avoid any financial bottlenecks, use the graph at the bottom of the Cash Flow Center to monitor your account balances. From there, you can track and compare the balance for one or multiple accounts, and for the current and future time frames. For example, if you want to see what your lowest account balance will be 30 days from the current day, you can forward to the next month using the arrows above the graph and/or calendar. Account balances are projections based on current bills, spending habits, account balances, and scheduled transaction trends.

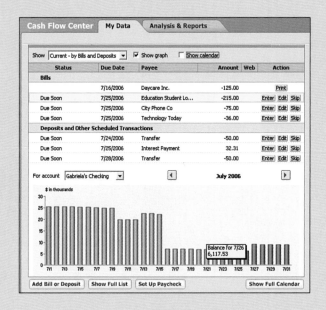

Analyze Your Income and Expense

The Analysis & Reports tab of the Cash Flow Center provides monthly expense pie charts, income and expense comparisons, and budget information, if you have a budget. This information allows you to take a bird's-eye look at your financial situation and assess where all your money is going and exactly how much you have coming in on a monthly basis or over any time frame you choose. In addition, you can run reports to further review your income, expenses, and budget.

View and Analyze Income and Expenses

1. If you don't already have the Cash Flow Center open, on the account bar, click **Cash Flow Center** and then click the **Analysis & Reports** tab.

2. The Expenses section provides a pie chart view of all your expenses for the current month. Hover your mouse over a slice of the pie to view the percentage and dollar amount for that category.

3. The color key shows the expense categories, the percentages for each category, the color the category represents, and your total expenses. Hover your mouse over a category to view what percentage of expenses the slice represents.

4. Click **Show Full Graph** to view the Expenses report as a pie chart or click **Show Expense Report** to view the Expenses report by category.

5. Click **View Last Month** to see how your expenses broke down for the previous month.

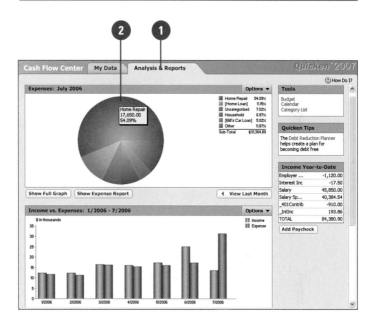

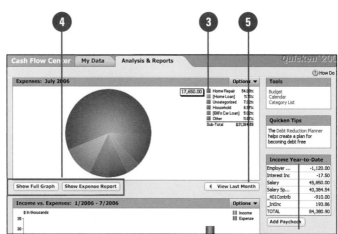

Your year-to-date income is listed here from all income sources. Click **Add Paycheck** to manage your income sources.

5

6 From the Income vs. Expenses section, you can view a bar graph of your total income and expenses over several months' time. Hover your mouse over a bar to view the total income or expenses for that month.

7 The color key shows the color the expenses and income represent. Hover your mouse over either Income or Expense to view your total income or total expense for the time period shown.

8 Click **Show Full Graph** to view the bar graph view of the Income vs. Expenses report or click **Show Income/Expense Report** to view the Expenses report by income and expenses categories.

9 The Budget section provides budget categories and budgeted amounts, what you actually spent for each category, and the difference between what you budgeted and what you spent.

10 Click **Show Budget** to review your budget or click **Show Monthly Budget Report** to view the budget report for the current month.

11 Click **View Current Month** to view budget information for the current calendar month.

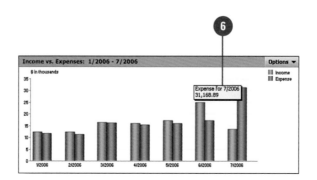

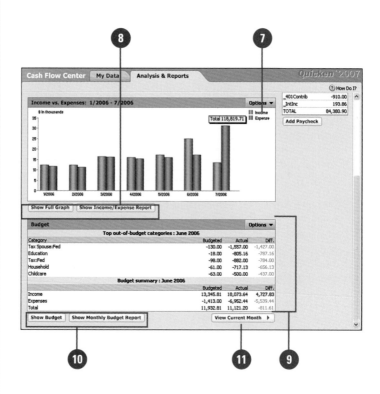

See Also

See "Setting Up a Budget" on page 196 and "Getting Out of Debt" on page 203 for more detailed information on creating and managing a budget.

Did You Know?

Check out all of the services available to you in the Cash Flow Center. The Cash Flow Services section, located on the right side of the My Data tab, contains several services that may be of interest to you. For example, you can access the Home Inventory Manager, get information on paying your bills online, downloading information from your bank, ordering Quicken checks, getting business tools, and how to use Quicken with your handheld. Click any of the links to get more information.

Analyzing Your Investments and Retirement Information

The Investing Center contains all your investment and retirement account information. This is where you can manage your accounts and portfolio, analyze investment performance, and run reports to further analyze your investments and securities. You can also download the latest quotes for your investments and securities, as well as historical quotes, to analyze how an investment or a security has performed over time.

Review Investment Accounts

1 On the account bar, click **Investing Center** and click the **Today's Data** tab.

2 Your existing investment and retirement accounts are listed in the **Investment & Retirement Accounts** section of the Today's Data tab. Click an account name to open that account's register.

3 The **Cost Basis** column provides a total for all of your security shares, which includes commissions, fees, and any income that has been reinvested in the security.

4 The **Gain/Loss** column provides the total dollar amount you have lost or gained for each security listed.

5 The **Gain/Loss (%)** column provides the percentage of the amount you have lost or gained for each security listed.

6 The **Day Gain/Loss** column provides the dollar value amount you lose or gain each day for each security is also listed.

7 The **Day Gain/Loss (%)** column provides the previous day's dollar value as a percentage for the amount you lose or gain each day for each security.

8 The **Market Value** column lists how much a security is worth and is listed for each security.

Continued, next page

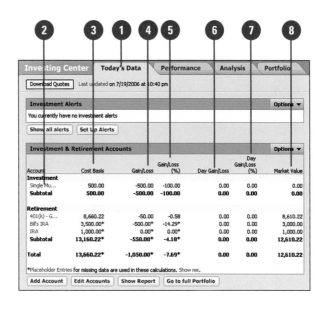

See Also

See "Setting Up Alerts" on page 118 for information on creating and editing alerts.

5

9 A subtotal for your investment accounts and a subtotal for your retirement accounts are provided, as is a total that includes both your investment and retirement accounts.

10 To add a new investment or retirement account, click **Add Account** and complete the Quicken Account Setup window.

11 To make changes to your investment, retirement, or any of your other accounts, click **Edit Accounts** to open the Account list window.

12 To review how your portfolio is doing, click **Show Report** to open the Portfolio Value report.

13 To view a list of all your securities, click **Go to Full Portfolio** to open the Portfolio tab in the Investing Center.

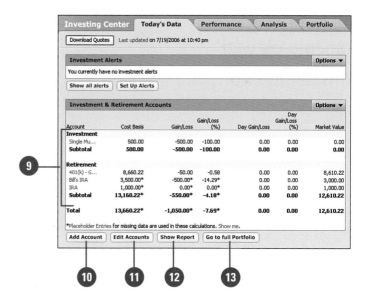

See Also

See "Adding New Investment or Retirement Accounts" on page 95 for more information on creating new investment or retirement accounts.

Tracking and Managing Investment Performance

To help you keep an eye on your investments or to keep an eye on investments you are considering, you can set up a watch list. A watch list provides easy access to investments of interest. Securities on your watch list appear in the Watch List section on the Today's Data tab in the Investing Center. You can add, edit, and delete securities from here.

Set Up a Securities Watch List

1 On the account bar, click **Investing Center** and click the **Today's Data** tab. Then scroll down to the Watch List section.

2 To add a security to your watch list, be sure that you are connected to the Internet and then click **Add a Security**.

3 Type the ticker symbol and/or name of the security and click **Next**. If you don't know the ticker symbol, click **Look Up** to locate, copy, and then paste it in the Ticker Symbol box. Quicken downloads the information for the security.

4 Click **Next**.

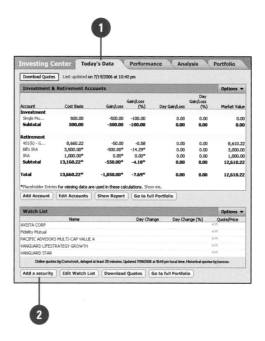

5

5. If you want to add another security, select **Yes** and repeat steps 1–4;if not, select **No**. Then click **Done**.

6. To make changes to your watch list, click **Edit Watch List**.

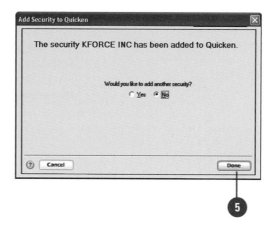

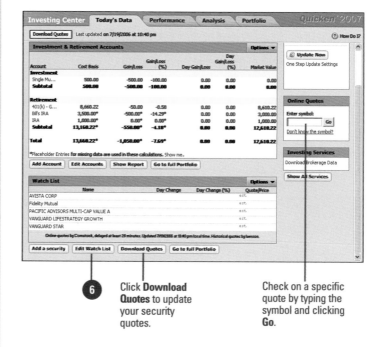

Click **Download Quotes** to update your security quotes.

Check on a specific quote by typing the symbol and clicking **Go**.

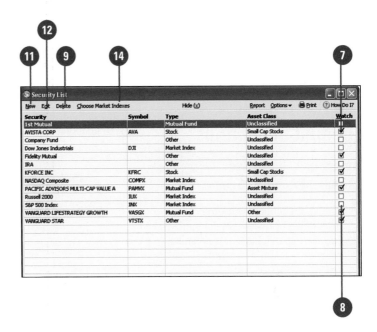

7 To add existing securities to your watch list, select the appropriate boxes in the Watch column. A check mark means the security is already on your watch list.

8 To remove securities from your watch list, clear the boxes next to the securities you want to remove.

9 To completely remove securities from your watch list, select the securities and click **Delete**. A message appears asking if you want to delete the security.

10 Click **OK** to remove it or **Cancel** to keep it.

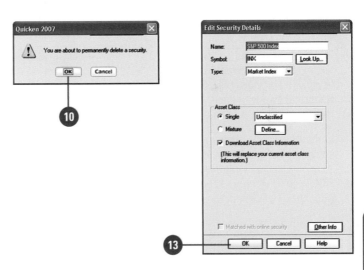

Did You Know?

You cannot delete securities that have existing transactions. Quicken does not allow you to delete a security that has transactions associated with it. To delete a security with transactions, you must first delete all associated transactions. If you no longer use a security, it is best to hide the security or simply remove it from your watch list.

11 To add new securities to your watch list, click **New** and complete the Add Security to Quicken setup process.

12 To change information about a security, select it and click **Edit**.

13 Make the required changes and click **OK**.

14 To select the market indexes you want to use in Quicken, click **Choose Market Indexes**.

15 Select the indexes you want and click **Done**.

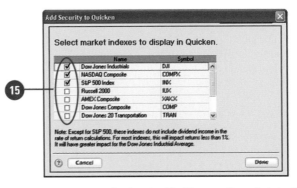

5

Reviewing and Analyzing Investment and Retirement Account Summaries

Review Investment and Retirement Account Summaries

1 On the account bar, click the investment or retirement account you want to review. In this example, we review a 401(k) account.

2 On the Summary tab, the Holdings section lists all your securities for the account, including the quote, shares, and so on. Click a security to open the Security Detail View window if you want to take a more detailed look at the security.

3 To select the timeframe and securities that you want to download and view, click **Download Historical Prices** to open the Get Historical Prices window.

4 In the Account Attributes section, you can view your account details. To update account information, click **Edit Account Details** to open the Account Details window.

5 To update online access information, if it's available, click **Change Online Services** and click the the **Online Services** tab on the Account Details window.

6 The Account Status section lists account status information, such as your account value, balance, market value, and so on.

7 To update statement information for the account, click the **Last Update** date link.

For each of your investment and retirement accounts, Quicken provides a summary for you to review and assess your account performance, security balances and values, account details, and activities. In addition, you can view reports to further analyze your account performance and attach documents, such as statements, to the account.

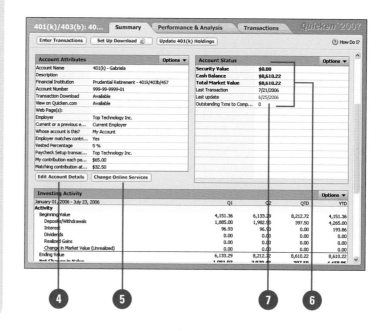

8 In the Investing Activity section, you can view activity and capital gains and losses for each quarter, quarter-to-date, and year-to-date.

9 To view and assess the activity for an investment, click **Show Full Report** to open the Investing Activity report.

10 To view any gains or losses for the account, if applicable, click **Capital Gains Report**.

11 The **Account Holdings** section provides security, share, and total value information. Click the security name to open the Security Detail View window, where you can take a more detailed look at a security, as shown previously in step 2.

12 In the Account Attachments section, you can add documents to the account by clicking **Add** and completing the Add Attachment window.

See Also

See "Flag and Attach Documents to Transactions" on page 165 for information on attaching files and images.

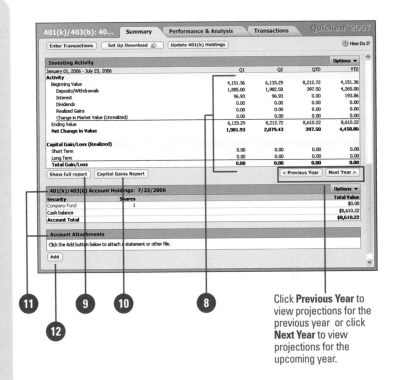

Click **Previous Year** to view projections for the previous year or click **Next Year** to view projections for the upcoming year.

5

Reviewing and Analyzing Investment and Retirement Performance

In each investment and retirement account, a Performance & Analysis tab is provided, with graphs and pie charts showing the account's overall performance. The information on this tab varies, depending on the type of investment or retirement account. Typically, the information you can expect to find includes the account value and a cost comparison, the asset allocation, and the security allocation. In addition, you can use this tab to view reports and different performance views; these options also vary by account type.

Analyze Investment and Retirement Performance

1. On the account bar, click the investment account for which you want to view investment performance.

2. Click the **Performance & Analysis** tab.

3. Click **Go to Portfolio Performance**.

4. In the **Growth** section, you can see how your investment or retirement account is doing over time, compared to common securities.

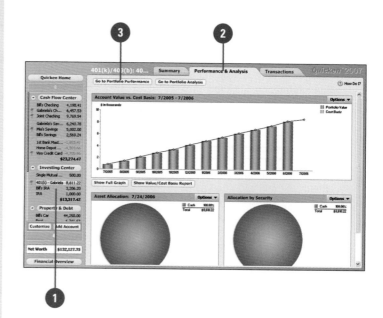

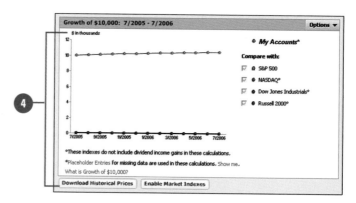

5 In the **Average Annual Return** section, you can analyze what kind of return you've been getting for your investment and retirement accounts.

6 In the **Portfolio Value vs. Cost Basis** section, you can view the value and cost of the security over a year's time. Hover (point, don't click) your mouse over the bar to view the value of the security for that month or over the point at the top of the bar to view the cost.

7 The color key provides the color that the value and cost represent. Hover your mouse over a key to view the totals for the value or cost.

8 Click **Show Full Graph** to view the graph view of the Account Value vs. Cost Basis report by account or click **Show Value/Cost Basis Report** to view the Account Value vs. Cost Basis report by security.

Continued, next page

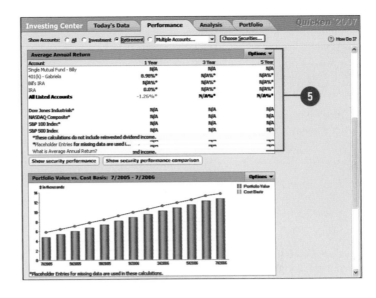

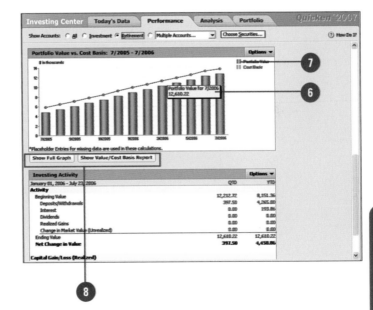

9 In the **Investing Activity** section, you can see all transactions for each investment, broken down by quarter, quarter-to-date, and year-to-date.

10 Capital gain and loss for short-term and long-term are listed for the same time periods as the investment activities.

11 Click **Show Full Report** to view the Investing report, which provides a complete compilation of all your investment activity.

12 Click **Capital Gains Report** to view detailed information on your capital gains and losses.

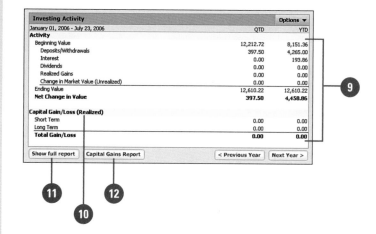

Investing Activity		Options ▼
January 01, 2006 - July 23, 2006	QTD	YTD
Activity		
Beginning Value	12,212.72	8,151.36
Deposits/Withdrawals	397.50	4,265.00
Interest	0.00	193.86
Dividends	0.00	0.00
Realized Gains	0.00	0.00
Change in Market Value (Unrealized)	0.00	0.00
Ending Value	12,610.22	12,610.22
Net Change in Value	**397.50**	**4,458.86**
Capital Gain/Loss (Realized)		
Short Term	0.00	0.00
Long Term	0.00	0.00
Total Gain/Loss	**0.00**	**0.00**

Show full report Capital Gains Report < Previous Year Next Year >

Analyze Asset Allocation

1 Click the **Analysis** tab.

2 The **Asset Allocation** section provides a pie chart view of how you have your assets allocated for the actual and target allocation. The chart is broken into slices that represent the allocation type.

3 Hover your mouse over a slice of the pie to view the percentage and dollar amount for that allocation.

4 The color key provides the color that each allocation type represents.

5 Click **Show Full Graph** to view the pie chart view of the Asset Allocation report or click **Show Allocation Guide** to view or make changes to the Asset Allocation Guide.

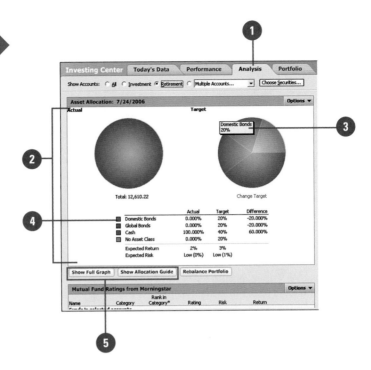

See Also

See "Getting Some Help with Asset Allocation" on page 288 for more information about the Asset Allocation Guide.

Continued, next page

5

6 For mutual funds accounts, the **Mutual Fund Ratings** section provides information about "the four Rs" for your funds: rank, rating, risk and return.

7 To add a mutual fund security, click **Add a Mutual Fund** and complete the Add Security to Quicken window.

8 To compare all securities side-by-side, click **Show Full Comparison** to open the Mutual Funds Ratings window.

9 To search for funds with specific ratings and returns, ensure that you are connected to the Internet and click **Find Top Funds**. Then complete the Mutual Fund Screener web page.

10 The **Allocation by Account** and **Allocation by Security** sections provide pie chart views of your account allocations and asset securities. Each chart is broken into slices that represent each account and security, respectively.

11 Hover your mouse over a slice of the pie or the color key to view the percentage and dollar amount for that security.

12 Click **Show Full Graph** in either section to view the Allocation by Account or Allocation by Security report.

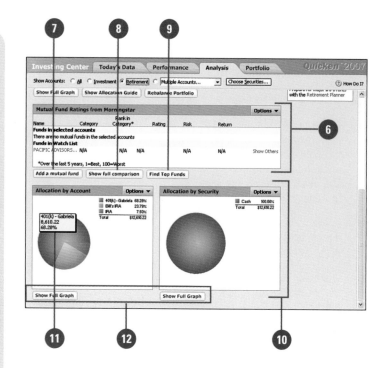

Reviewing and Analyzing Your Property and Debt

The Property & Debt Accounts section of the Property & Debt Center lists all your asset- and liability-related accounts. Accounts are divided between liability and asset accounts. When you set up a property (asset) and there is a loan associated with it, Quicken also creates a debt (liability) account for it. Both are listed in this center so that you can manage all property and debt accounts from one location. In addition, you can manage alerts specific to your property or debt accounts, add new loans, edit existing loans, and record loan payments.

Review and Analyze Property and Debt Accounts

1. On the account bar, click **Property & Debt**.

2. Click an account name to go to the register for that account.

3. Use the **Options** menu in any of the Property & Debt sections to take action on your accounts.

4. The ending balance for each property or debt account is provided.

5. The subtotal is provided for your assets and your liabilities. The subtotal is the sum of all your assets or the sum of all your liabilities.

6. The total is determined by subtracting your liabilities from your assets.

7. To add a new property or debt account, click **Add Accounts** and complete the Quicken Account Setup window.

8. To change account information, click **Edit Accounts** to open the Account List window.

Continued, next page

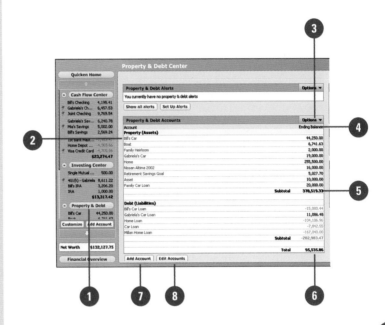

See Also

See "Setting Up Alerts" on page 118 for information on creating and editing alerts.

5

9 The **Loan Accounts Summary** section lists all of your loans. In addition, you can view the interest rate, principal paid, interest paid, how many payments you have left, and the balance for each of your loans. Comprehensive totals are also provided.

10 To add a new loan, click **Add Loan** and complete the Loan Setup window.

See Also

See "Managing Your Loan Accounts" on page 87 for information on how to add a new loan.

11 To view, edit, or manually make a loan payment, click **Make a Payment**.

See Also

See "Setting Up Alerts" on page 118 for information on managing loans.

12 The **Auto Expenses** section of the Property & Debt Center lists your auto-related expenses totals for year-to-date, month-to-date, monthly averages, and totals by category.

13 To view a report of all your auto-related expenses for a specific period of time, click **Show Auto Expense Report**.

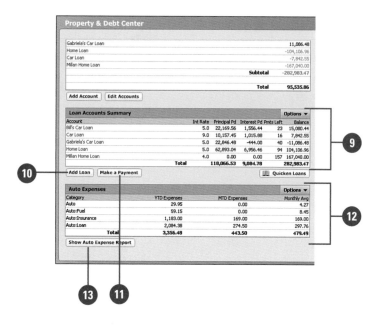

Did You Know?

It is important to track your car maintenance expenses. If you don't assign categories to transactions that are associated with car maintenace, you won't see anything in the Auto Expenses section of the Property & Debt Center. In addition, you won't have a record of the repairs and maintenance of your auto. When you enter transactions into your registers and select one of the auto-related categories, such as fuel or insurance, Quicken tracks this information in the Auto Expenses section. You can run the Auto Expenses report, which lists all of your auto expenses in detail for a specific period of time for tax deductions, budgeting, for insurance purposes, or to show proof of the upkeep of the vehicle. See "Recording Transactions in Your Account Register Manually" on page 167 for information on assigning categories to a transaction.

Managing Your Bills and Transactions

6

Introduction

All of your accounts contain transactions that need to be managed. Whether you download your transactions or enter them manually, they require your time and attention. Using alerts, you can monitor and manage when your transactions and bills are due, which you can review and update from each account center. You can manage your account transactions from several places in Quicken: from the Quicken Home page, from the account centers, and from the individual account registers. For example, the Scheduled Bills & Deposits section of the Cash Flow Center allows you to view all of your bills that are due, enter them in your account registers, edit the transaction information, and choose to skip individual instances of transactions. In addition, you can add new transactions and paychecks.

Using the account centers to manage your bills and transactions is beneficial because all your bills and transactions for your similar accounts (cash flow, investment, or property and debt) are listed in one place. Therefore, you don't have to open individual account registers to view and manage the bills or scheduled transactions that are due for each of your accounts. Each account center provides one-stop access to all your bills and account transactions that are due for the accounts in that center.

You also have the option of managing your account transactions by going into each individual account register. In the account registers, you can add, edit, or delete transactions; add downloaded transactions to the register; set up scheduled transactions; search for transactions; transfer funds between accounts; and balance your account. In addition, you can view spending averages for transactions and reports for each of your accounts.

This chapter covers everything you need to know about transactions to help you manage and take control of your bills and transactions.

Managing Alerts

The first section of each of the account centers is Alerts; for example, Cash Flow Alerts is the first section of the Cash Flow Center. This is where your alerts that are associated with your cash flow accounts are listed. You should review the alerts to ensure they are working for you. Is the timing good? Are there too many or too few? Remember, alerts are only as current as the information in Quicken. Therefore, it is important to keep Quicken up-to-date with the latest transactions and quotes using One Step Update or if you manually enter information, with your latest statement information. You can review, update, or remove alerts from any of the account centers. The process is the same. The example provided here shows you how to review and update your cash flow alerts from the Cash Flow Center.

Manage Cash Flow Alerts

1. From the account bar, select the account center for which you want to review and manage alerts.

2. To take action on an alert, click the links within the **Message** column.

3. To see a list of all alerts that are currently active, click **Show All Alerts**.

4. To remove an alert, select the box next to the alert and click **Delete**. A message appears, asking if you want to delete the alert; click **OK**.

5. To make changes to alerts, click the **Setup** tab.

6. Review and change all alerts as needed, and then close the window when you are finished.

> ### See Also
>
> *See "Setting Up Alerts" on page 118 for information on how to set up and change alerts.*

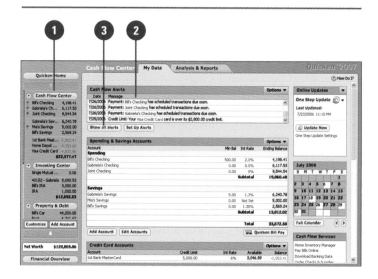

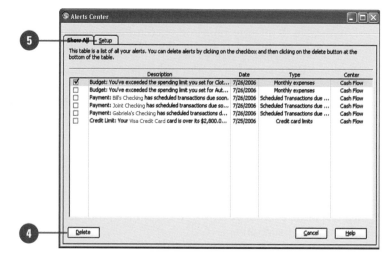

Record and Edit Transactions Using Scheduled Bills & Deposits

As your bills and scheduled transactions become due, you can add them to your account registers, unless you indicated when you set them up for Quicken to automatically enter them in your account registers. You can also edit them or skip an instance of a transaction. When you enter account transactions from the Scheduled Bills & Deposits section of the Cash Flow Center, they are automatically added to the appropriate account register. If you download transactions, the transactions appear on the Downloaded Transactions tab in the account register. You can then add the transactions to your register. You designate when bills and scheduled transactions show up on the list when you set up the account.

Record Transactions Using Bills and Scheduled Transactions

1 From the account bar, click **Cash Flow Center** and then scroll down to the **Scheduled Bills & Deposits** section.

2 To record a transaction in the account register, click **Enter**.

3 Review the transaction information to ensure it is correct and make changes, if needed. For example, if you make online payments, click **Add a Web Page Address** to enter the web address. You can then go online to make your payment by clicking the address.

4 Click **Enter Transaction** or **Enter** (what you click depends on the transaction type). Any changes you make apply to only the current transaction, not to all future transactions.

5 Click **Cancel** to take no action. The transaction remains on the list until you are ready to record it.

6 Click Skip to remove a transaction from the list for this period. It reappears the next time it is due.

7 Repeat steps 1–5 for each bill or transaction you want to add to your account registers.

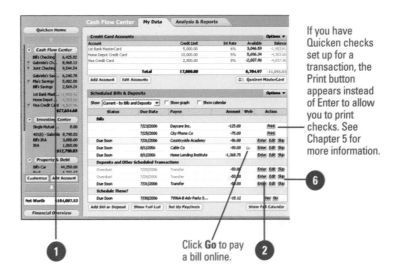

If you have Quicken checks set up for a transaction, the Print button appears instead of Enter to allow you to print checks. See Chapter 5 for more information.

Click **Go** to pay a bill online.

Edit Future Instances of Transactions

① To edit all future instances of a transaction, from the Scheduled Bills & Deposits section of the Cash Flow Center, click **Edit** next to the transaction you want to update.

② Make any changes needed; for example, adding a web address for a bill that is paid online.

③ To add or change scheduled transaction options, such as changing from calendar days to business days for the number of days before you are reminded the transactions is due, click **Options**.

④ To disregard any changes you made, click **Cancel**. The transaction remains as it was before you opened the Edit All Future Transactions window.

⑤ To save changes you made, click **OK**. Quicken applies the changes you made to all future instances of the transaction you edited.

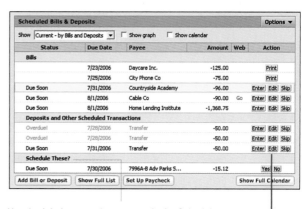

Unscheduled transactions appear in the Schedule These? section. If there are transactions that have not been scheduled, for example, a transaction that you have downloaded a few times, but for which you have not created a scheduled transaction, Quicken creates a temporary section in your Scheduled Bills & Deposits list called "Schedule These?." You can click **Yes** to schedule a transaction or **No** to leave it unscheduled.

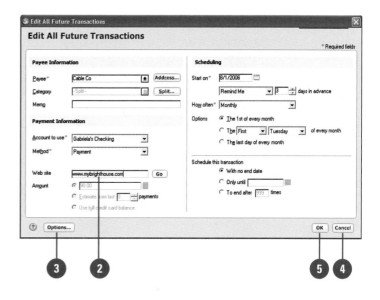

See Also

See "Managing All Your Scheduled Transactions" on 147 for more information on adding and editing scheduled transactions.

For Your Information

To delete a transaction, you use the Scheduled Transaction List window. Refer to the task "Manage All Your Scheduled Transactions," later in this chapter, for more information.

Managing All Your Scheduled Transactions

To create new, make changes to, or delete scheduled transactions, you use the Scheduled Transaction List window. All your transactions are included in the Scheduled Transaction List window. You can access this window from the Scheduled Bills & Deposits section of the Cash Flow Center, from any account register, or from the Tools menu.

Manage All Your Scheduled Transactions

1 If you don't already have the Cash Flow Center open, on the account bar, click **Cash Flow Center** and then scroll down to the Scheduled Bills & Deposits section.

> **TIMESAVER** *As an alternate way of opening the Bills & Deposits window, you can select* **Scheduled Transaction List** *from the Tools menu or use the shortcut key,* **Ctrl + J**.

2 Click **Show Full List**.

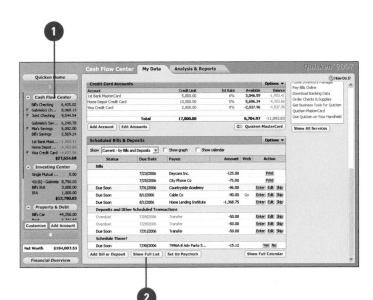

Did You Know?

You can enter and skip transactions using the Bills & Deposits window. Like the Scheduled Bills & Deposits section of the Cash Flow Center, you can enter transactions in your account registers and skip transactions using the **Enter** and **Skip** options located on the menu of the Bills & Deposits window.

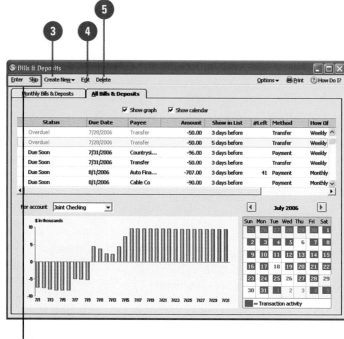

3 To add a new scheduled transaction or paycheck, click **Create New**, and select **Scheduled Transaction** or **Paycheck** from the list. Depending on which option you choose, either the Add Scheduled Transaction window or the Manage Paychecks window opens.

4 To update information about a transaction, select the transaction from the list and click **Edit**.

5 To delete a transaction—for example, if you no longer use the account for the transaction—select the transaction and click **Delete**.

Click to enter or skip transactions.

See Also

See steps 2–5 of the previous task, "Edit Future Instances of Transactions" on page 146 for more detailed information on editing transactions. See the next task, "Add a New Bill" for more detailed information on adding new scheduled transactions. See "Using Scheduled Bills & Deposits," on page 68 for information on using the calendar and graph.

Adding New Bills

You can add recurring bills in the form of scheduled transactions from several places in Quicken, including the Scheduled Bills & Deposits section of the Cash Flow Center. The process here is the same as in other areas of Quicken. This is just another convenient way to enter new transactions while you are managing your bills and other transactions. Scheduled transactions are added manually, unless you indicated when you set the scheduled transaction up for Quicken to automatically enter it for you.

Add a New Bill

1. If you don't already have the Cash Flow Center open, on the account bar, click **Cash Flow Center** and then scroll down to the Scheduled Bills & Deposits section.

2. Click **Add Bill or Deposit**.

See Also

See "Add a New Transaction" on page 73 for more detailed information on adding new transactions.

Did You Know?

You can add the payee address from the Add Scheduled Transaction window. To add the address for a payee, click the **Address** button next to the Payee drop-down menu and complete the Address window.

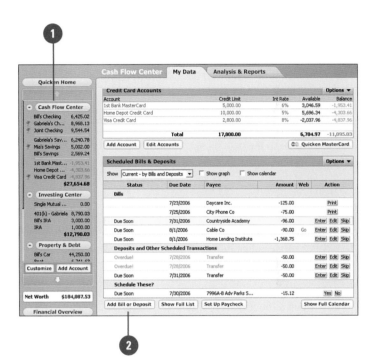

③ In the **Payee Information** section, enter the recipient name, for example a creditor name, select the category you want to track, and enter a memo, if needed.

④ In the **Payment Information** section, provide the account information, payment type, website address (if applicable), and transaction amount.

TIMESAVER *You can visit the website listed in the Web Site field by clicking the **Go** button on the Add Scheduled Transaction window. **Go** will also appear in the Web column of the Scheduled Bills & Deposits list in the Cash Flow Center and the Quicken Home page. This is a quick and convenient way to access your online payment websites from Quicken.*

⑤ In the **Scheduling** section, select when the transaction is to begin and how often you want to be reminded of the transaction. If this is a one-time transaction, from the **How Often** drop-down menu, select **Only Once**.

⑥ If the transaction occurs on a regular basis (for example, monthly) select the time of month the transaction is to occur.

⑦ Select **With No End Date** if the transaction is continuous or type a date when the transaction will end.

⑧ Click **OK**. The transaction is added to the appropriate account and will appear in the Scheduled Bills & Deposits list and on both the Cash Flow Center and the Quicken Home page when it is due.

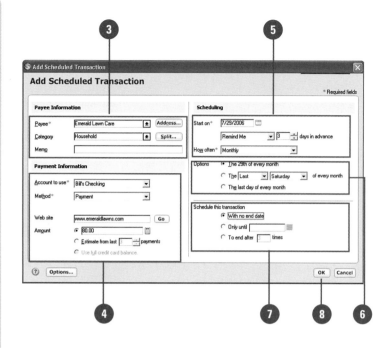

Did You Know?

Some information is automatically updated. If you use a split transaction, the amount is already updated but is grayed out so that you can't change it. In step 3, if you selected a payee you've used previously, the amount that you used previously is automatically entered, but you can change it.

You can use scheduled transactions to set up transfers. If you transfer money from one account to another on a regular basis, for example, from your checking to savings, set up a scheduled transaction. To do this, from the **Method** drop-down menu, select **Transfer**. Then use the **Transfer TO** and **Transfer FROM** drop-down menus to specify the accounts from which the money is credited and debited. Complete the rest of the information as shown in this task. This transaction is added to your scheduled transactions list.

Adding and Editing Paychecks

As with scheduled transactions, there are several places from which you can add new paychecks, for example, the Scheduled Bills & Deposits section of the Cash Flow Center. Also, like scheduled transactions, as you manage and work with your bills and transactions, you can add new paychecks, edit existing paycheck information, and add one-time payments. Before you begin, get your paycheck stub. You will need it when entering your deduction information.

Add a New Paycheck

1 If you don't already have the Cash Flow Center open, on the account bar, click **Cash Flow Center** and then scroll down to the Scheduled Bills & Deposits section.

2 Click **Set Up Paycheck**.

3 Click **New**.

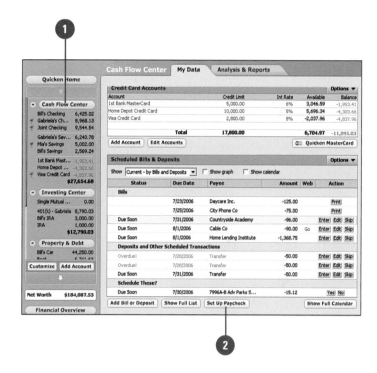

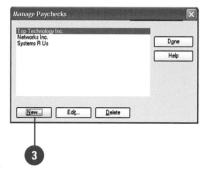

6

4 Click **Next**.

5 Specify whose paycheck this is—yours or your spouse's.

6 In **Company Name**, type the source of the income. If the source is an individual, you can use their name. If the income is from a company already in use, Quicken does not allow you to use the same name twice. Therefore, you will have to use a unique name or identifier.

7 If you'd like to make a notation about the income—for example if the income is from the same source as a paycheck that is already set up—click in **Memo** and type a notation. Then click **Next**.

8 Select whether you want Quicken to track taxes and other deductions taken from the income, or if you want to track the net deposits only. Click **Next**.

IMPORTANT *If deductions are taken out of this income, it is wise to have Quicken track the earnings, taxes, and other deductions. Quicken can use this information to forecast your taxes and when it comes time to do your taxes, you can export this and all other tax-related information to use in TurboTax, other tax software, or to give to your accountant.*

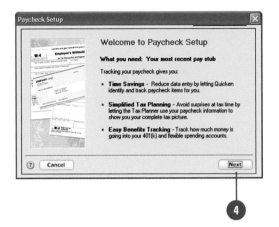

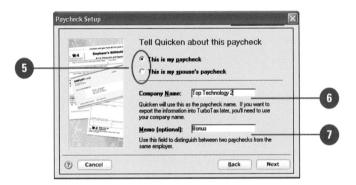

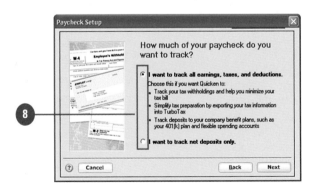

9 Select the account into which the income is deposited.

10 Select or type the date you begin receiving the income and how frequently, if the income is continual. If this is a one-time deal, select **Only Once** from the Frequency drop-down menu.

11 To create a scheduled transaction for this deposit, select **Remind Me** or select **Automatically Enter** to have Quicken enter this deposit in your account register for you. Then enter the number of days in advance you want for this transaction to either show up in Scheduled Bills & Deposits or be recorded in your account register.

Click to collapse the Scheduling section.

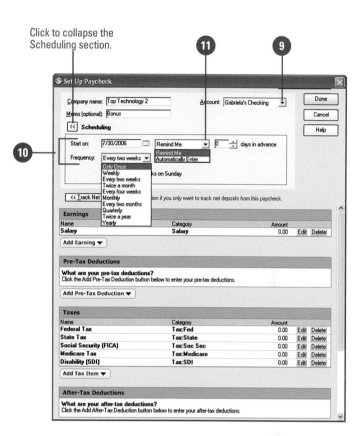

For Your Information

If you choose to track taxes and other deductions in step 8, the Track Net Only button appears in the top portion of the window. You can click this button to hide the deductions portion of the window so that you can track only net earnings. Or, if you choose to track only net deposits, the Track Deductions button appears in the top portion of the window. Clicking this button allows you to enter deductions for the paycheck.

For Your Information

If you don't want to be reminded of this transaction or the income is a one-time occurrence, type "0" in **Days in Advance**.

6

Add Earnings Information

1. If the income you are adding is you or your spouse's salary, click in **Amount** and type the salary amount.

2. If the income is not salary, from the **Add Earning** drop-down menu, select the type of income you are adding.

3. The **Name** and **Category** fields are already completed for you. However, you can change them, if needed.

4. Type the amount of the income and click **OK**.

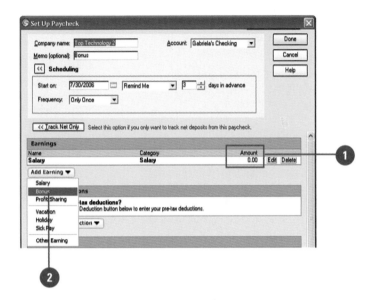

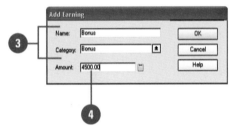

For Your Information

If you opted to track only the net earnings, you do not see the Earnings, Pre-Tax Deductions, Taxes, or After-Tax Deductions sections of the Set Up Paycheck window.

Add Pre-Tax Deduction Information

1. If the income you are adding has any pre-tax deductions, for example, insurance or flex-spending, from the **Add Pre-Tax Deduction** drop-down menu, select the deduction you want to add.

2. The **Name** field is already completed for you. However, you can change it, if needed.

3. If applicable, select the account associated with the deduction.

4. Type the amount and in the case of a 401(k) match, type the company's contribution in the **Employer Match** field. Click **OK**.

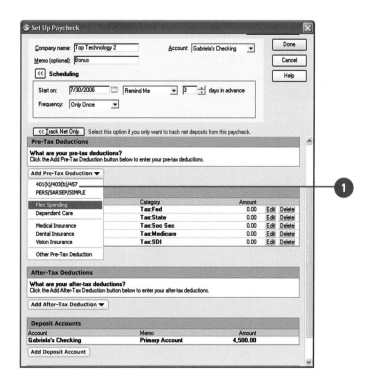

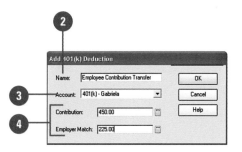

6

Add Taxes and After-Tax Deductions Information

1. To enter the tax deductions, click in the **Amount** column for each applicable tax category and type the appropriate amounts.

2. If a tax category is not listed, click **Add Tax Item**, select the tax item you want to add. If it is not listed, select **Other Tax** to add it.

3. If you have any after tax deductions to apply, such as a stock purchase, click **Add After-Tax Deduction** and select the deduction you want to add. The process works the same as adding pre-tax deductions.

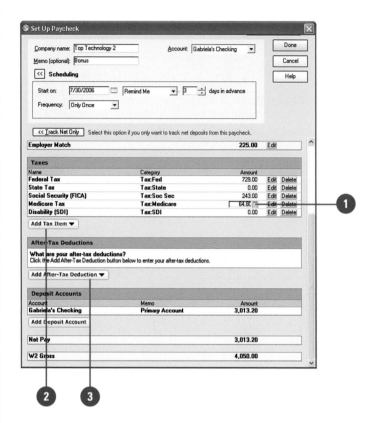

Add Deposit Accounts Information

① The account you selected from the Account drop-down menu at the top of the Set Up Paycheck window is automatically listed in the Deposit Accounts section. To add another account to which some of the income is deposited, click **Add Deposit Account**.

② Select the account you want to add.

③ Type the dollar amount that is deposited into the account you selected in the previous step and click **OK**. Quicken adds the account to the list and automatically adjusts the amount deposited into the primary account.

TIMESAVER *After the account is added to the Deposit Accounts section, you can change the deposit amount, if needed, by clicking in the **Amount** column for that account and typing over the amount. You can also delete the account by clicking the **Delete** button next to the account. This does not delete the account itself; it only tells Quicken that no money is going into this account for this income.*

④ When you are finished adding all the information for the new paycheck, click **Done**. A message appears asking if you want to add year-to-date information for the income.

⑤ Select **I Want to Enter Year-to-Date Information** to enter the year-to-date deductions information. Otherwise, select **I Do Not Want to Enter This Information** to bypass this step.

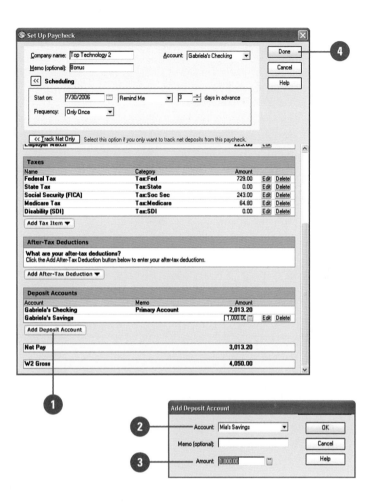

For Your Information

If this is a one-time payment, you don't need to enter year-to-date information because the deductions you entered when it was set up are all that are needed. However, if this is an ongoing salary, you should enter the information. Quicken uses this information for your taxes for forecasting and tracking purposes, which is used in reports and can be used to file your taxes.

6

Edit or Delete a Paycheck

1 If you don't already have the Cash Flow Center open, on the account bar, click **Cash Flow Center** and then scroll down to the Scheduled Bills & Deposits section.

2 Click **Set Up Paycheck**.

3 To edit an existing paycheck, select it and click **Edit**.

4 Change any of the information by clicking in the fields and typing, using the Edit and Delete buttons, and using the drop-down menus. When you are finished making changes click **Done**.

5 To remove a paycheck, select it click **Delete**.

See Also

See the previous task, "Add a New Paycheck" for more detailed information on completing paycheck information.

6 When you are finished with paychecks, click **Done**.

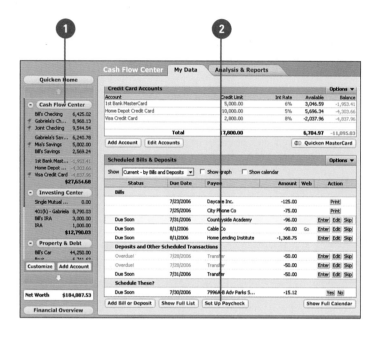

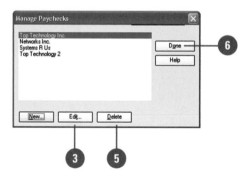

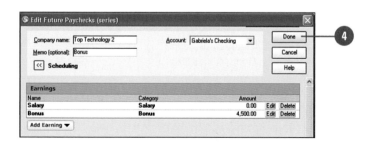

Recording Scheduled Transactions in Your Account Register

When you set up your accounts and tell Quicken about any regularly scheduled transactions for your accounts, Quicken creates a scheduled transactions list for you. The scheduled transactions for your all your accounts appear on the Scheduled Bills & Deposits tab in each of your account registers. They also appear on the Scheduled Bills & Deposits section in the Cash Flow Center, the Quicken Home page, and on the master list in the Bills & Deposits window. You can record transactions from any of these locations. The following task shows you how to record scheduled transactions from an account register.

Record Scheduled Transactions in Your Account Register

1. On the account bar, select the account to which you want to record scheduled transactions.

2. If it's not already visible, click the **Scheduled Bills & Deposits** tab. The number in parentheses represents the number of transactions waiting to be added to your register.

3. If you pay this bill online through a website, ensure that you are connected to the Internet, and click the **Go** link to open the website. After you're finished, you can return to Quicken and enter the transaction in your register.

4. To add a scheduled transaction to your register, click **Enter**.

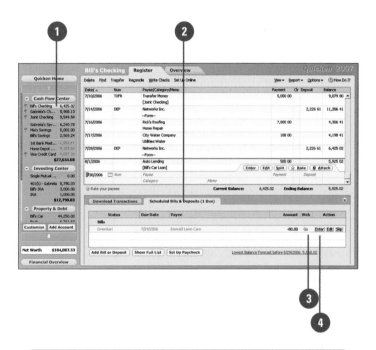

For Your Information

You can edit transaction information for all future instances of this transaction by selecting it from the Scheduled Bills & Deposits tab and clicking **Edit**. Then from the Edit Future Transactions window, make your changes and click **OK**.

6

5. Review the information to ensure that it is correct and make changes, if needed. Any changes you make here do not apply to all future transactions—only to the current transaction.

6. To add the transaction to your register, click **Enter Transaction**.

7. If you are not ready to enter the transaction in your register, click **Cancel** to take no action on the transaction and return to the scheduled transaction list. The transaction remains in the scheduled transaction list until you are ready to record it or skip it.

8. If the transaction does not apply for this transaction period, click **Skip** to remove the transaction from your scheduled transactions for the current period. It will reappear the next time it is scheduled to show up.

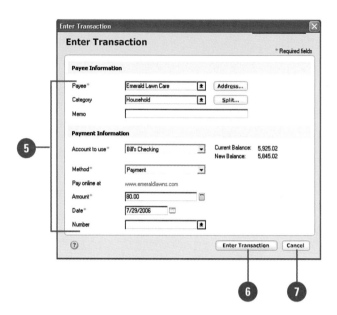

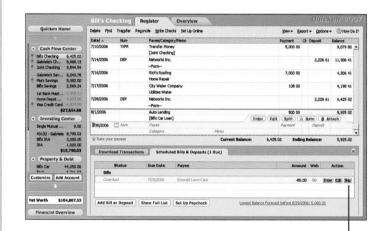

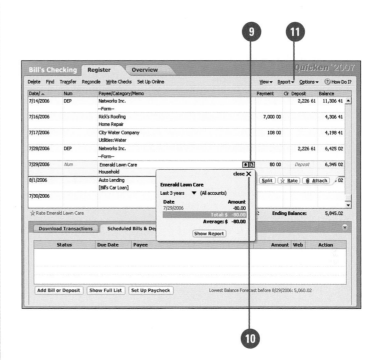

9 To view the average amount spent for a transaction, select the transaction and click the **Report** icon. You can view a complete report by clicking the **Show Report** button.

10 To close the pop-up window, click **Close**.

11 You can also use the **Report** drop-down menu to view other information about the selected transaction and the categories associated with it.

12 Enter all scheduled transactions until you are finished. Transactions you record are entered into your register, and your balance is adjusted accordingly.

Did You Know?

Unscheduled transactions appear under the Schedule These? section. If there are transactions that have not been scheduled, Quicken creates a temporary section on the Scheduled Bills & Deposits tab called Schedule These? (not shown here). You click **Yes** to schedule a transaction or **No** to leave it unscheduled. This does not remove it from your scheduled transactions. If there are no unscheduled transactions, you do not see this section.

6

Downloading and Adding Transactions from Your Account Register

Download Transactions from Your Account Register

1 On the account bar, click the account to which you want to add downloaded transactions.

2 To download account transactions, connect to the Internet and on the Downloaded Transactions tab, click **Update Transactions**.

3 In the Online Update for this Account window, select the account you want to download (if there are multiple accounts), type your password, and click **Update Now**.

See Also

See "Editing Accounts" on page 103 for information on setting up online services for accounts and "Using Online Updates" on page 79 for information on setting up a PIN.

Did You Know?

Your account must be set up for online access before you can download transactions. In order to download account transactions, the account must already be set up for online access, your financial institution must provide download capability in to Quicken, and you must have a login ID and password already set up.

If you set up any of your accounts for online access, each time you use One Step Update, your most recent account transactions download to the appropriate account in Quicken. You can then review and add the transactions to your register, edit transactions before you add them to your register, or delete them if needed. If you don't use the online updates, you can add transactions manually.

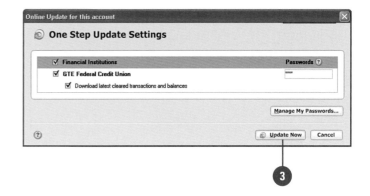

4 If the Online Update Summary window opens, review the information that was downloaded and click **Close**.

5 To add all transactions to your register, click **Accept All**.

IMPORTANT *Be aware that if you have scheduled transactions set up and have already entered them in your account register, and you then download the same transactions, duplicate transactions can be created. You should match up the transactions so that duplicate transactions are not entered in your account register. To do this, before you accept the transaction, click the **Edit** drop-down next to the transaction and select **Match Manually**. From the Manually Match Transactions window, select the scheduled transaction you want to replace with the downloaded transaction. Then click **Accept**.*

6 To add only individual transactions to your register, click each transaction you want to add and click **Accept**. A message appears, asking if you want to assign a category to each transaction.

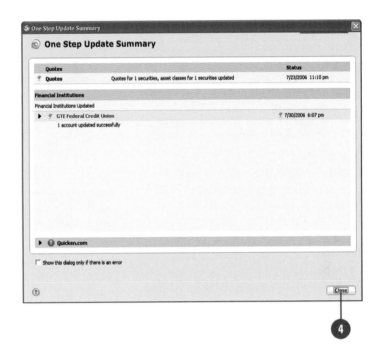

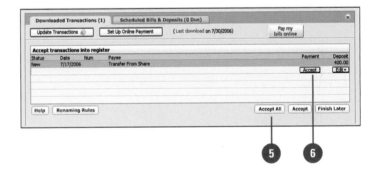

7. Click **Yes** to assign a category or **No** to enter the transaction without assigning a category.

8. To assign a category, select the category you want to use or click **Split** to assign more than one category to a transaction.

9. Click **Enter**. The status of the transaction changes to Accepted on the Downloaded Transactions tab. After you add all transactions to your register, the transactions no longer appear on the Downloaded Transactions tab.

10. To remove a transaction, select the transaction, click **Edit**, and then select **Delete**.

11. To view spending totals and averages for the category, click the **Report** icon.

TIMESAVER *You can also view payee spending totals by clicking in the Payee column and clicking the Report icon.*

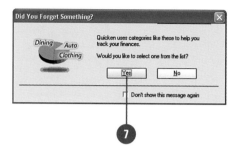

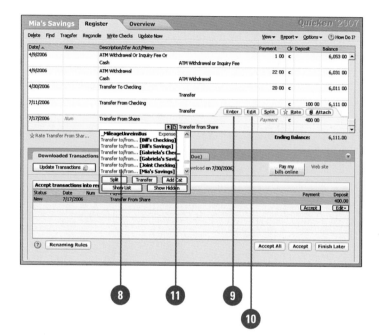

Did You Know?

Assigning categories can help you track your spending. By assigning categories to all your transactions, you can see exactly where your money is going when you run transaction reports, as shown in step 11. Quicken tracks categories across all your accounts so that when you run a report, it can show you exactly how much you've spent in a specific category.

Flag and Attach Documents to Transactions

You can flag transactions in your account registers; for example, as a reminder to follow up on the transaction at a later time. In addition, you can attach documents to transactions in your account registers, such as an electronic or scanned receipt to keep with the transaction. There's no losing an attached receipt!

Flag Transactions

1. Open the account register that contains the transaction(s) you want to flag or attach documents.

2. To flag a transaction, select a transaction and click **Attach**.

3. Click **Add Follow-Up Flag**.

4. Type a note or message about the follow-up, select the color you want for the flag, and type a date when you want to be reminded of the follow-up. Then click **OK**.

5. To review or delete a follow-up message, click the flag.

6. To delete the message, click **Delete**.

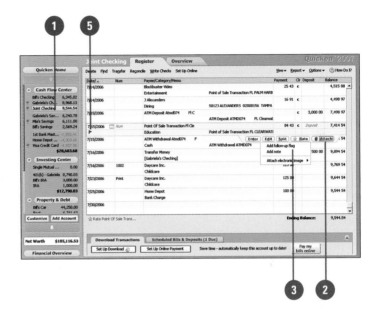

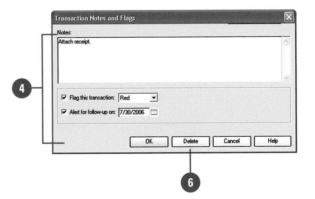

Attach Documents to Transactions

1. To attach a document, click **Attach** and select **Attach Electronic Image**. Then select the type of file you want to attach.

2. Select the type of attachment.

3. Click the source of the attachment you want to add.

4. Locate and select the document you want to attach and click **Open**. The attachment appears in the Transaction Attachments window.

5. Click **Done**. The Attachment button appears next to the transaction.

6. To remove an attachment, click the attachment.

7. From the Transaction Attachments window, select the attachment you want to remove and click **Delete**. A message appears, asking if you want to delete the attachment.

8. Click **Yes** to remove the attachment or **No** to keep it.

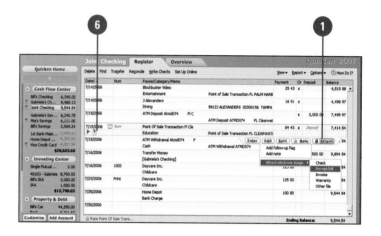

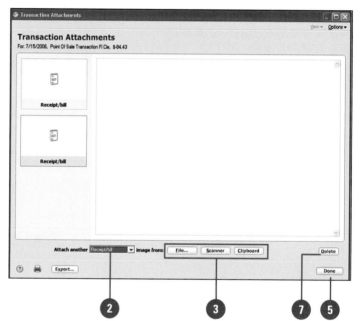

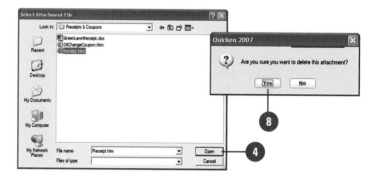

Recording Transactions in Your Account Register Manually

Record Transactions in Your Account Register Manually

1 From the account bar, select the account to which you want to add a transaction.

2 Click in the **Date** column of an empty row and type the date of the transaction.

3 In **Payee**, type the payee name.

4 Click **Category** and select a category to assign to the transaction. Or if the category does not exist, type the name of the category you want to track for this transaction.

5 Click in the **Memo** column to type a note about the transaction.

6 Click in the **Charge** or **Payment** columns and type the amount of the transaction.

7 To flag this transaction to follow up on later, or to attach a document, click **Attach**.

8 Click **Enter**. Quicken adjusts your account balance and if you selected other accounts in step 4, the balance of any other accounts are adjusted as well.

See Also

See "Flag and Attach Documents to Transactions" on page 165 for more information on flagging transactions for follow-up and attaching documents to transactions.

If you don't have online access to download transactions into your account registers or you don't have a scheduled transaction set up, you can add transactions manually. The process works the same for all types of accounts. A credit card account is used in this task to show you how to add transactions manually. If you add transactions to investment or retirement accounts, the process is slightly different. See the "Record and Edit Investment Transactions" in the next task for more information.

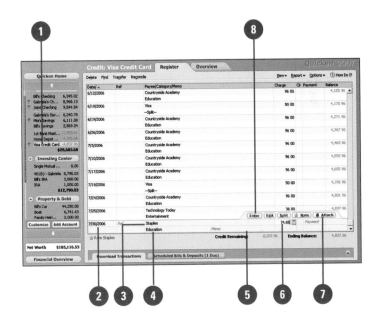

See Also

See "Tracking Transactions with Multiple Categories" on page 71 for more information on splitting transaction categories.

Did You Know?

You can assign more than one category to a transaction. To track more than one category for a transaction, click **Split**. Then from the Split Transaction window, specify the categories you want to track. Be aware that if you select another account for the category—for example, if you are entering a payment that is being applied to your credit card, but is coming out of your checking account—Quicken automatically enters a transaction in the register of the other account.

6

Record and Edit Investment and Retirement Transactions in Your Account Register Manually

1. In the activity bar, from the **Investing Center** section, click the account for which you want to add scheduled transactions.

2. Click the **Transactions** tab.

3. Click in the **Date** column and type the date of the transaction.

4. Click the drop-down arrow in the **Action** column and select the reason for the transaction. If the action you want to use is not listed, type a new one.

5. Click the drop-down arrow in the **Description** column and select or type a explanation for the transactions.

6. Click the drop-down arrow in the category field and select or type a new category for the transaction.

7. Click in the **Inv. Amount** column and type the dollar amount of the transaction.

8. Review the information to ensure that it is correct, make changes, if needed, and add it to your register by clicking **Enter**. Your balance is adjusted accordingly.

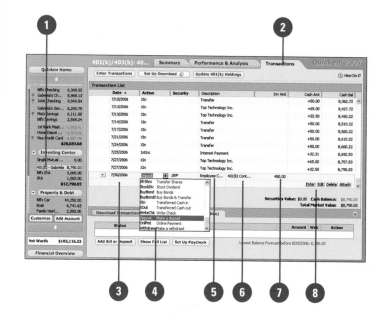

> ### Did You Know?
>
> *Assigning categories can help you track your spending.* By assigning categories to your transactions, you can see exactly where your money is going when you run transaction reports. In addition, when it comes to tax time, you can utilize the information to file your taxes.

Editing and Deleting Transactions

Edit and Delete Transactions

1 From the account bar, select the account for which you want to edit or delete transactions.

2 Click the area you want to change (for example, the category) and type or select the new information.

3 Click in any of the other fields in the transaction to change the information, as needed.

4 Click **Enter**.

5 To delete an entire transaction, select the transaction and click **Delete**. A message appears, asking if you want to delete the transaction.

6 Click **Yes** to delete it or **No** to keep it.

See Also

See "Use the Memorized Payee List to Manage Your Renaming Rules" on page 174 for information on renaming payees and assigning categories.

If you set up your accounts to use One Step Update, the transactions download and appear in the Downloaded Transactions tab of your account registers. You can then review and add the transactions to your register. However, because downloaded transactions often come in with a series of numbers, symbols, or names that probably don't make a lot of sense, you may prefer to rename them. To do this, you can edit the transaction, rename it to something that makes sense to you, and assign a category so you can track it. One of the nice things about Quicken is that when you do rename transactions and assign categories, Quicken remembers so the next time a transaction is downloaded or entered into your register with the same, original name, Quicken automatically renames it for you and assigns the category. In the meantime, refer to the following task to learn how to edit and delete transactions.

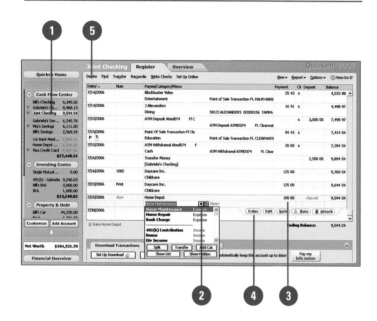

Searching for Transactions

As you use Quicken, your transactions grow in number. The more transactions you have, the harder it can be to find what you're looking for (for example, if you need to update a specific transaction). If you have hundreds of transactions, it could be like trying to find a needle in a haystack. Luckily, Quicken has a search tool that is available in all account centers to locate specific transaction information.

Search for Transactions

1 From the account bar, select the account you want to use to search for transactions.

2 Click **Find**.

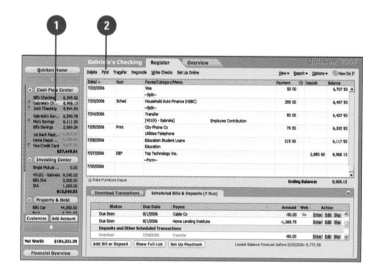

Did You Know?

Sorting transactions is another way of finding transactions. You can sort your transactions by clicking the column headings. For example, clicking the Payee/Category/Memo heading sorts the transactions list in alphabetic order by the payee name. The current sort for the transactions list is indicated by an arrow that appears next to the column title.

③ From the Search drop-down menu, select the focus of your search. For example, if you want to find a transaction that cleared your account for 1546.25, but you don't know the payee's name, select **Amount**.

④ From the **Match If** drop-down menu, select the criterion you want to use to narrow the search further.

⑤ Click in **Find** and type the word or number you are searching for. For example, using the example here, you type 1546.25.

⑥ If you want Quicken to search backward from the current date, select the **Search Backwards** box.

⑦ Click **Find** to locate transactions in the current register. Quicken locates and highlights the transaction that contains the search criteria you specified

⑧ To locate transactions in all registers, click **Find All**. Quicken displays the results in the Search Results window, where you can select and edit the transactions, if needed.

⑨ If you don't find the information you are looking for, perform the search again, using different search criteria by repeating steps 3–8.

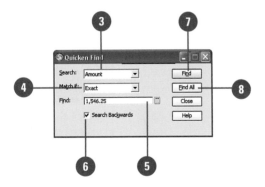

Did You Know?

The Match If and Find criteria work together to locate the transaction. What you select from the Match If menu corresponds with what you type in the Find box. For example, because you know that the amount cleared your account for $1546.25, you can select Exact because you know that the transaction will include 1546.25.

6

Transferring Funds Between Accounts

Transferring funds between accounts means withdrawing money from one account and depositing it into another. When you transfer funds between accounts, Quicken automatically logs the transaction in the register from which the money is being removed and creates a parallel transaction in the register for the account to which the money is being deposited. Transferring funds between accounts happens only within Quicken, though; it does not affect the accounts at your bank or other financial institution. If you use your financial institution's online features to transfer money from one account to another, there is no need to perform a transfer in Quicken because the transactions for the transfer will automatically appear in your downloaded transactions. However, if you are not using the online features or are experimenting with moving your funds around, you can use the following task to step through a transfer.

Transfer Funds Between Accounts

① From the account bar, select the account you want to use to transfer funds. It does not matter which account you open first (the one from which you are removing the funds or the one to which the funds are being deposited).

② Click **Transfer**.

Did You Know?

You can use scheduled transactions for frequent transfers. If you have a transfer that takes place on a regular basis, you can use a scheduled transaction to set up an automatic transfer. You can also set the dates and amounts of the transfer. When it comes time for the transfer to occur, Quicken automatically updates your scheduled transactions list. Refer to the task "Record Scheduled Transactions in Your Account Register," in this chapter, for more information.

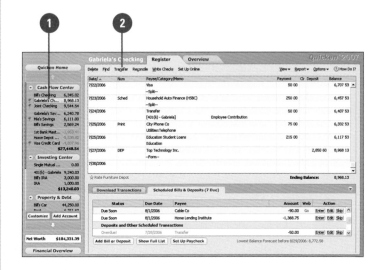

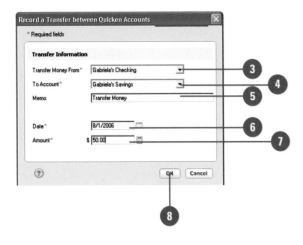

3 Select the account from which you want to transfer the funds; the money will come out of this account.

4 Select the account to which the funds are going; the money will be deposited into this account.

5 In the **Memo** field, type a description or reason for the transfer.

6 Type the date that the transfer is to take place. You can future-date the transaction; however, the balances for each account are immediately adjusted.

7 Type the dollar amount of the transfer.

8 Click **OK**. The transfer shows up as TXFR in the Num column of the account register from which the money is taken. In the register to which the money is deposited, the transaction shows up as Transfer Money. Quicken automatically adjusts the balances accordingly.

6

Use the Memorized Payee List to Manage Your Renaming Rules

Whenever you change the payee name or memo for transactions, Quicken remembers what you rename the payee or memo and the category you assign. It keeps this information in the Memorized Payee List window, along with the renaming rules. You can use the Memorized Payee List window to review and edit the list, which is advisable because the list grows over time and can be get out of control. To review and trim up the memorized payee names:

1. From the **Tools** menu, select **Memorized Payee List** (or press Ctrl+T).

2. To add a new payee to the list, click **New** and complete the information on the **Create Memorized Payee** window.

3. To review or change the renaming rules, click **Renaming Rules**.

   See "Set Downloaded Transactions Preferences" on page 47 for more information on creating and editing renaming rules.

4. To change all information for a memorized payee, such as the associated category, select the transaction and click **Edit**.

5. On the **Edit Memorized Payees** window, make your changes and click **OK**.

6. To change the name of a payee, select it and click **Rename**.

7. On the Merge and Rename Payees window, type the new name and be sure to select **Create Renaming Rules for Future Downloaded Transactions** so that Quicken will rename the payee to the new name next time. However, changing a payee name does not change the name for transactions that are already downloaded.

8. To create a new renaming rule, click **Rename** and complete the Merge and Rename window.

9. To remove a name, select it and click **Delete**.

10. To inhibit a payee from being renamed, select it and click the lock button. To remove the lock, click it again.

11. To add the renamed payee to your transaction calendar, select the transaction and click the calendar button. To remove it, click the button again.

12. To search for a specific payee name and replace it with a new name for all your transactions, click **Go to Find and Replace**. Then complete the information on the Find and Replace window to locate and rename transactions.

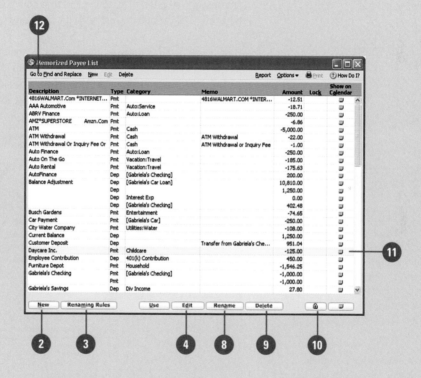

Balancing Accounts

TIMESAVER *To save time in comparing and clearing each transaction manually, you can click **Reconcile** on the menu, enter all of your statement information, and let Quicken reconcile all transactions for you. When Quicken is finished and there are any discrepancies, Quicken provides a list for you to review and resolve.*

Balancing or reconciling accounts in Quicken is very similar to balancing your accounts by using your paper register and monthly statement. You should balance your accounts in Quicken as often as you normally would manually using your monthly statements. If the account has online access, each time you download your transactions, Quicken automatically clears each transaction in your register.

If the account you are balancing does not have online access, you need your monthly bank statement to compare against your Quicken register. If you find discrepancies, you can reconcile your balance by adding missing transactions, downloading the latest transactions, and so on to ensure that your ending balance matches that on your paper statement. You need to keep in mind that some transactions may not have cleared yet and therefore might not show up on your statement.

Before you begin to balance your accounts, you should make sure that all transactions (deposits, withdrawals, purchases, payments, interest, and so on) have been downloaded and recorded or entered in your account register. Depending on which account you are balancing, what you see in the examples that follow may differ from your experience.

Balance Your Account Manually

① On the account bar, open the account you want to balance.

② Compare the transactions on your statement to those that appear in your Quicken account register. When you find a match, double-click in the **Clr** column to tell Quicken that this transaction has cleared. A message appears, asking if you want to reconcile this account.

③ Click **Yes** to enter your statement information and have Quicken reconcile your account or click **No** to continue clearing each transaction manually.

④ If you choose to clear the transaction manually, Quicken places a C in the Clr column to indicate that the transaction has cleared. You must then click **Enter** to save the cleared transaction.

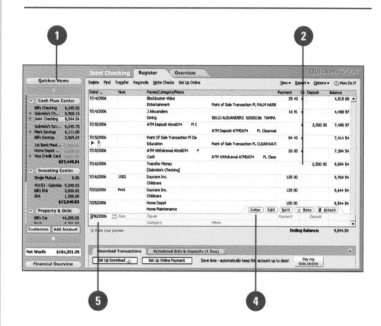

5 To add a missing transaction, click in the next empty transaction row and type the information. Then click **Enter**.

6 To edit a transaction, select the transaction, click **Edit**, make your changes, and click **Enter**.

7 Continue comparing transactions and clearing each transaction, as needed. When you are finished, compare your statement balance to your register. If there is a difference, determine the reason for the discrepancy (for example, maybe fees and interest were added).

8 When you are ready to enter the balance, click **Reconcile**.

9 Type the ending balance and date from your statement, type any bank charges and interest, and select a category to associate with the charges and interest. Then click **OK**.

Did You Know?

You can reconcile when you want to update your balance or to skip clearing the transactions individually in your register. You can reconcile an account when there is a discrepancy between your statement balance and your Quicken register balance. Reconciling the balance gives you the opportunity to synch the two balances. When you reconcile your balance, the next time you balance your account, Quicken works from the reconcile balance. You can also check off your cleared transactions using the Statement Summary window by selecting **Yes** in step 3.

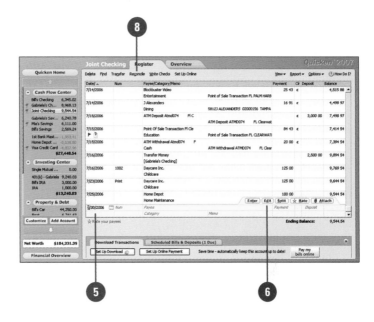

Continued, next page ▶

10 The Statement Summary window shows you which transactions have cleared by placing a green check mark next to each cleared transaction. You can select transactions that have cleared by clicking in the **Clr** column.

11 If there are discrepancies, you can add missing transactions and edit or delete transactions by using the menu options to balance your account.

12 To complete the balance at another time, click **Finish Later**.

13 If the difference is zero, the account is balanced. Click **Finished**. Quicken places an R in the Clr column to show that your transactions have been reconciled.

14 If the account balanced, the Reconciliation Complete dialog box opens, asking if you want to view a reconciliation report. Click **Yes** if you want to view the report; otherwise, click **No**.

15 If the account did not balance and you clicked Finished instead of Finish Later, a message appears asking if you want for Quicken to adjust your balance to reconcile it. Click **Adjust** to adjust your balance or **Cancel** to return to the Statement Summary window.

Balance Your Online Accounts

1 On the account bar, open the account you want to balance and click **Update Transactions** to download the most recent transactions.

2 If you use the Password Vault, you may be prompted to enter your Password Vault password. If not, the Online Update window appears. Type your password and click **Update Now**.

3 After the download is complete, the Online Update Summary window may appear (unless you have opted for it to appear only if there are errors). Click **Close** to close it.

4 Add any downloaded transactions to your register by clicking the transaction's **Accept** button.

5 Click **Reconcile**.

6 Select **Online Balance**.

7 To let Quicken compare your transactions and reconcile your account, select **Auto Reconcile After Compare to Register** and click **OK**. The Statement Summary window opens, where you can clear, add, edit, or remove transactions to balance your account.

See Also

See steps 10-15 on the previous page for information on using the Statement Summary window.

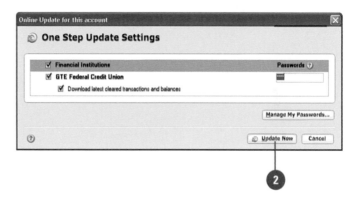

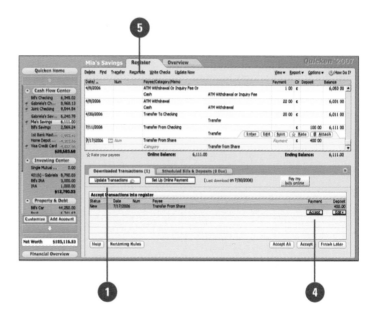

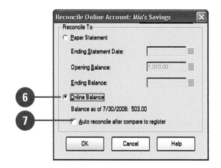

6

Paying the Bills

7

Introduction

Quicken provides several convenient tools you can use to pay your bills. A bill payment tool called Quicken Bill Pay allows you to pay your bills and carry out nonbill transactions, such as sending money to a family member or a babysitter, from your Quicken software through Quicken Bill Pay. You can also pay bills through the Bill Pay website. Your accounts don't have to offer online services for you to use Quicken Bill Pay, though. If the payee or financial institution can receive electronic transfers, the money is electronically taken out of your account and deposited into the payee's account. However, for payees or financial institutions that cannot receive electronic transfers, Quicken prints a check and sends it the old-fashioned way, via U.S. mail.

If you pay some of your bills by writing checks, Quicken offers the convenience of printing checks directly from Quicken so that you don't have to hand-write your checks. In this chapter you will learn how to use Quicken Bill Pay and order, create, and print Quicken checks.

Using Quicken Bill Pay

There is, of course, a fee to use Quicken Bill Pay. Currently, the fee is $9.95 per month for up to 20 transactions. However, Quicken is offering the first month free for the first 20 payments. You will be billed $2.49 for every five payments over the initial 20.

To enroll, you must fill out an application and provide your personal information, such as your name, address, phone number, Social Security number, and payment (for example, checking) account information. When you are approved, you can start setting up your payee and bill information and start paying bills and conducting other payment transactions. You receive your login information by email so that you can log in and access Quicken Bill Pay anytime you want. There are some limitations. If you are interested in using Quicken Bill Pay, check out the details by using this task to determine if this service is for you.

Review Quicken Bill Pay Details

1. From the **Online** menu, select **Quicken Bill Pay** and then click **Learn About Quicken Bill Pay**.

2. Review the information about the Quicken Bill Pay service by clicking the tabs. Be sure to carefully read all information so that you can determine whether this service meets your needs.

3. If you decide you want to enroll, click the **Sign Up** tab.

IMPORTANT *Be aware that you must provide your credit card number up front when using the trial service. If after using Quicken Bill Pay for the 30-day trial you decide you don't want the service, you must cancel it. Otherwise, your credit card will automatically be charged for a service you aren't using. To cancel Quicken Bill Pay services, contact Metavante at 877-486-8844.*

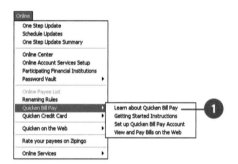

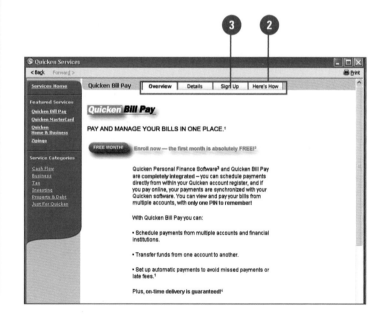

Enroll in Quicken Bill Pay

1 Click **Sign Up Now**.

2 Review the introduction information, click any of the links to get more information, and then scroll down to complete the application. Required fields are bolded.

3 Type your personal and demographic information.

For Your Information

You must complete all bolded fields to successfully sign up for Quicken Bill Pay. Nonbolded fields are optional.

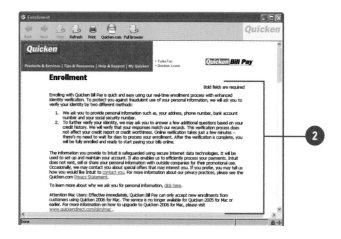

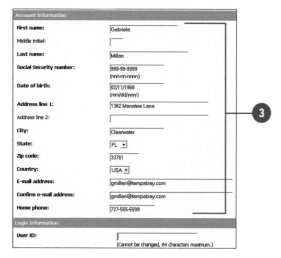

4 Type the login and password you want to use, select a secret question, and type the answer to the secret question. The secret question is used to identify you when you inquire on your account.

5 Enter all your banking information. Be sure to enter your entire account number, including any leading or trailing zeros.

6 Select the type of email messages you can receive, text or HTML, and then select the version of Quicken that you use.

7 Read the privacy statement and select the box **I Have Read and Accept the Terms and Conditions of the Subscriber Agreement**.

8 Click **Sign Me Up!** Quicken processes your enrollment.

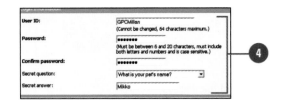

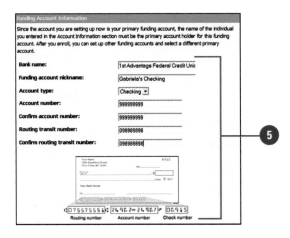

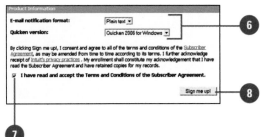

9. Answer the confirmation questions by selecting the appropriate answer and then click the **Submit** button at the bottom of the page.

10. Click the **Here** link to set up your payees and bills.

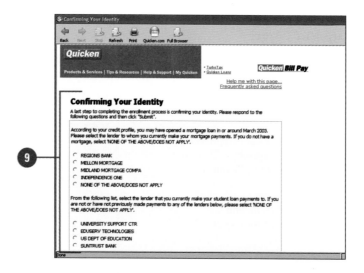

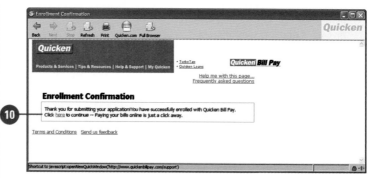

Set Up Your Payees

① To set up your payees, from the **Quicken Bill Pay** web page, click **Payee Setup**.

② Click **Add New Payee**.

③ Type the payee name or, to view and select a payee from Quicken's list, click **View Our Payee List**.

④ Type the account number, the payment ZIP code, and the nickname or alternate name.

⑤ Select the type of account or category for the payee. If the category you want to use is not listed, you can either select **None** or select **Add a New Category** to create one.

⑥ Click **Add Payee**.

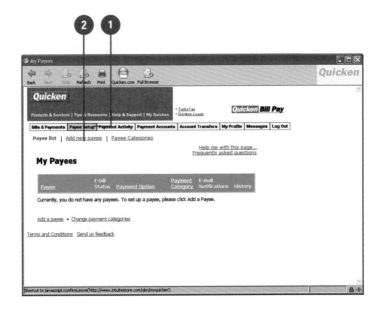

If this account does not have an account number, select this box.

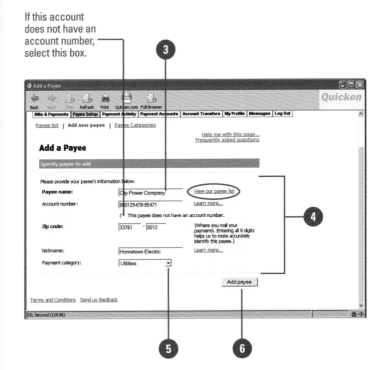

7 Type the payee address and phone number and then click **Add Payee**. Quicken adds the payee information to your payee list and displays a confirmation page, letting you know that the payee was added successfully.

8 To add additional payees, click the **Add Another Payee** link and repeat steps 3–7. Select any of the other links to make a payment or add additional information for this payee.

Did You Know?

You can set up bill payment options, such as notifications and recurring payments. To have Quicken Bill Pay send you an email message when your bills have been paid, click the **Add E-mail Notification** link, shown in step 8 and complete the information. You can also set up recurring payment, by clicking the **Add Payment Options** link and completing the Payment Option section.

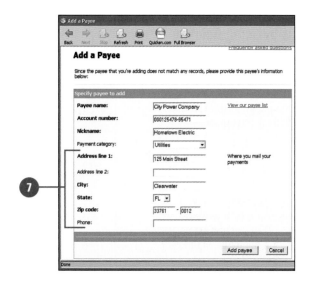

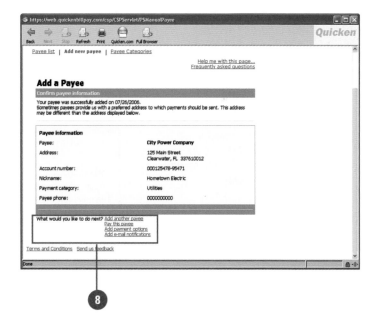

Pay Your Bills by Using Quicken Bill Pay

① To pay a bill by using one of the payees you set up in Quicken Bill Pay, from the menu in Quicken Bill Pay, click **Bills & Payments**.

② To make non–e-bill payments (payments that are received via postal mail, not online), click **Make a Payment to Any Payee**.

③ Type the amount(s) you want to pay for each of your bills and the dates you want the bills paid.

④ Click **Make Payments**.

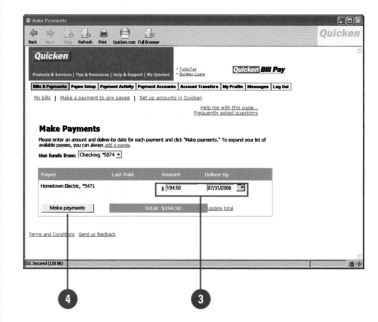

To review the bills scheduled for payment, click **Payment Outbox**. The My Bills page opens.

Click **Payment Detail** to review payment information.

Click **Edit** to make changes to the payment.

Click **Cancel** to stop and remove the payment.

Click **Notes** to add a comments for the payment. If you don't have any changes, the payment(s) will be sent out in time to reach the payee by the designated time.

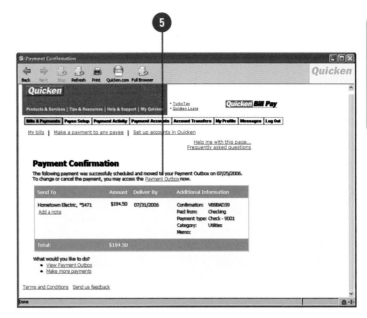

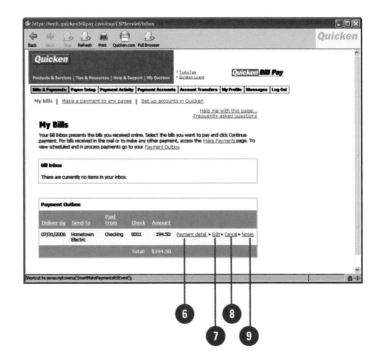

Ordering and Printing Quicken Checks

You can order Quicken checks through the Quicken program and then print them on your printer. Currently, checks start at $59.99 for 250 standard checks. You can also order envelopes, labels, deposit slips, and more. When you receive the checks, you can enter the transactions you want printed on checks, and then print the checks through Quicken on your printer. You can use the payee information that's already in Quicken, or you can add it if you don't have the payee set up, to print your checks.

Order Quicken Checks

1. From the **Cash Flow** menu, select **Quicken Services**, **Order Checks & Supplies**.

2. Ensure that you are connected to the Internet and click the **www.intuitmarket.com** link. The Intuit Checks, Forms & Supplies web page opens.

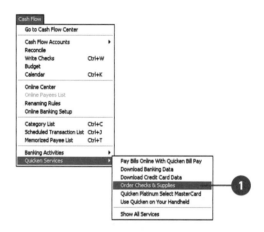

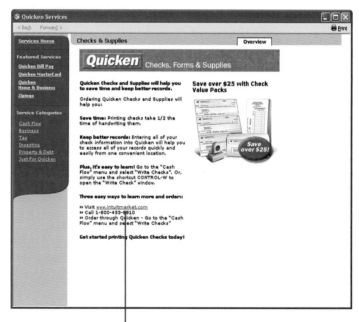

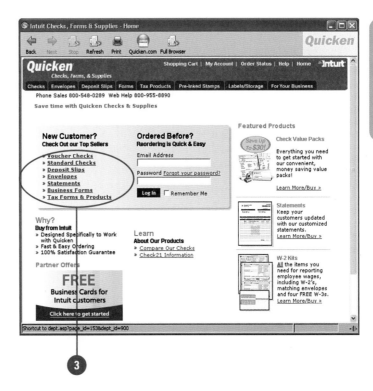

Select the type of checks you want to order.

Review the information about your printer type check options and then scroll down to select your check options.

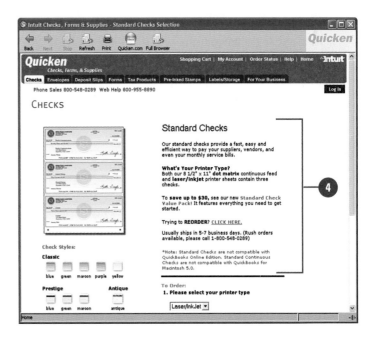

5. Select your printer type, the number of sheets of checks, and the quantity of checks. Then click **Continue**.

6. Proceed through the check-ordering process by completing all the steps. When you are finished ordering, your checks will be mailed to you in the designated timeframe.

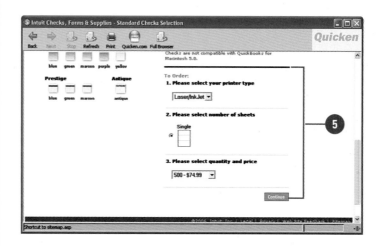

Set Up Transactions to Use Quicken Checks

1. Open the Quicken Cash Flow Center and scroll down to the **Scheduled Bills & Deposits** section. If you already have transactions set up for Quicken checks, a Print button already appears next to the transaction.

2. To set up transactions to print Quicken checks, click **Enter** next to the transaction.

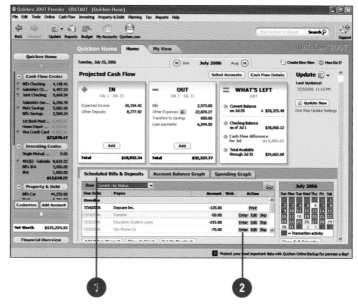

For Your Information

You can also go to the Cash Flow Center to access Scheduled Bills & Deposits.

Did You Know?

You can change your payment method. When you set up your accounts and scheduled transactions, you specified how you would make your payments or which printing method you would use for your payment transactions. There are four payment methods: Payment, Deposit, Print Check, and Online Payment. The payment method you selected when you set up the account is what automatically appears for the account transactions. You can change the payment method when you enter the transaction into your account register to change only that one transaction, or you can edit the transaction to change all future payments to another method.

From the Method drop-down list, select **Print Check**.

To have the payee address print on the check, click **Address** and enter the address of the payee.

Click **Enter Transaction** or **Record Payment** (whichever applies). A Print button appears next to the transaction.

Repeat steps 2–5 for each transaction that requires a printed check.

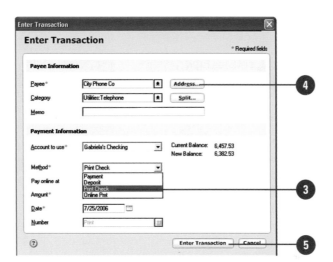

Print Quicken Checks

1 To print checks, click the **Print** button next to the transaction.

2 Type the check number you want printed for this check.

3 Select the check(s) you want to print. If you want to select only specific checks to print (if you have more than one), click **Choose**.

4 Select or clear the checks you want to print or not print and click **Done**.

5 Select the style of the check you want to use.

6 Select how many checks you want to print on a page.

7 Click **OK**. If the following messages appear, take the appropriate actions:

• **Do the Checks Have a Tear-Off Strip?**—It is recommended that you leave the tear-off strip on.

• **Did the Check(s) Print OK?**— Click **OK** if the checks printed correctly. If the checks did not print correctly, type the number of the first check that printed incorrectly and click **OK**. Then determine what the problem is (for example, the checks jammed or the printer is out of checks). If the check information did not print correctly (for example, it is not aligned correctly), adjust the alignment.

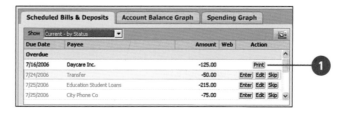

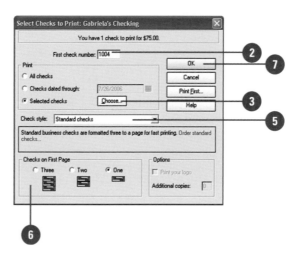

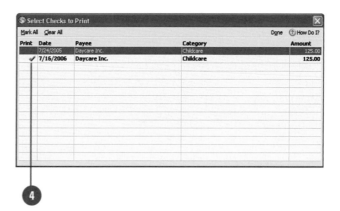

For Your Information

You can also print checks from the Write Checks window by selecting **Write Checks** from the Cash Flow menu.

Managing Your Property and Debt

Introduction

The Property & Debt Center contains account information for your property or assets, such as your home or car, and your liabilities or debt, such as your home and car loans. You can access and manage all of your property and debt accounts from the Property & Debt Accounts section of the Property & Debt Center, just as you manage your spending and savings accounts from the Cash Flow Center. For example, you can add, edit, or delete property or debt account transactions, update the roster with transactions that have been downloaded, review, add, or edit scheduled transactions, balance your register, and manage your loans. In addition, you can set up alerts and access reports.

However, there are a few other features that are not like the other financial centers. The Property & Debt center contains planners and tools that can help you better monitor and manage your finances. For example, to better manage your debt, you can set up a budget and create a plan to get out of debt. To help you manage your property, you can track your auto expenses, record and track your home inventory, insurance policies, claims, and other important records.

Setting Up a Budget

Creating a budget can be a time-consuming and not-so-fun task. But Quicken provides a fast way of creating a budget for you, unless you prefer to create it yourself, one painstaking step at a time. You have three choices for how you want to create your budget. You can either create one manually; you can let Quicken create one for you, using all your existing information; or you can import one that you've used in a previous version of Quicken. If you're like me, the less effort expended, the better. Therefore, the following task steps you through the second choice, letting Quicken create a budget for you. You can tweak the budget later if needed.

Set Up a Budget

1. In the **Planning** menu, click **Budget**.

   TIMESAVER *Once you get your budget set up, you can quickly access it by using the toolbar. You can add the Budget button to the toolbar by right-clicking the tool bar and selecting **Customize Toolbar**. Then from the Add to Toolbar section, select **Budget** and click **Add**. Click **OK** to save your changes.*

2. Select **Automatic** to have Quicken automatically create a budget for you and then click **Create Budget**.

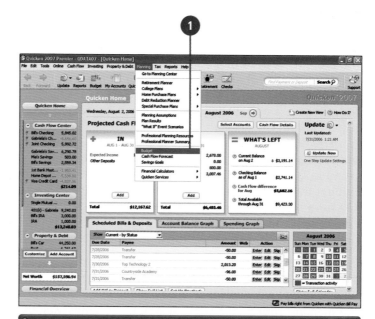

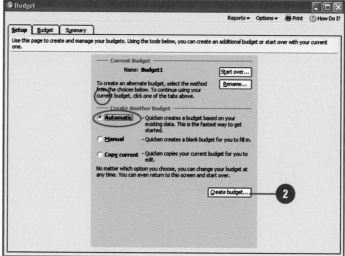

③ Type a name and description for the budget and select the date range that you want Quicken to use to scan your transactions. Quicken uses this information to create your budget.

④ If want to use another time frame besides monthly for your budget, select a different budget method.

⑤ To select the categories Quicken uses to create your budget, click **Categories**.

⑥ Select or clear the categories you want Quicken to use for your budget; for example, your salary. Then click **OK**.

⑦ Click **OK**. A message appears telling you that your budget has been created.

⑧ Click **OK**. Quicken creates a budget based on the transaction and information you've entered thus far for the categories you selected and displays it on the Budget tab.

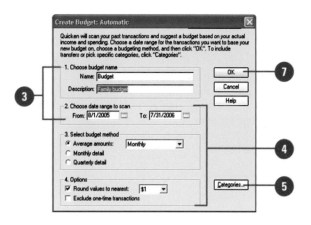

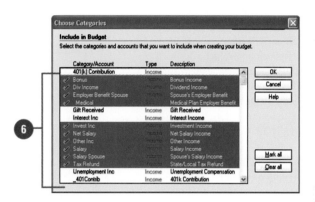

Adjust Your Budget

1 The **Budget** tab contains all the categories you selected, the period, and the average amounts for each category. To change the categories included in your budget, click **Choose Categories** and select or remove the categories.

Did You Know?

You can change the view of your budget. You can view your budget broken into separate tabs for your income, expenses, and savings on separate tabs, rather all combined on one tab. To do this, click **Options** and select **Separate View**. The Income/Expense view shows just your income and expenses on the Budget tab.

2 To change the budget method used for a category or account, select the category or account and then select **Average Amount** to use the average amount spent for the time period; select **Monthly Detail** to set a specific dollar amount for each month; select **Quarterly Detail** to set a specific dollar amount for each quarter.

3 To change the budgeted amount, select the category or account, click in **Amount**, and type the new dollar amount.

4 To change the time period for a budgeted amount, from the **Period** drop-down menu, select the timeframe you want to use. You can use different time periods for each category or account, if needed.

5 To view the average amount spent for a category, click **Analyze**. The Analyze window opens.

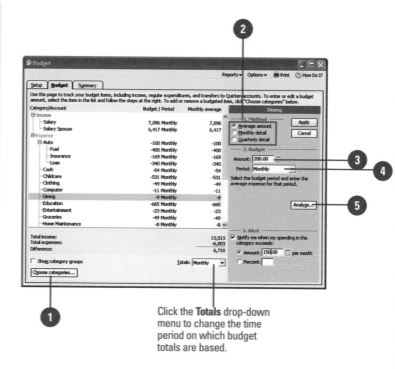

Click the **Totals** drop-down menu to change the time period on which budget totals are based.

For Your Information

You can view and change the groups that categories belong to by selecting the **Show Category Groups** option located in the lower left corner of the Budget tab.. Then click the **Category Groups** button to open the Assign Category Groups window. From there, you can remove or assign categories to or from groups, create new groups, or remove groups.

6 The graph shows you the amount spent for a category or account budget period. For example, if Monthly appears in the Period drop-down list on the Budget window, the Expense graph shows the actual average amount spent each month. Click **Done** to close the window.

7 To set up a reminder to notify you when you exceed the budgeted amount or the percentage of the budgeted amount, select **Notify Me When My Spending in This Category Exceeds**. Then type a dollar amount in **Amount** or select **Percent** and type the percentage of the budget you want to use.

8 Click **Apply** to save the changes you made to a category or account or click **Cancel** to disregard any changes you made.

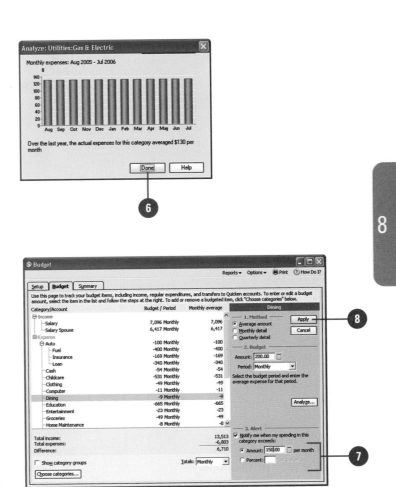

Review Your Budget

1. Click the **Summary** tab to view your entire budget and see whether your budget works for you.

2. The Monthly Budget Summary window provides a breakdown, by month, of your income and expenses. To view the budgeted amounts for a specific month, select it and click **Details**.

3. Click **Done** to close the window.

4. The pie chart shows a yearly view of how your budget breaks down. To view a different breakdown, click the drop-down list and make a selection.

5. To make further adjustments to your budget, click one of the tabs.

6. To print the budget, click the **Print** button.

7. To view a budget report or set savings goals, click the links.

8. Go to the next task to set up a savings goal or close the Budget window if you are finished with your budget.

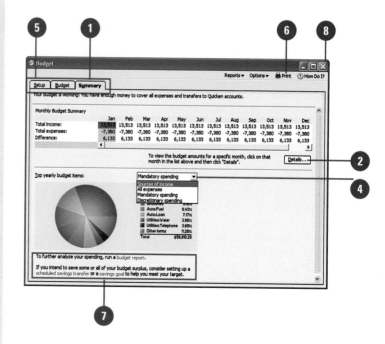

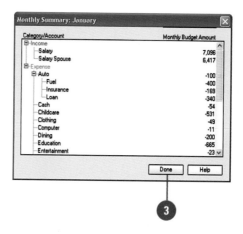

For Your Information

The Budget report shows you how your budget compares to actual totals and how much over you went, if at all for a specific period of time. This report also provides line-by-line detail comparisons of your budget versus actual amounts spent for each category or account and any difference. To learn more about using reports, refer to Chapter 11, "Working Reports" on page 309.

Set Up Savings Goals

1. If your budget shows that you have extra money (shown in the Difference row of the Summary tab) that you can squirrel away for a rainy day, set up a savings plan. To do this, from the Summary tab of the Budget window, click the **Savings Goal** link.

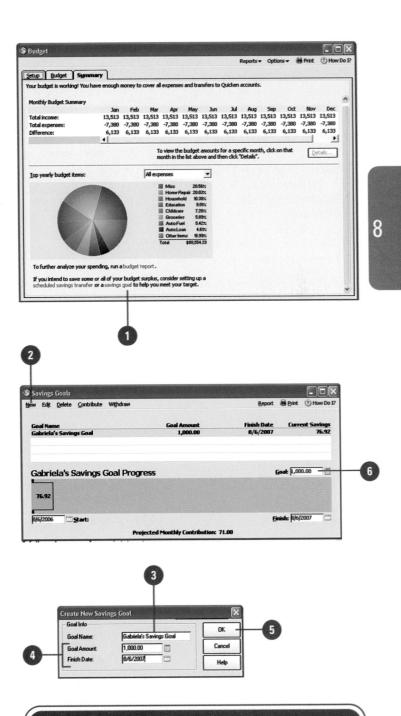

Did You Know?

You can use multi-currency for your savings goals. If you are using multi-currency in Quicken (this is set up in Quicken Preferences), a drop-down list appears (not shown) to allow you to select the currency you want to use for your savings goal.

2. Click **New**.

3. Type a name for your savings goal. Quicken uses this name to create an account to track your savings goal.

4. Type the total amount you want to save and then select or type the date by which you want to save the goal amount.

5. Click **OK**. Quicken creates a savings goal account and displays at the bottom of the window the monthly amount you should save in order to reach your goal.

6. To edit the savings goal amount, ensure that the goal is selected (if there is more than one goal set up), click in **Goal** and type the new amount.

For Your Information

To make changes to a savings goal, you can also click **Edit** on the Savings Goal menu bar.

7. To change the begin and end dates for the goal, in the **Start** and **Finish** boxes, type or select the new dates.

8. To make a contribution to your savings goal, click **Contribute**.

9. Select the account from which you are withdrawing funds to put in your savings account, change the date and amount, if needed, and click **OK**. Your progress and balance are adjusted on the Savings Goals window.

10. To remove money from your savings goal, click **Withdraw** and type the amount you want to remove. Then click **OK**.

11. To remove a savings goal, select it and click **Delete**. A message appears asking if you want to keep the account.

12. Click **Yes** to remove it from your savings goal but keep it as an asset account; click **No** to remove it altogether; or click **Cancel** to take no action.

13. To create additional savings goals, repeat steps 2–5, or if you are finished, close the Savings Goal window.

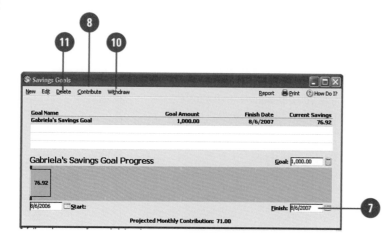

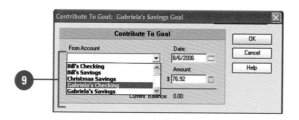

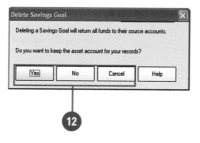

Did You Know?

Deleting a savings goal does not remove it from Quicken. When you delete a savings goal by clicking **Yes** in step 11, it is removed from the Savings Goal window. However, it still appears on the Account List window as an asset account. You can keep it to use for historical tracking. If you decide later that you want to remove it altogether, you have to delete it from the Account List window.

For Your Information

When you withdraw money from an account in Quicken, your account balance is adjusted accordingly within Quicken and a transaction is added to your account register. However, the withdrawal does not affect your account at your financial institution. You still have to make this adjustment to your account at your financial institution.

Getting Out of Debt

Is it hard to breathe under all that debt? Don't despair; help is available. Quicken's Debt Reduction planner can help you create a plan to get yourself out of debt and, hopefully, stay out of debt. I know it's more fun to go shopping than work on your improving your financial status, but the Debt Reduction planner is easy to use and does a lot of the work for you by importing your debt information from your accounts in Quicken. You have nothing to lose but your debt, so follow the steps here to get started.

Set Up a Debt Reduction Plan

1. If you're not already there, open Property & Debt Center by clicking **Property & Debt** on the account bar.

2. From the Tools section, click **Debt Reduction Planner**.

3. Review the introduction and click **Next** to get started with the plan.

Did You Know?

View multimedia clips as you go through the Debt Reduction planner. You can view multimedia clips as you create your debt reduction plan. The clips provide an animated demonstration on how to create a debt reduction plan so that you can see how it is done before doing it yourself. However, you must insert your Quicken CD in your CD drive to view the clips. If you do not want to watch the clips or you don't have your CD near by, click **Next** two times to proceed through the planner and bypass the clips. This task does not show the multimedia clips.

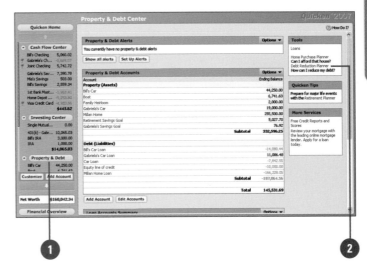

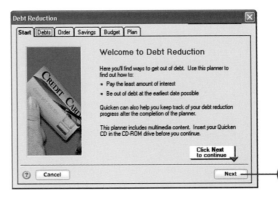

Set Up Your Debt Accounts

① Review your debt accounts. To ensure that all your debt accounts are included and up-to-date, click **Update Debts**. A message appears asking if you want to update.

② Click **Yes**. Quicken queries your accounts and imports any additional accounts and updates those already listed.

③ Click **OK**.

④ To add an account manually, click **Add**.

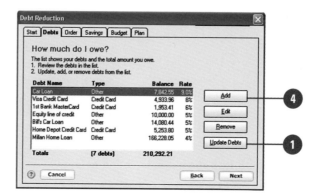

⑤ Complete the account information and click **OK**. If there is no account in Quicken that is associated with this debt, a message appears asking if you would like to set up an account.

⑥ Click **Yes** to set one up (recommended).

⑦ Click **Next** and complete the Loan Setup window.

See Also

See "Add an Auto Loan" on page 108 for information on completing the Loan Setup wizard.

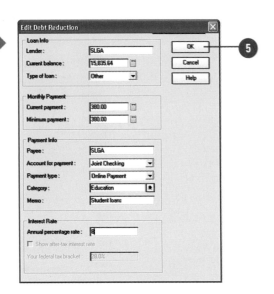

8. To remove an account from your plan, select it and click **Remove**. A message appears asking if you want to delete it.

9. Click **Yes** to remove it or **No** to keep it in the Debt Reduction plan.

10. To update account information, select the account and click **Edit**. Then update the account information and click **OK**.

11. When you are finished setting up the accounts to include in your Debt Reduction plan, click **Next**. If a message appears, asking for more information about the debt accounts, complete the information and click **OK** (not shown).

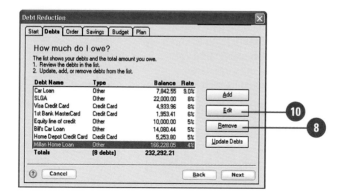

Determine How to Reduce Your Debt

1. Review your total debt situation and click **Next**.

2. Review the order in which you should pay off your debt. You can change the order by selecting **Change Payment Order**, but doing so is not recommended. Quicken uses a specific order to ensure that you pay off your debt quickly and save as much money as possible. Click **Next**.

3. Quicken displays what you currently have in your savings. If you are able to apply part of your savings to your debt, type that amount.

4. Click **Recalculate**. Your debt amount is adjusted accordingly. You can change the amount and click **Recalculate** again to see how the change affects your debt.

5. When you are finished, click **Next**.

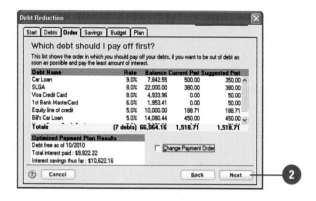

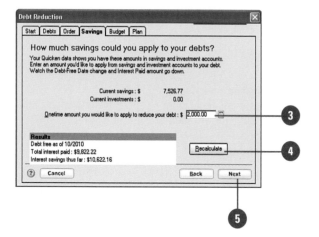

8

6 To reduce the amount you are spending in a specific category, from the **Quicken Category** drop-down lists, select a category. The average spending amount for that category is listed in the Average Monthly Spending column.

7 For each category, type the dollar amount you are willing to cut back for each category listed and then click **Recalculate**. You can change the amount and click **Recalculate** again to see how the change affects your debt.

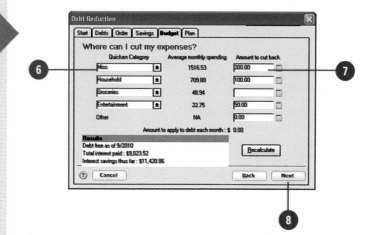

Did You Know?

The Results section provides a running tally of your plan. As you enter the amounts you are going to cut back on, Quicken provides a running tally of when you will be debt free, how much you are currently paying in interest, and how much you will be saving in interest in the Results section of the Budget tab. In addition, a monthly amount that will be applied to your debt is provided just above the Results section.

8 When you are finished selecting categories and entering the amount you are going to cut back on, click **Next**.

Finalize Your Plan

1 Scroll through your plan to review the plan of attack. The **Congratulations** section shows you how much money you can save if you stick to this plan.

2 Sections **Step 1** through **Step 5** and **Other Steps** provide advice, resources, and tips on getting and staying out of debt. For example, Step 2 provides recommendations on where to apply any savings you want to apply to your debt.

3 Scroll down to the **One Year's Payment Coupons**. All your debt accounts are listed by month for a year's time with the payment and balance information for each account. In addition, your total monthly debt balance is listed.

4 If needed, you can go back and make adjustments by revisiting the other tabs in the plan.

5 You can print it by clicking **Print This Action Plan**.

6 When you are ready to finalize the plan, click **Next**.

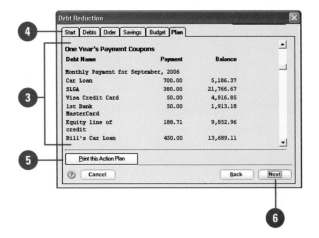

8

7 To set up reminders to keep you on track with your plan, select the **Alert Me If I Fall Behind** option.

8 If you want Quicken to automatically set up your scheduled transactions, select the **Set Up Scheduled Transactions for My Monthly Payments** option. Then click **Next**.

9 Click **Done** (not shown).

10 Review your plan and the steps you should take to update it. Close it when you are finished. The plan now appears at the bottom of the Property & Debt Center.

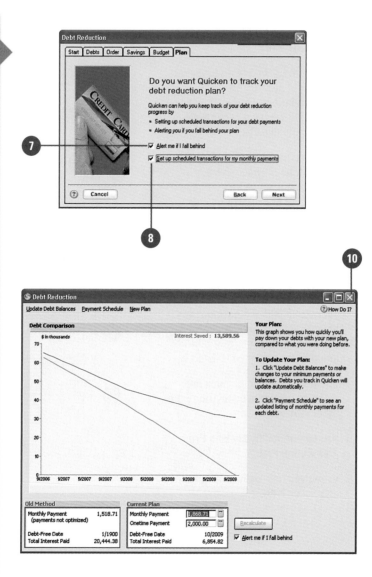

For Your Information

You can review and make adjustments, if needed, to your Debt Reduction plan by repeating the steps in this task.

Keeping Track of Your Home Inventory

I must admit that taking and keeping inventory of my belongings is not one of my favorite things to do. That's right up there with doing taxes, as far as I'm concerned. However, after enduring such destructive and action-packed hurricane seasons the past few years, it behooves everyone to take inventory of his or her belongings. No matter where you live, accidents and disasters can happen. Since luck favors the prepared, everyone should take inventory of their homes and the Quicken Home Inventory tool makes keeping track of your belongings easy and painless. This tool steps you through a process of logging your belongings, room-by-room, and even tracks the contents of your safety deposit box, and anywhere else you might have important belongings and papers. In addition, you can log claims that you've filed and details of your insurance policies.

After you have the information in Quicken, if ever you need to file a claim due to loss of any of your belongings, all the information is at your fingertips. However, I highly recommend that you run an inventory report that contains all of your items after you are finished and keep it with your insurance and other emergency papers. You may not have access to your computer in some emergency situations.

Record Inventory Items

1 From the Property & Debt menu, select **Quicken Home Inventory Manager**.

2 From the **View by Location** drop-down menu, select the room or area you would like to start the inventory.

3 To enter items in the inventory log for the room you selected, click in the first row and from the **Suggested Items For** section, select the name of the item and click **Add Selected Item**.

4 From the **Item Category** drop-down menu, select the category for the item you added.

> ## Did You Know?
>
> ***Create categories to meet your needs.***
> If the categories, policies, or claims you have to choose from do not meet your needs, you can create new ones, edit existing ones, or delete the ones you don't need. To change categories, from the button bar, click **Categories**. Click **New** to create a new category, type the name, and click **OK**. To change the name of a category, select the category, click **Edit**, change the name, and click **OK**. To remove a category, select it and click **Delete**. Click **Close** when you are finished.

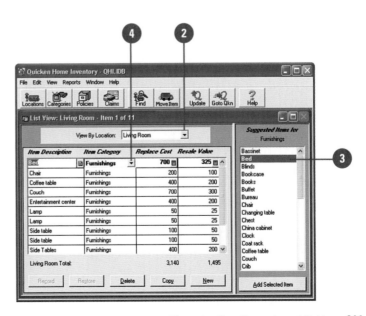

5 If you selected the item from the **Suggested Items For** list, an estimated replacement cost and resale value are already filled in for you. Don't worry about the replacement and resell costs just yet. We will cover costs and other details later.

6 To delete an inventory item, select it and click **Delete**. Or to copy an item to a new line to use some of the same information for another inventory item, click **Copy**.

7 Continue entering all the items for the room and when you are finished, click the detail view icon in the **Item Description** column next to the first inventory item.

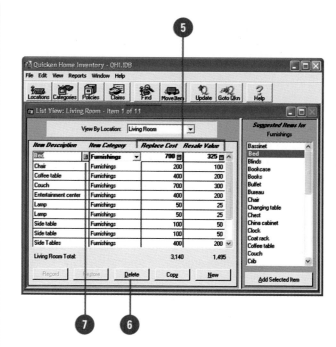

Record Inventory Item Details

1 Enter as much information as you can for the item. If you are unsure of some of the information, leave it blank for now. You can always update it later.

2 To track any paperwork, such as receipts, you have for the item, click **Receipts & Records**.

3 Select the types of receipts and paperwork you have for the inventory item. Then, in **Location of Records**, type where you keep the paperwork, and click **OK**.

Did You Know?

Use the calendar and calculator icons to insert dates and amounts. You can use the calendar icon next to Purchase Date to select the date for the purchase date. Use the calculator icon to calculate and select amounts for Original Price, Replace Cost, and Resale value fields.

4 To add or change resale value information, click **Resale Value History**.

TIMESAVER *To quickly change the resale value of an item, you can click in* **Resale Value** *in the Detail View window and change the amount.*

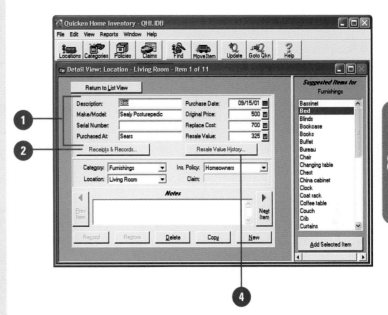

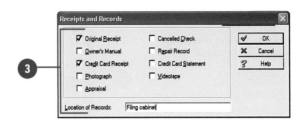

5. To add a new resale value, keeping the old one for historical tracking, click **New**.

6. Type the new value and click **OK**.

7. To edit an existing value instead of creating a new one, select it, click **Edit**. Then change the value and click **OK**.

8. Click **Close**.

9. Click the **Ins. Policy** drop-down list and select the policy under which the inventory item is covered. If the item is not covered, select **Unassigned**.

10. If you have any additional information you want to add about the item—for example, information about the warranty—click in the **Notes** field and type it.

11. Click **Record** to save the changes.

12. Click **Next Item** to enter information about the next inventory item.

13. Complete each item in the inventory and when you are finished, click **Return to List View**.

14. Repeat steps 2–13 for each room or location. When you are finished, Quicken saves all of your inventory items in a QHI.IDB file, which you can back up for safekeeping.

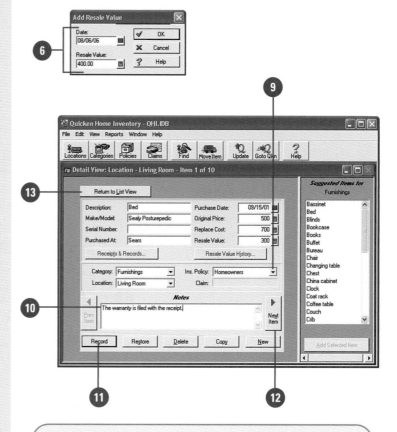

Did You Know?

Search for inventory items. After you get all of your items in the Quicken Home Inventory tool, the list can be long. Trying to find a specific item could be time-consuming, because you have to scroll through all the lists. Using the Find Item window is a much quicker way of finding what you are looking for. To search for an item, from the toolbar, click **Find**. In the Search For box, type the name of the item you want to find, for example, `chair`. Ensure that **Item Description** and **Notes** are selected (this provides a better chance of finding the item) and then click **Find All**. The items found are listed in the List of Found Inventory Items window. Select an item and click **View** to go to that item.

Manage Policies

① To add a new policy, change an existing one, or delete one, from the toolbar, click **Policies**.

② To create a new policy, click **New**.

③ Complete the policy information.

④ To add information about the claims adjuster, click **Claims** and enter that information. Click **OK**.

⑤ To make changes to a policy, select it, and click **Edit**. Then make your changes and click **OK**.

⑥ To delete a policy, select it and click **Delete**. A message appears telling you that any items currently assigned to this policy will be reassigned to the Unassigned policy.

⑦ Click **OK** to go ahead and remove the policy or click **Cancel** to keep the policy.

⑧ When you are finished making changes to policies, click **Close**.

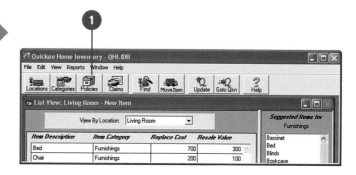

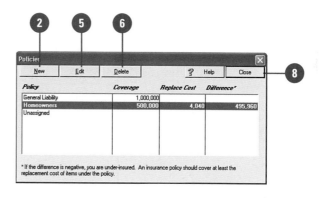

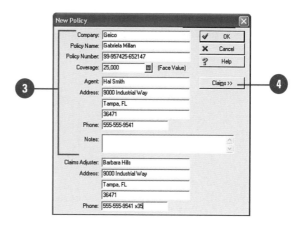

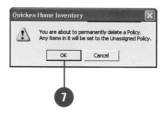

Create a New Claim

1. From the toolbar, click **Claims**.

2. To create a new claim, click **New**.

3. Review the claim instructions (not shown) and click **OK**.

4. Complete the claim information.

5. To add the item(s) for which the claim is being made, click **Items**.

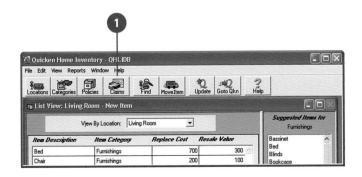

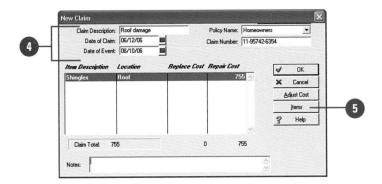

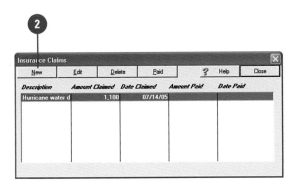

6. Select the item(s) you want to include and click **OK**.

7. To change the repair or replacement costs, click **Adjust Cost**.

8. Select whether the cost is for replacement or repair, type the amount, and then click **OK**.

9. To add more detail about the claim, click in the **Notes** field and type the information.

10. Click **OK** to save the claim. A message appears asking if you want to create a report for the claim.

11. Click **Yes** to create the report. You can print the report to keep in your records or to send to your insurance company.

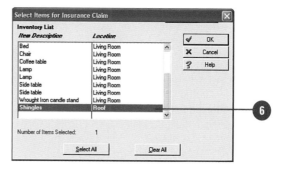

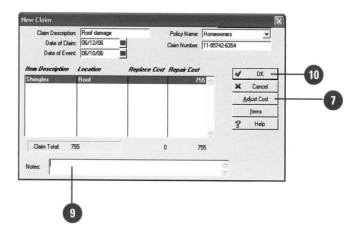

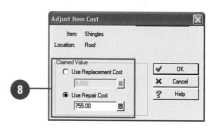

Manage Claims

1. To edit a claim, select it, click **Edit**, make your changes, and click **OK**.

2. To remove a claim, select it and click **Delete**. A message appears asking if you want to remove the claim.

3. Click **OK** to remove the claim or Cancel to keep the claim.

4. When a claim is paid, select the claim and click **Paid**.

5. Type the date the claim was paid and the amount you received, and then click **OK**. A message appears asking if you want to create a report for the claim.

6. Click **Yes** to create the report or **No** to not create it (not shown).

7. When you are finished managing your claims, click **Close**.

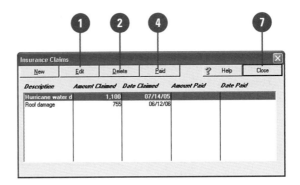

Viewing Home Inventory Reports

There are reports that you can run to get specific information about your inventory. For example, a summary of the value of your items, a detailed report about every item—including specifics about each item—or reports about insurance and claims. These reports come in handy for insurance or claims purposes, or to keep in a safe place with your emergency papers. To view Home Inventory Reports, from the menu, click **Reports** and select a report you want to view.

Keeping Track of Your Emergency Records

Whether you're challenged in the area of organization, or you are meticulously organized and like to keep all of your ducks in a row, you'll love the organizer tool. The Emergency Records Organizer tool allows you to create emergency contact, medical, and hospital records for you and all of your family members. In addition, you can create records for your finances, legal matters, and insurance. Creating and keeping these records up-to-date ensures that you have all of your most important information in one place for you or anyone else to access whenever it's needed. In addition, you can run reports for specific records, print, and share them with whomever needs the information.

1. Click Property & Debt and select **Emergency Records Organizer**.

2. Review the Introduction tab and click **Next Tab**.

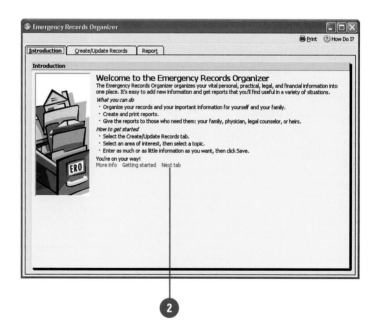

③ The first record defaults to your contact information under the Adults' Emergency Info. Review your information, make any necessary changes, and click **Save**. A green check mark next to the topic means it is saved.

④ To create a new contact record, for example, for each of your emergency contacts, click **New Record**.

⑤ Enter all the information and click **Save**. Create additional records for any other emergency contacts.

TIMESAVER *To quickly clear a record—for example, if you need to update all the information—click* ***Reset Form****.*

⑥ To create records for doctors and dentists, click **Physicians/Dentists**.

⑦ Enter the information for each doctor or dentist record and click **Save**. Click **New Record** to create additional records for each of your doctors and dentists.

⑧ To create a medical record, click **Medical History**.

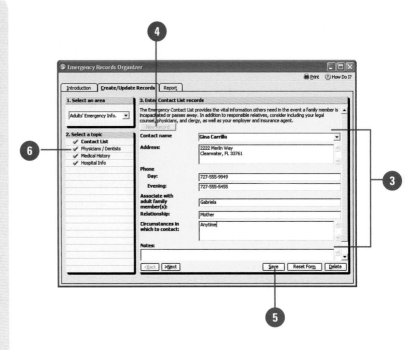

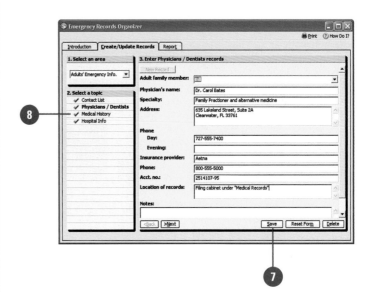

⑨ Enter all the medical information and click **Save**.

⑩ Click **New Record** and repeat step 9 for each adult family member. Then click **Save** after you are finished with each record.

⑪ To create a record with all of your hospital information, click **Hospital Info**.

⑫ Enter all the information about your hospital. You might want to include directions in the Notes field in case someone else has to take you to the hospital and doesn't know how to get there. Then click **Save**.

⑬ When you are finished entering all of the records for each adult in your family, from the **Select an Area** drop-down menu, select the next area for which you would like to create records.

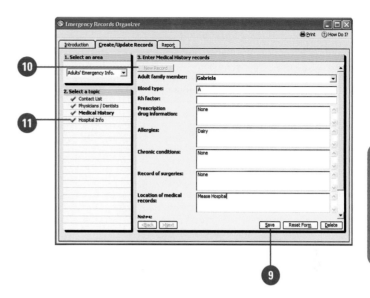

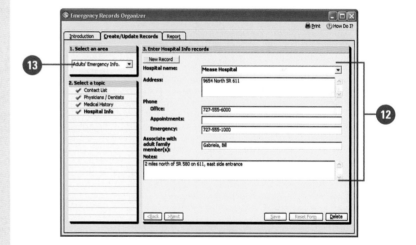

14 Click a topic to create the record, enter the record information, and click **Save**.

15 To remove any of the records, open the record and click **Delete**.

16 Repeat these steps until you've completed all the emergency records you want to create.

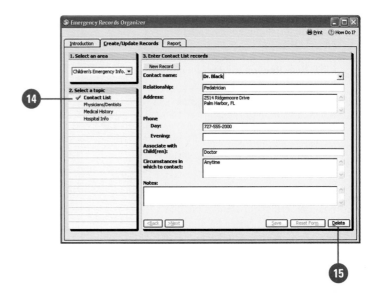

Planning for the Future

Introduction

Quicken provides planners for just about everything, with the exception of honey-do planners and how-to-get-a-spouse planners (those enhancements are coming in a future release, I think). But, for everything financial, Quicken has made it fairly painless to plan for most of life's financial events, including college and retirement. Quicken also has planners that can help you plan for buying a home and making special purchases, such as home remodeling, taking a dream vacation, or planning for a wedding. In addition, Quicken provides special calculators that allow you to get preliminary estimates for events such as retirement, college, or refinancing your home.

If planning is something you don't care to spend too much time on, the planners are for you. Quicken makes it easy to set up and manage plans because you have already done most of the work; all the account, investment, banking, and other financial information you have entered in Quicken is utilized by the planners. All plans are flexible, in that you can change them, remove them, and create new ones to compare. You are in full control.

Setting Up New and Editing Existing Planning Alerts

Planning alerts work just like the other alerts in Quicken, except instead of setting alerts for balances and due dates, you can set alerts for bigger things, such as saving for your retirement. Creating and editing planning alerts works the same as creating and editing alerts in the other centers.

Set Up New and Edit Existing Planning Alerts

1. From the **Planning** menu, select **Go to Planning Center**.

2. Click the **Planning** tab.

3. To create or edit planning alerts, click **Set Up Alerts**.

4. To view and manage all your alerts, click **Show All Alerts**.

See Also

See "Setting Up Alerts" on page 118 for more information on creating or changing alerts.

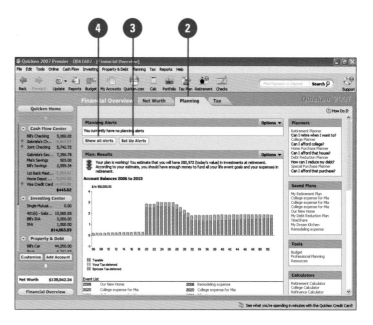

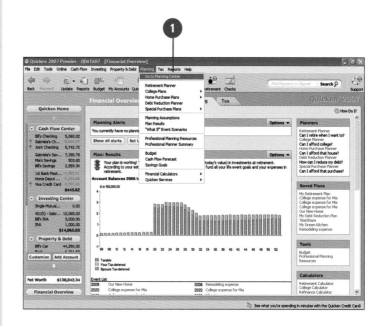

Setting Up and Changing Your Planner Assumptions

Quicken gathers certain information about you and your finances to help you set up the different planners. For example, your age, income, and expenses are used to determine how much you need to save in order to retire. You can set up, change, and review your assumptions at any time. You should review your assumptions on a regular basis—for example, every six months or whenever your financial situation changes—so that Quicken can make adjustments, as needed, to ensure that your goals and plans are as accurate as possible.

Review Planner Assumptions

1 From Planning menu, select **Go to Planning Center** and then click the **Planning** tab.

2 Scroll down to the **Plan Assumptions** section to review your assumption information. Click any of the links to view or change the information.

3 To set up or change all assumptions, click **Change Assumptions**.

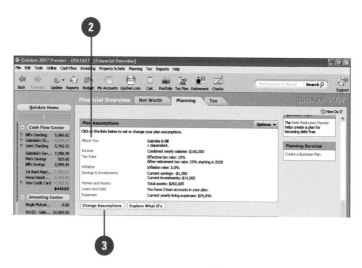

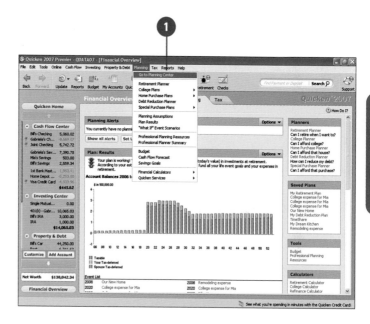

9

Review and Change Your Personal Information

1. In the **About You** section of the Planning Assumptions window, review your age, retirement, and dependent information. To change any of the information, click **Edit**.

2. Change any of the information about yourself or your spouse.

3. To add new dependent information, click **New**.

4. Enter the new dependent information and click **OK**.

5. To change dependent information, select the dependent you want to update and click **Edit**, make the changes and click **OK**.

6. To delete a dependent, select the dependent you want to remove and click **Delete**. A message appears asking if you want to remove the dependent.

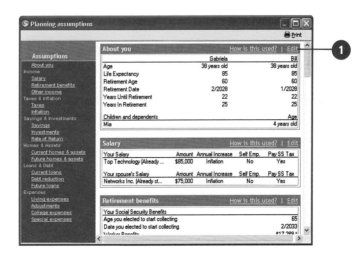

Click to add or remove a spouse from your plan assumptions.

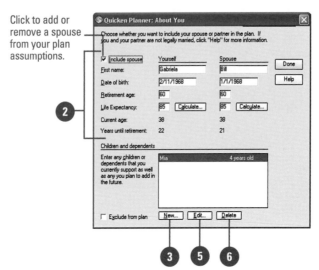

For Your Information

To determine your life expectancy, click the **Calculate** button. From the Calculate Life Expectancy window, select the answers to the questions. Quicken determines your life expectancy based on the options you choose. You can choose to use this age or change it. Click **OK** to return to the Quicken Planner: About You window.

7 Click **Yes** to remove the dependent or **No** to keep it.

8 When you are finished making changes, click **Done**.

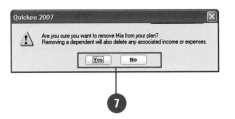

Did You Know?

You can exclude specific information from your plan. If you don't want certain information (for example, dependents or a specific salary) to be used when calculating your plan, you can select the **Exclude from Plan** option. If you later decide you want that information included, you can go back and clear Exclude from Plan. This option appears throughout the planner.

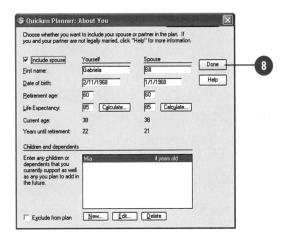

9

Review and Change Your Salary Information

1. Scroll down to the **Salary** section of the Planning Assumptions window and review your salary information. To change any of the information, click **Edit**.

2. To make changes to a specific salary, select the salary and click **Edit**.

3. Make the changes and click **OK**.

4. To add a new salary, click **New**.

Did You Know?

Adding and editing salaries does not change your paychecks in Quicken. The salary information you enter in the Planning Assumptions window does not affect the paychecks you have already set up in Quicken. Quicken uses the information in the Planning Assumptions window solely to make projections for plans, such as your

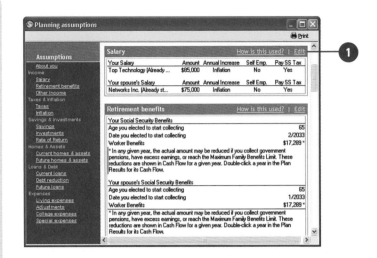

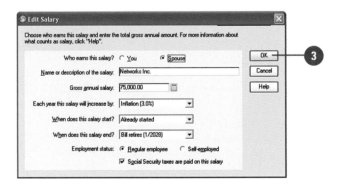

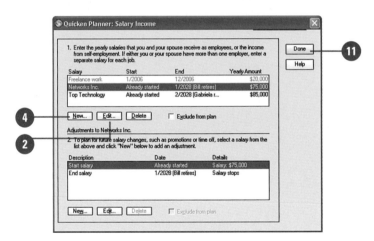

5 Select to whom the salary belongs.

6 Type the source of the salary and enter the yearly salary amount.

7 Leave the inflation amount as is. Quicken updates the inflation rates on a regular basis when you update your accounts and download quotes.

8 Select salary beginning and ending dates.

9 Select the employment status, and whether Social Security is taken from the salary.

10 Click **OK**.

11 When you are finished with the salaries, click **Done**.

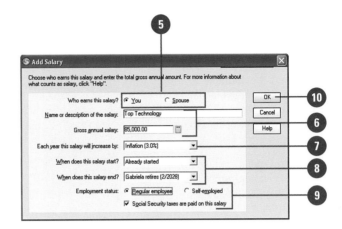

Did You Know?

You can add future salary adjustments to see how they affect your bottom line. If you anticipate your salary or work schedule being affected—for example, working part-time instead of full-time, or visa versa—you can add a salary adjustment. To do so, in section 2 of the Quicken Planner: Salary Income window, click **New**. From the Add Salary Adjustment window, select an adjustment option, complete the information, and click **OK**. If you decide to change or remove the adjustments, you can go back to the Planning Assumptions window and edit or delete the adjustments.

9

Review and Change Retirement Information

① Scroll down to the **Retirement Benefits** section of the Planning Assumptions window and review your retirement information. To make changes, click **Edit**.

② Type the age at which you and your spouse (if applicable) would like to retire and the amount of Social Security you will be receiving per year. If you are not sure of the amount, click **Estimate**.

③ Complete your estimated Social Security benefits information and click **OK**.

④ If you do not want to count on Social Security being there by the time you retire, select **Yes** and enter the reduction figure. Otherwise, click **No** for Quicken to estimate the Social Security you could receive.

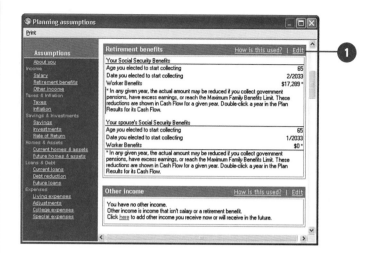

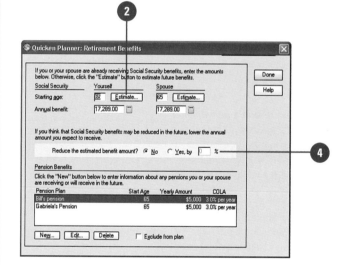

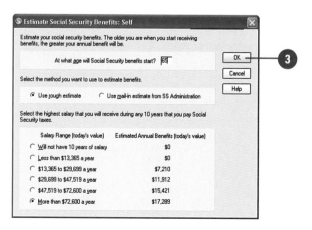

5 If you and/or your spouse have a pension, click **New**.

6 Complete the pension information. Be sure to use the standard inflation rate and click **OK** when you are finished.

7 To change pension information, select it and click **Edit**.

8 To remove a pension, select it and click **Delete**.

> ### Did You Know?
>
> ***Exclude pensions to view the impact to your overall plan results.*** You can exclude a pension from your plan by selecting the **Exclude from Plan** option so that Quicken does not add the income from that pension into your overall plan. You can use this to view the impact to your retirement plan and then make adjustments to your plan, if needed. Excluding the pension does not remove it. You can return to the Retirement benefits section of the Planning assumptions window to add it back into the plan totals by clearing the option.

9 When you are finished setting up and changing retirement information, click **Done**.

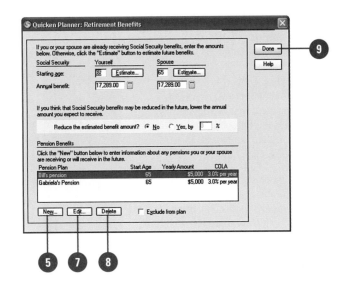

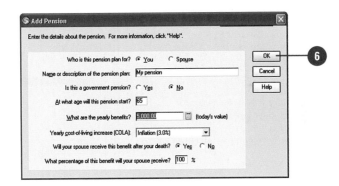

Review and Change Other Income

1. Scroll down to the **Other Income** section of the Planning Assumptions window and review your other types of income: for example, one-time payments. To make changes, click **Edit**.

2. If you have income that is not retirement or salary-related but that you will be receiving through your retirement, click **New** to add it.

3. Select the type of income and then complete the information for that income type. When you are finished, click **OK**.

4. Repeat steps 2–3 to add additional income sources.

5. To change income source information, select the source and click **Edit**.

6. To remove an income source, select it and click **Delete**.

7. When you are finished, click **Done**.

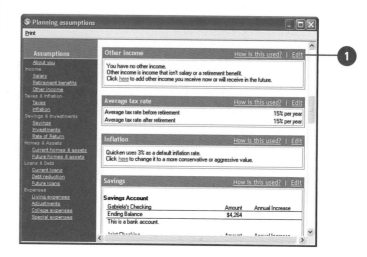

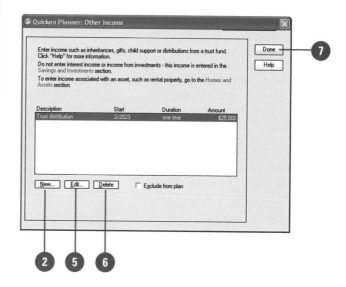

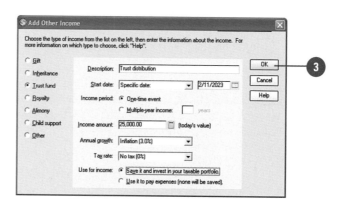

Review and Change Tax and Inflation Rates

① Scroll down to the **Average Tax Rate** and **Inflation** sections of the Planning Assumptions window and review your tax and inflation information.

Did You Know?

It is recommended that you use the standard tax and inflation rates.
However, to see how changing either the standard tax and/or inflation rates might affect your plans, you can experiment with different rates in the Average Tax Rate and Estimated Inflation windows.

② To make changes to the average tax rate, from the Average Tax Rate section, click **Edit**.

③ To change your tax rate information, select **Demographic Average** to use an average rate based on where you live or select **Tax Returns** to enter the tax information from your last tax return.

④ Select or change the state you live in and select the range for your total household income.

⑤ If you know the adjusted rates you want to use, you can change the percentage rates that Quicken has estimated for you.

⑥ When you are finished, click **Done**.

⑦ To change the inflation rate, from the Inflation section of the Planning assumptions window, click **Edit**.

⑧ To change the inflation rate, type the adjusted percentage rate and click **Done**.

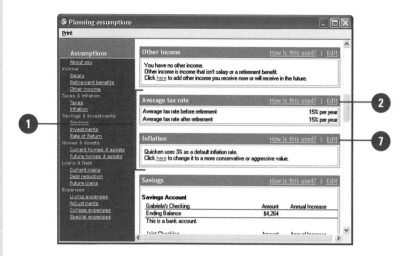

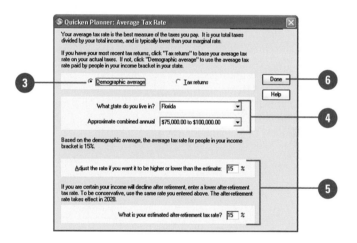

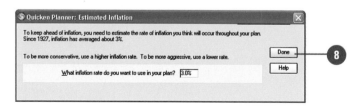

9

Review and Change Savings Information

1. Scroll down to the **Savings** section of the Planning Assumptions window and review your savings account information. To make changes, click **Edit**.

2. To exclude an account from this plan, select the account and select **Exclude from Plan**. To view excluded accounts, select **Show Excluded Accounts** or clear it to see the accounts that are used in the plan.

3. To change the category for which an account is used, select the account and click **Details**.

4. Change the category and click **OK**.

5. To enter regular contributions to a savings account (Quicken uses these contributions to figure your future retirement, debt, and savings goals), select the account and click **New**.

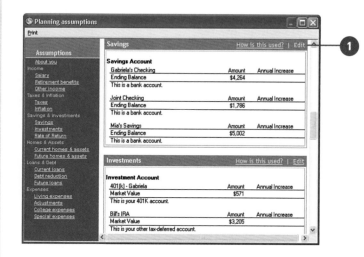

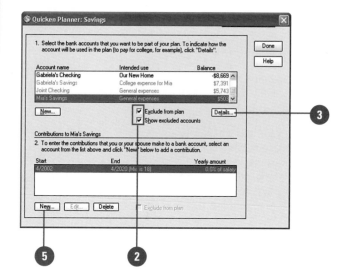

6 Select how contributions will be made to this account (using a percentage of a specific source of income or an inflation percentage). Your options after this step differ depending on which option you choose. Then click **Next**.

7 Type the contribution amount.

8 Select when the contributions are to begin or enter a specific date, if applicable.

9 If this is a one-time contribution, select **One-Time Contribution**: otherwise, enter an end date.

10 Click **Done**.

11 When you are finished making changes to your savings accounts, click **Done**.

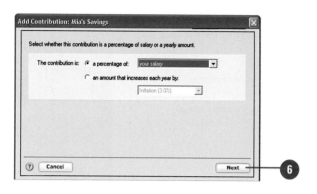

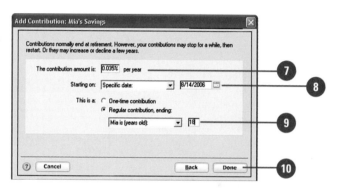

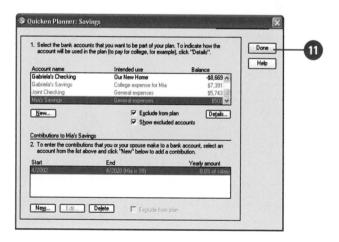

Review and Change Investment Information

1 Scroll down to the **Investments** section of the Planning Assumptions window and review your investment information. To make changes, click **Edit**.

2 To exclude an account from this plan, select the account and select **Exclude from Plan**. To view excluded accounts, select **Show Excluded Accounts** or clear it to see only the accounts that are used in the plan.

3 To change the intended use for an account, select the account and click **Details**.

4 From the **Account Will Be Used For** drop-down menu, select another option, if desired, and click **OK**.

5 To enter regular contributions to an investment account (Quicken uses these contributions to figure your future retirement, debt, and savings goals), select the account and click **New**.

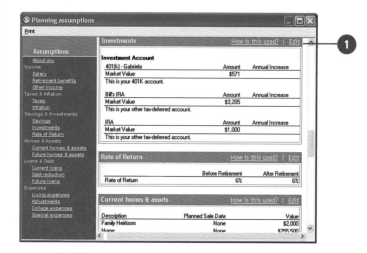

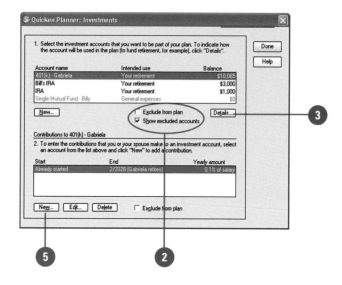

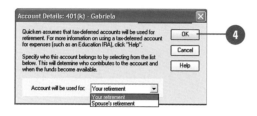

6 Select how contributions will be made to this account (using a percentage of a specific source of income or an inflation percentage). Your options after this step differ depending on which option you choose. Then click **Next**.

7 Type the contribution amount, enter start and end dates, and click **Next**.

8 Enter the employer contribution information and click **Done**.

9 When you are finished making changes to your investment accounts, click **Done**.

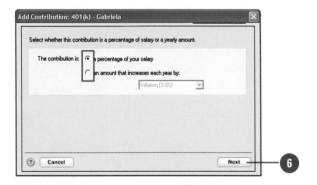

9

For Your Information

Financial experts recommend you save 10% of your salary to ensure that you have enough money for retirement. In step 8, you can choose to save 10% of your salary (or another percentage if you can't save 10%) or a set amount that will change with inflation. Choosing the second option ensures that you save the appropriate amount even though inflation increases the cost of living.

Review and Change Rate of Return Information

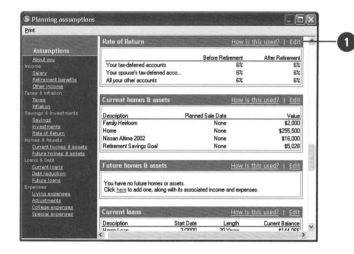

1 Scroll down to the **Rate of Return** section of the Planning Assumptions window and review your return rates for before and after retirement. To make changes, click **Edit**.

2 Type the rate of return you expect to receive for your investments and savings accounts. If you and your spouse expect different rates, select **Use Separate Rates of Return for Taxable and Tax-Deferred Accounts** and enter the rates for each of you.

Did You Know?

Quicken uses the rate of return to help determine how much money you need in order to retire. The rate of return you enter is used to determine whether you will have the money you need to cover your expenses when you retire. The higher the rate, the more risk you should take with your investments.

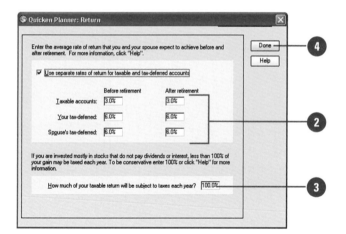

3 To err on the side of caution, keep 100% for the taxable return. This ensures that you plan adequately for taxes on your returns.

4 Click **Done**.

Review and Change Current and Future Asset and Property Information

1. Scroll down to the **Current Homes & Assets** section of the Planning Assumptions window and review your assets information. To make changes, click **Edit**.

2. If you are planning to sell any of your property or assets, select the asset or property and click **Sale Info**. The option you select determines the options you see in the Asset Account Sale Information dialog box. This example uses a home.

3. Change any of the purchase or inflation information, if needed, and click **Next**.

Continued, next page

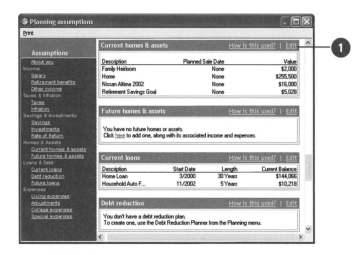

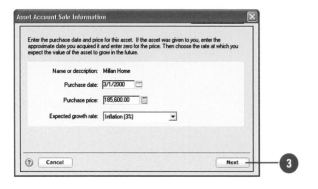

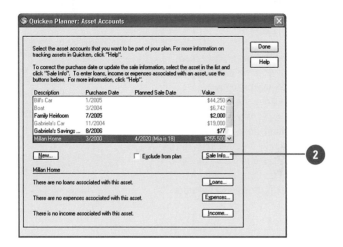

9

4 If the property is your primary residence, select **This House Is or Will Be My Primary Residence** and then select whether you intend to sell the property.

5 If you intend to sell the property, select approximately when you will sell it or enter an approximate date. Click **Next**.

6 Type an approximate total amount for home improvements between now and when you plan to sell and the expected sales fee. Use the defaults for both the tax rate and exemption, and click **Next**.

Did You Know?

Holding on to your property for at least two years and renovating pays off. You can exempt up to approximately $250,000.00 if you keep your primary residence for at least two years before selling it. In addition, home improvements can drastically improve your selling price and are tax deductible when you sell your house. Consult with an accountant or tax professional for more information.

7 Select whether you intend to use the money you make from the sale to purchase another home and then click **Done**.

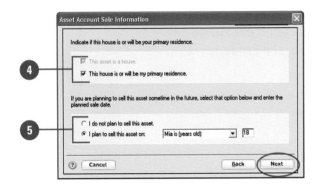

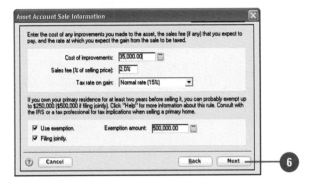

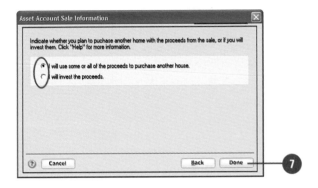

8 To exclude an asset or property from the plan, select the asset or property and then select **Exclude from Plan**.

9 To add a loan, expenses (for example, upkeep for a rental property), or income (for example, rent you receive from a rental property) for an asset or property, select the asset and click **Loans**, **Expenses**, or **Income**.

10 To add a new asset, click **New** and complete the Quicken Account Set Up dialog box.

See Also

See "Add New Property or Debt Accounts" on page 99 for more information on adding new assets.

11 When you are finished making changes to your assets and properties, click **Done**.

12 To add property as future purchase, from the **Future Homes & Assets** section of the Planning Assumptions window, click **Edit** and then click **New**. Follow the prompts to add the new property.

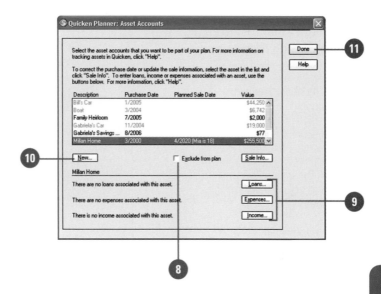

Did You Know?

Use the Future Homes & Assets section to set up homes or assets you are thinking of purchasing. To see how a new home or asset would affect your plan, in the Future Homes & Assets section, click **Edit** and set up a new home or asset. After you see the results, you can remove it or save it to use in your plan.

9

Review and Change Current and Future Loan and Debt Information

1. Scroll down to the **Current Loans** section of the Planning Assumptions window and review your loan information. To make changes, click **Edit**.

2. To review loan details, select the loan. The loan detail appears at the bottom of the Loan Accounts window.

3. To exclude a loan from the plan, select the loan and then select **Exclude from Plan**.

4. To adjust payoff information, select the loan and click **Payoff**.

5. Select whether there will be a balloon payment for early payoff and click **OK**.

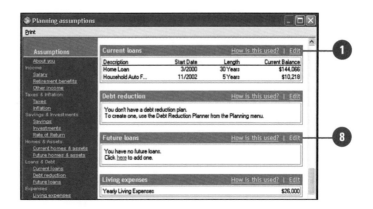

See Also

See "Getting Out of Debt" on page 203 for information on using the Debt Reduction section of the Planning Assumptions window.

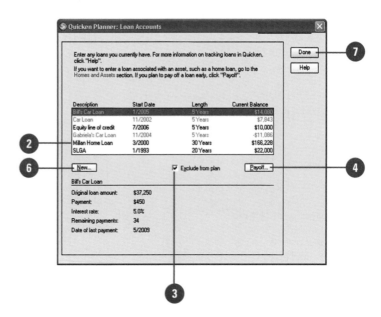

6. To add a new loan, click **New** and complete the Loan Setup dialog box.

7. Click **Done** when you are finished reviewing and making changes to your loan accounts.

8. To add potential future loans that are not related to any property or asset, from the **Future Loans** section of the Planning Assumptions window, click **Edit** and then click **New**. Follow the prompts to add the new loan.

See Also

See "Managing Your Loan Accounts" on page 107 for information on adding new loans.

Review and Change Living Expenses Information

1 Scroll down to the **Living Expenses** section of the Planning Assumptions window and review your yearly living expense information. To make changes, click **Edit**.

2 To use an estimate that Quicken has predetermined (this is based on your current bills and expenses), select **Rough Estimate** and change the yearly living expenses amount.

Continued, next page

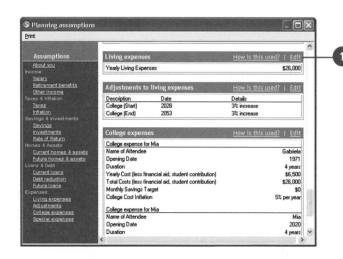

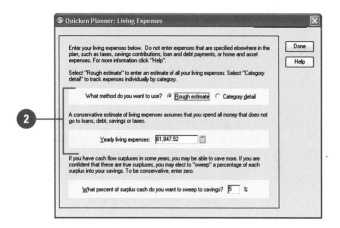

3 To use the total derived from amounts you enter for all expense categories, select **Category Detail** and then click **Details**.

4 To have Quicken create an estimate for each category, based on your spending habits thus far, click **Estimate**.

5 Quicken provides a date range for the past year. If needed, you can enter a new date range, and then click **OK**.

6 To view only living expense categories, select the **Only Show Living Expense Categories** option.

7 To change the living expense amounts, click in the **Monthly Amount** column for each category and type the amount that you use each month. Then click **OK**.

8 To indicate that you want to save a percentage of your excess income, type the percentage of the excess amount. Otherwise, leave it at zero.

9 Click **Done**.

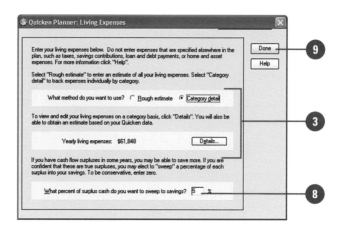

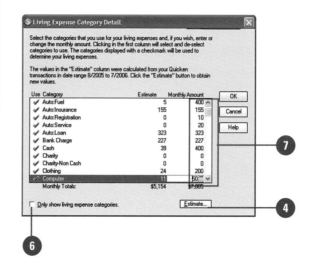

For Your Information

The amounts that appear in the Category Detail dialog box are based on information you've entered in Quicken thus far. The categories are the same as those that appear in the budget planner. However, if you set up a budget, the budgeted amounts you set up for each category are not the same as those amounts that appear in this dialog box. For more information on budgets, see "Setting Up a Budget" on page 196.

Review and Change Adjusted Living Expenses

1. Scroll down to the **Adjustments to Living Expenses** section of the Planning Assumptions window and review any adjustments you are planning on making to your yearly living expenses. To make changes, click **Edit**.

2. To add a life event, such as retirement or college, click **New**.

3. Select whether or not the event is for a specific person, complete the adjustment information, and click **OK**.

4. To update an adjustment, select it and click **Edit**.

5. To remove an adjustment, select it and click **Delete**.

6. To exclude an event from your plan, select the event and select the **Exclude from Plan** option.

7. When you have completed the adjustments, click **Done**.

See Also

See "Planning for College" later in this chapter for information on using the College Expenses section of the Planning Assumptions window.

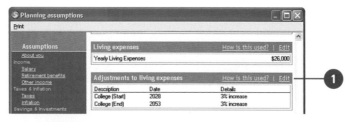

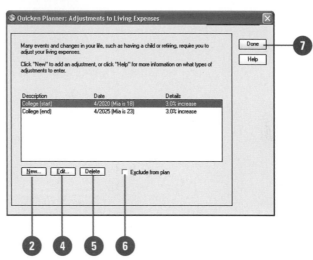

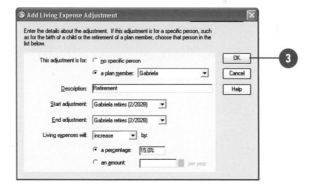

For Your Information

Living expenses usually change when you retire. To help you determine what percentage your living expenses will increase or decrease, see "Planning for Retirement" later in this chapter. You can enter an arbitrary amount for now, if you like. After you determine the expected increase or decrease in living expenses, you can go back to the Planner Assumptions window to change the percentage.

9

Review and Change Special Expenses

1 Scroll down to the **Special Expenses** section of the Planning Assumptions window and review any additional expenses you are planning. To make changes, click **Edit**.

2 To add a new expense, click **New**.

3 Select whether or not the expense is for a specific person, type a description for it, and then click **Next**.

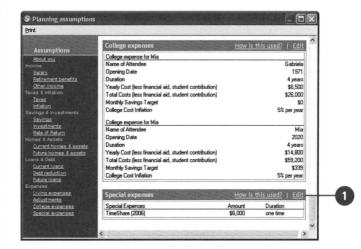

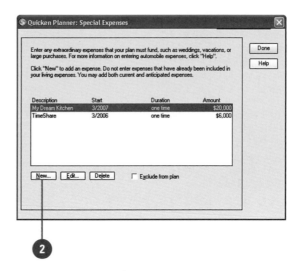

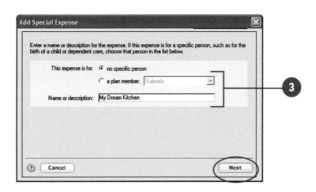

4 Type the approximate date for the expense, the duration, and the expense amount, and then click **Next**.

5 To select the account you plan to use to fund the expense (if any), click **Choose Accounts**.

6 If you do not have a specific account to fund the expense, select **General Expenses** (shown in this example); otherwise select **Specific Accounts** to select the account. The option you select determines what you see in the next step.

7 If you have money to apply toward the expense, enter that amount and type the date you plan to have the money. (If you selected Specific Accounts in step 6, you would select the account you want to use in this step.)

8 Click **OK**. Quicken fills in the top portion of the Add Special Expense dialog box with the account information.

9 In the **Amount from Loans** box, enter the loan amount you need for the expense, if a loan will be used. The amount you need to save monthly to pay for the expense appears in the Monthly Savings Target box.

10 To change how you would like to fund the expense, repeat steps 5–9; otherwise, click **Done**.

Continued, next page

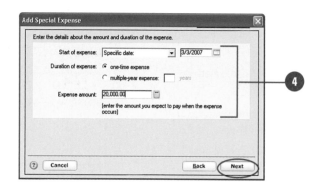

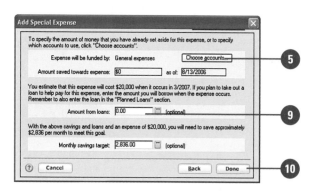

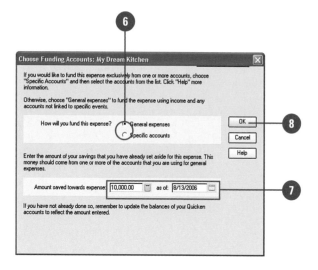

9

11 To update an expense, select it and click **Edit**.

12 To remove an expense, select it and click **Delete**.

13 When you are finished with special expenses, click **Done**.

14 If you are finished with all your assumptions, close the Planning Assumptions window.

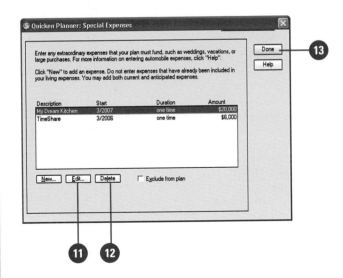

For Your Information

Remember, you can exclude this event from your planner assumptions by selecting the event shown in step 11 and selecting **Exclude from Plan**. For example, if you entered an expense to see how it affects your finances, but don't plan on acting on the expense right away, you can exclude the expense until you are ready to act on it.

Review and Change Planner Assumptions and What If Scenarios

1. If you don't already have the Planning tab open, choose **Planning**, **Go to Planning Center**, and then click the Planning tab.

2. Review the **Plan Results** section to see how the information you entered in the Planning Assumptions window affects your financial outlook.

3. Scroll down to the Plan Assumptions section to review details for each of the planner assumption categories. To make any adjustments to any of the categories, you can click a category link.

   TIMESAVER *You can also click the* ***Change Assumptions*** *button to open the Planner Assumptions window to make changes to all of the assumptions*

4. Make your changes and click **Done** when you are finished.

5. To explore different scenarios or situations to see how they change the outcome of your plans, click **Explore What If's**.

Continued, next page ▶

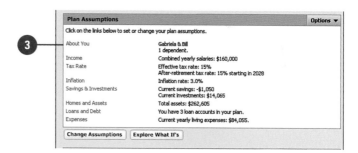

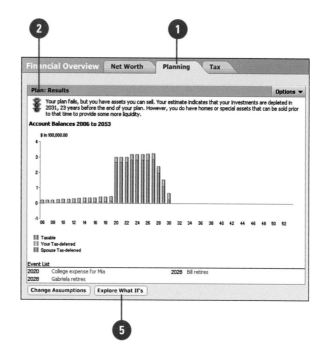

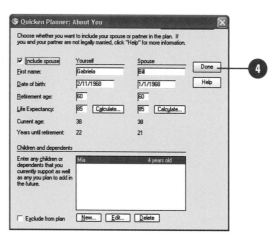

9

6. From the **Choose a Goal Type** drop-down menu, select a goal, such as Retirement, and then click a what-if scenario, such as changing your retirement age.

7. Make changes (in this example, the retirement age) and click **Done**. Quicken adjusts the outcome and shows you the impact, using a line chart in the What If window.

8. Repeat steps 6–7 to play with other what-if scenarios.

9. To save a scenario, click **Save What If as Plan**.

10. To revert to the original information, click **Reset What If**.

11. To close the window without saving anything, click **Close Without Saving**.

12. When you are finished, close the window.

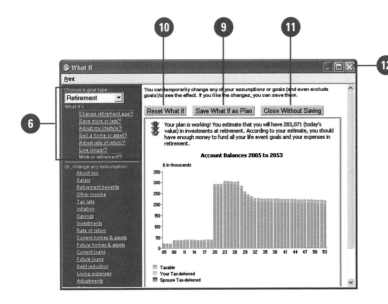

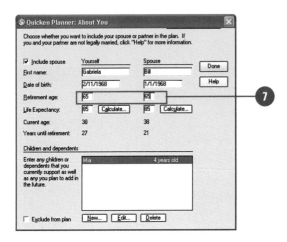

Using Calculators

The Calculators section of the Planning tab in the Financial Overview center provides a series of calculators that can help you crunch numbers for retirement, college, refinancing, savings goals, and loans. Each calculator is customized to determine the potential for the particular situation. For example, if you want to see whether it would be advantageous to refinance your home, you can use the Refinance Calculator to find out. Using the Refinance Calculator as an example, let's step through how the calculators work:

1. In the **Calculators** section of the Planning tab, click **Refinance Calculator**.

2. Type the current payment and escrow amounts for your existing mortgage.

3. Enter the principal amount, the number of years, and the interest rate for the new mortgage.

4. Type any closing costs and points you will be charged.

5. Click **Calculate**.

6. If needed, you can change any of the information in steps 2–4 and click **Calculate** again to see how different figures affect the outcome.

7. If you are finished, click **Done**. You can use the other calculators in a way similar to what is shown here.

> ### Did You Know?
>
> ***You can print from the calculators.***
> You can print the calculations to save for reference later by clicking the **Print** button.

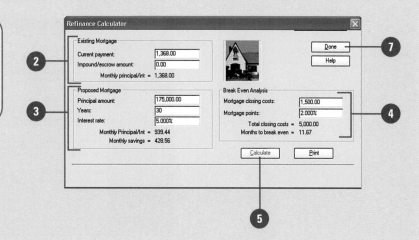

Planning for Retirement

No matter your age, it's never too early to plan for your retirement. One of the many great planners you can use in Quicken is the Retirement planner. You can set up a retirement plan to determine when you can retire and how much you need to start saving in order to retire. Setting up a retirement plan ensures that you will be comfortable during that period of your life. The information contained in the retirement plan is derived from the assumptions you set up in the Planning Assumptions window, so most of the information is already completed for you. You can, however, change it if needed.

Plan for Retirement

1. From the **Planning** menu, select **Retirement Planner**. The My Retirement Plan window opens.

   TIMESAVER *If you are already on the Planning tab, you can click the **Retirement Planner** link in the Planners section to open the My Retirement Plan window.*

2. Review the introduction and click **Next** to get started with a plan.

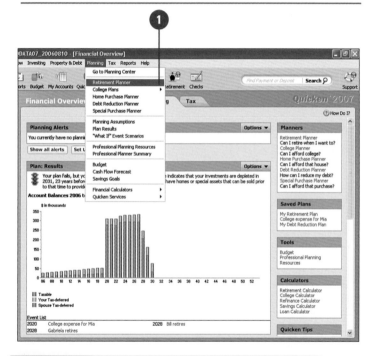

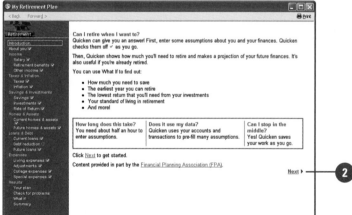

3 Review the **About You** section. To change any of the information, click **Edit**.

4 After you've made any necessary changes, click **Next** to move on.

5 Continue reviewing each section, making any changes, if needed, by clicking the **Edit** links, and then clicking **Next** to proceed through the retirement planner.

TIMESAVER *As you proceed through the Retirement planner and complete each section, a checkmark appears next to the sections titles in the menu (on the left). This helps provide a visual queue as to where you left off, should you have to close the planner and return to it later.*

Continued, next page ▶

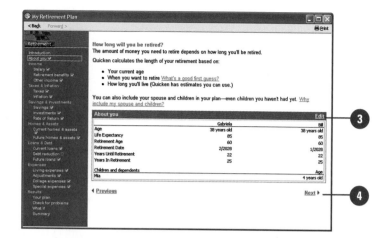

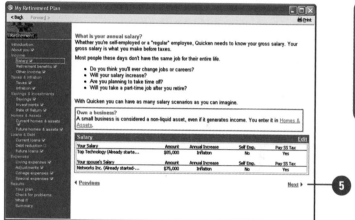

6 When you reach the **Results** section, Quicken shows you a bar graph of your account balances from the current year through the remainder of your life. In addition, Quicken lets you know if you will be able to retire when you want to. To make adjustments to your assumptions, click **Change Assumptions**.

7 To play with different scenarios to determine the impact to your retirement plan, click **Explore What If's**.

8 To have Quicken check for any potential weaknesses or problems with your plan, click **Check for Problems**.

9 Review any potential problem areas and go back and make adjustments, if needed, by clicking a specific area in the planner or clicking the **Previous** link.

10 To play some more with what-if scenarios, click **Next**.

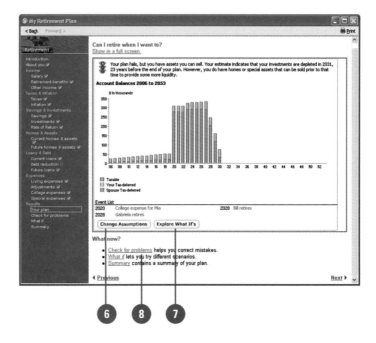

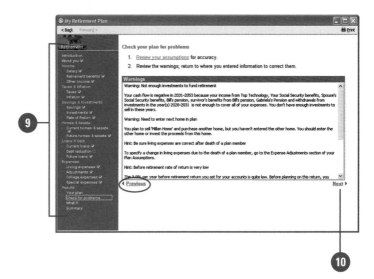

11 Click **What If Event Scenarios** to open the What If window, where you can explore what–if scenarios.

See Also

See "Review and Change Planner Assumptions and What If Scenarios" earlier in this chapter on page 249 for information on working with what–if scenarios.

12 When you are satisfied with the plan, click **Next** to view the plan summary.

13 When you are finished with the plan, close the window. The results of your retirement plan appear in the Plan: Results section on the Planning tab of the Financial Overview center.

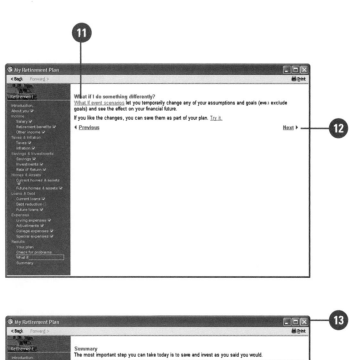

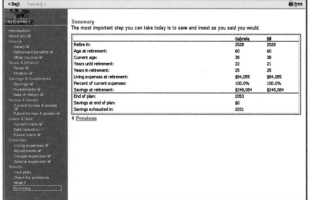

Planning for College

Whether you are planning on going to college or have a family member you are sending or helping to send to college, the College planner can help you plan for it. With the rising costs of higher education, planning for college is getting tougher and tougher. By using the College planner, you can see exactly what you need to do to plan for college expenses.

Plan for College

1. If you're not already there, open the Planning tab in the Financial Overview center and in the Planners section, click **College Planner**.

2. Review the introduction and click **Next** to get started with the plan.

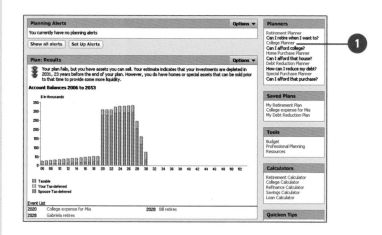

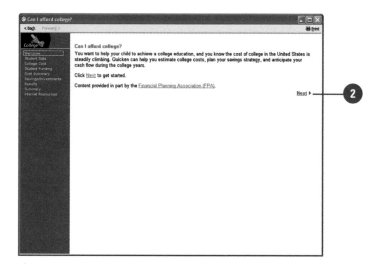

Add or Edit Student Data

① To add or change information about the person going to college, click **Edit**.

② Select the name of who is going to college.

③ Type a description of the event.

④ Specify when the student is to begin college.

⑤ Type the number of years he or she will attend college.

⑥ Click **Done**.

⑦ Click **Next**.

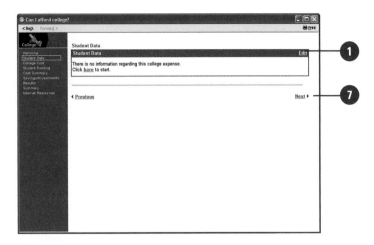

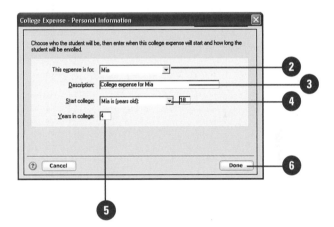

Add or Edit College Costs

1 Click the links to read more about different college expenses. This will help you determine the costs you need to enter in the next step. Some links require Internet access.

2 Click **Edit** to add college expenses.

3 Enter the annual costs for tuition, any out-of-state fees, room and board, books and supplies, and other (personal) college expenses. Then click **Done**.

4 Click **Next**.

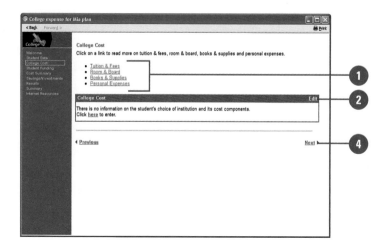

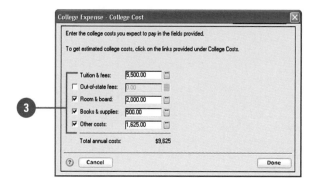

Add or Edit Student Funding Options

① If you anticipate needing financial assistance to fund college expenses, review all the information about different financial aid sources by clicking the links. Most sources require Internet access.

② To add financial aid information, such as student loans or financial contributions from other sources, click **Edit**.

③ Type the potential funding amounts for all applicable types of financial contributions and click **Done**.

④ Click **Next**.

Did You Know?

You may make too much money to get financial aid. Be aware that in a household with income more than $70,000 per year, a student most likely will not be eligible for financial aid. You can, however, obtain student loans to help with the cost of tuition, room and board, and so on.

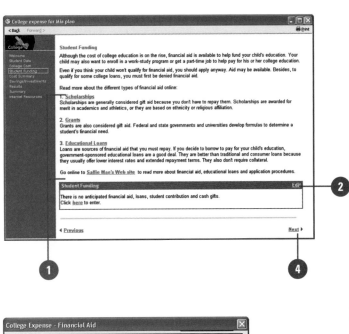

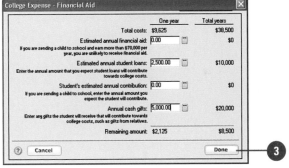

9

Review the Cost Summary

① Review the cost summary information. To go back and make any changes, click **Previous**.

② When you are ready to proceed, click **Next**.

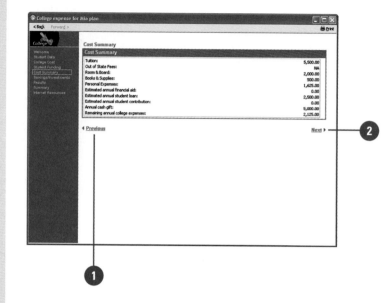

Review and Change Savings and Investment Information

1 Click the links to read more about saving for college expenses. Some links require Internet access.

2 Click **Edit** to set up a savings plan.

3 Use the default inflation rate and select the account you want to use to save for the college expenses. You can change it, if needed. However, it is recommended that you use the default rate.

4 To specify the account you want to use to save for college expenses, click **Choose Accounts** and complete the Choose Funding Accounts dialog box.

5 Depending on the account balance you chose to use (if any), Quicken determines how much you need to save monthly to meet the college expenses. Click **Done**.

6 Click **Next**.

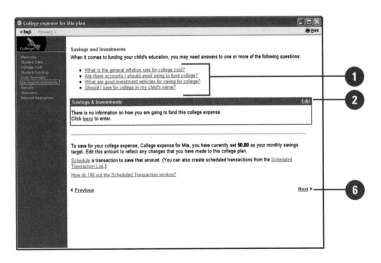

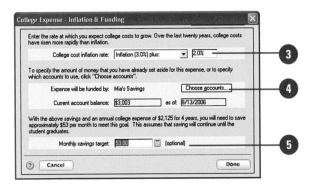

9

Did You Know?

Set up a plan to save for college. Once you know how much you need to save for college, you can set up a savings plan by clicking the **Schedule** link at the bottom of the Savings and Investments window. You can also get help with setting up scheduled transactions using the Create Scheduled Transaction window by clicking the **How Do I Fill Out the Schedule Transaction Window?** link, also located at bottom of the window.

For Your Information

If the account you want to use to save for the college expense is not listed, it most likely has been excluded from your plan assumptions. To make it available, from the Planner Assumptions section of the Planning tab, click **Change Assumptions**. From the Planning Assumptions window, click the **Savings** link and click the **Edit** button in that section. Then select the account that has been excluded and clear the **Exclude from Plan** option. Click **Done**, close the Planning Assumptions window, and return to the College Planner.

Review Plan Results

1 Review the results. If you need to go back and make any changes, click **Previous** or click any of the menu links in the upper-left portion of the window.

2 To review any of the plans you already have in place, click one of the links.

3 To change your plan assumptions, click **Change Assumptions**.

4 To change the what-if scenarios, click **Explore What If's**.

See Also

See "Review and Change Planner Assumptions and What If Scenarios" earlier in this chapter on page 249 for information on changing assumptions and what-if scenarios.

5 If you are not able to obtain or save the money required for college expenses, click the **What Options Should I Consider If I Can't Fund This College Goal?** link to get more information.

6 Click **Next** to review the plan summary.

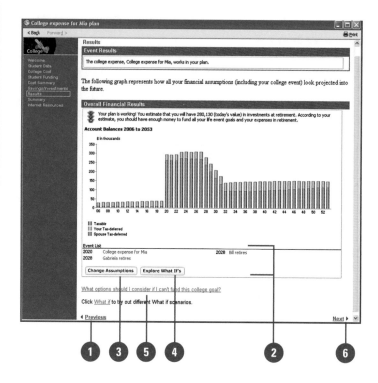

Review the Plan Summary and Internet Resources

1 Review the summary. If you need to go back and make any changes, click **Previous** or click any of the menu links in the upper-left portion of the window.

2 Click **Next** to review the Internet resources.

3 Click any of the links to view helpful Internet resources related to preparing for college and its expenses.

4 When you are finished with the College planner, close the planner. The plan results appear in the Plan: Results section of the Planning tab, along with any other plans you have.

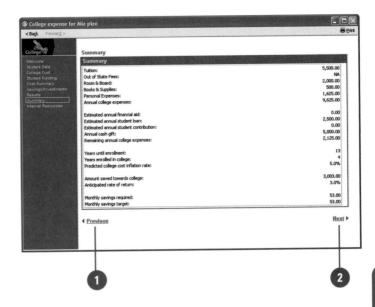

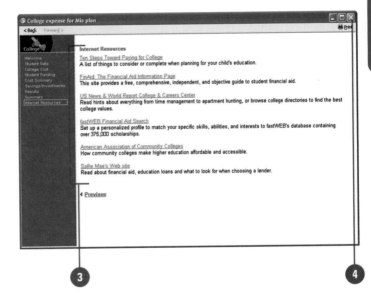

Planning to Purchase a Home

One of the biggest milestones in a person's life is being able to buy his or her first home. It's an exciting and fulfilling time, but also a very serious time. How do you determine how much you can afford? How much will you need to put down? What type of home do you need? There are so many questions and concerns related to buying a home. No matter if this is your first home or your fifth home, the Home Purchase planner can help you prepare for purchasing a home. As soon as you're finished with the planner, you'll be able to see how much you can afford, how much you need to put down, and other important information you need to consider when planning to purchase a home.

Plan to Purchase a Home

1. If you're not already there, open the Planning tab in the Financial Overview center and in the Planners section, click **Home Purchase Planner**.

2. Review the introduction and click **Next** to get started with the plan.

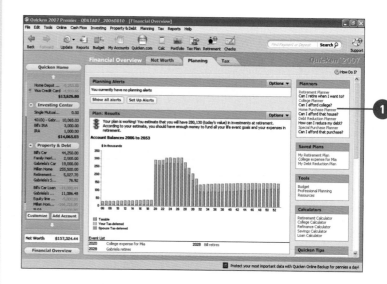

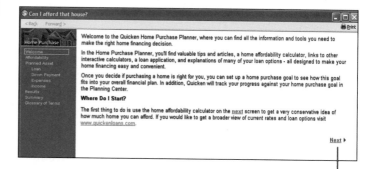

Determine How Much House You Can Afford

1 Enter your income or you and your spouse's combined gross income. From the drop-down menu, select how often you receive this income.

2 Enter your total monthly debt payments.

3 Type the amount of money you have to put down on a house.

4 Type the current interest rate. You can click the **Get Current Mortgage Rates Online** to access the latest mortgage rates on the Internet.

5 Select the mortgage term you are considering.

6 Type the maximum payment you want.

7 Click **Calculate**. Quicken calculates what you can afford and lists the information under the What a Lender Would Typically Let You Borrow section in the middle of the window.

8 To view information on how Quicken determines how much you can afford and other information to help you determine how much you should spend, click the links.

9 If needed, adjust the figures you entered in steps 1–3 to see how it affects the final outcome. When you are finished, click **Next** to proceed.

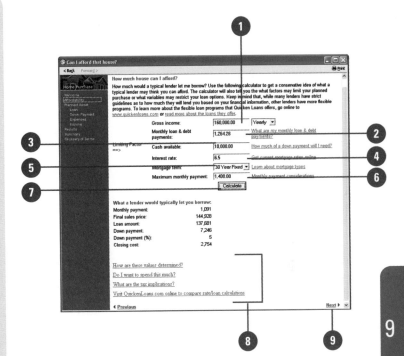

Did You Know?

You can use the Income and Expense Comparison by Category report to help complete the Affordability section of the planner. To help determine what your gross income and monthly loan and debt payments are, you can run an income/expense report. To do this, from the Reports menu, select **Comparison, Income and Expense Comparison by Category**. The report is broken down into income and expense categories so that you can see what your monthly income and debt payments are. You can also use the links on the right of the How Much House Can I Afford? section of the Home Purchase planner to get more information.

9

Add or Edit Planned Asset Information

1. If you don't already have a specific house at a specific price in mind, you can go online to search for a home or click **QuickenLoans.com** to get help finding a home.

2. Click **Edit** to add information about the house you want to purchase.

3. Type a description, an approximate date you want to purchase the house, and an approximate amount. Leave the inflation percentage as it is. Click **Next**.

4. Select whether this house will be your primary residence and whether you plan to sell the home anytime soon, and then click **Done**.

5. Click **Next**.

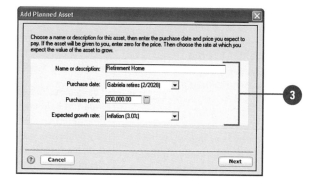

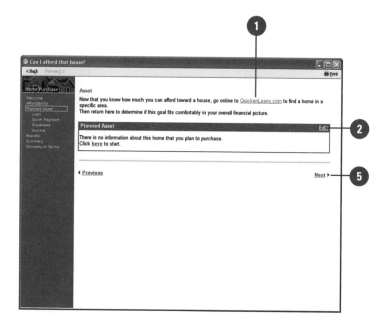

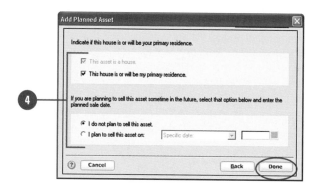

Add or Edit Loan Information

① Click **Edit** to add estimated loan information.

② Click **New**.

③ Enter the approximate amount you are thinking of borrowing (you can use the amount provided in the Loan Amount field of the Affordability section if you are unsure) and the term of the loan (30 years is standard).

④ Select the frequency of your payments.

⑤ Click **Next**.

Continued, next page ▶

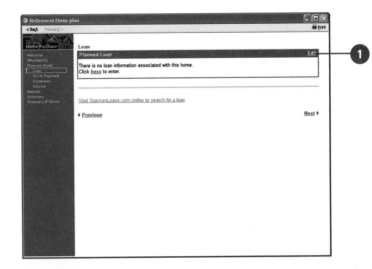

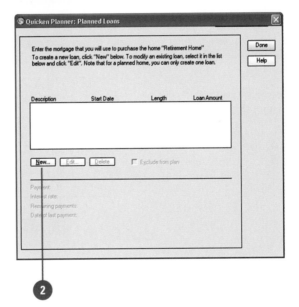

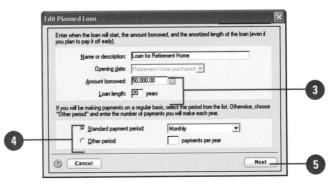

9

6 Enter the interest rate you anticipate and click **Calculate**. Quicken calculates your monthly payment.

7 If you anticipate an early payoff, select whether there will be a balloon payment and then click **Done**.

8 To go back and make any changes to the loan, select the loan and click **Edit**.

9 To remove the loan, select it and click **Delete**.

10 To exclude the loan from your plan, select the loan and click the **Exclude from Plan** option. If you exclude the loan, it does not show up on the Loan section in the Home Purchase planner.

11 If you are finished making changes to the loan information, click **Done**.

12 On the Loan page of the plan, click **Next**.

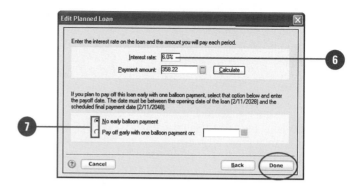

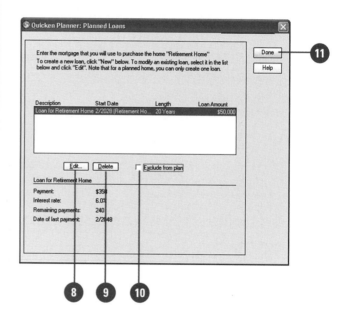

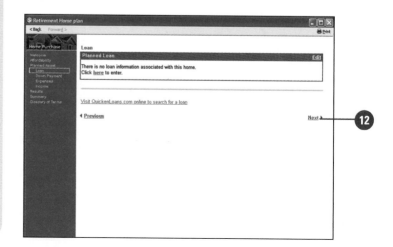

Set Up or Edit a Down Payment Savings Plan

1 Click **Edit** to add down payment and savings information.

2 Click **Choose Accounts** to open the Choose Funding Accounts dialog box, where you can specify the accounts you want to use to save for the new home.

See Also

See "Review and Change Special Expenses" on page 246 for more information on completing the Choose Funding Accounts dialog box.

3 Quicken determines how much you need to save monthly to meet the savings goal and lists the amount in the **Monthly Savings Target** box on the Asset Funding dialog box. Click **OK**.

4 If needed, you can adjust any information in the planner by clicking **Previous** or any of the links in the menu. Otherwise, click **Next** to proceed.

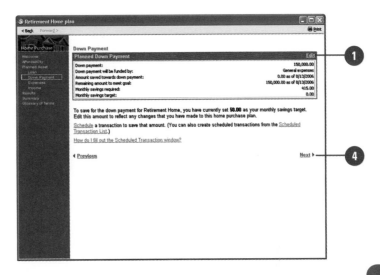

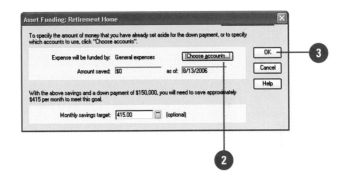

Did You Know?

Set up a plan to save for your new home. After you know how much you need to save for the new home, you can set up a savings plan by clicking the **Schedule** link at the bottom of the Down Payment section. You can also get help with setting up scheduled transactions using the Create Scheduled Transaction window by clicking the **How Do I Fill Out the Schedule Transaction Window?** link, also located at bottom of the section.

Add or Edit Expenses

1 Click **Edit** to add expense information for your new home.

2 Type the tax amount you expect to pay; if you are unsure, use the amount that Quicken has estimated for you in the paragraph above the How Much Tax Do You Pay on This Asset? box.

3 To add new expenses (for example, for remodeling), click **New** and follow the prompts to enter the information.

4 To go back and make any changes to expenses, select the expense and click **Edit**.

5 To remove an expense, select it and click **Delete**.

6 To exclude an expense from your plan, select the expense and click the **Exclude from Plan** option. If you exclude an expense, it does not show up on the Expenses section in the Home Purchase planner.

7 When you are finished, click **Done**.

8 Click **Next**.

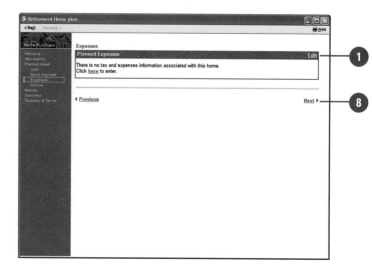

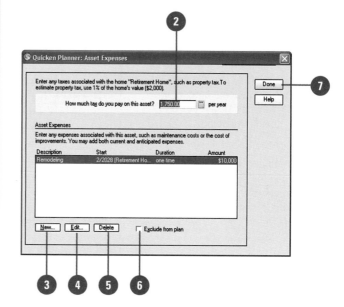

Add or Edit Income

① Click **Edit** to add income you expect to receive from the new property (for example, if it is a rental property). If you don't expect any income, skip this section and click **Next**.

② If you expect to receive income from the house, click **New** and follow the prompts to add the income information.

③ When you are finished, click **Done**.

④ Click **Next** to review the results of the plan.

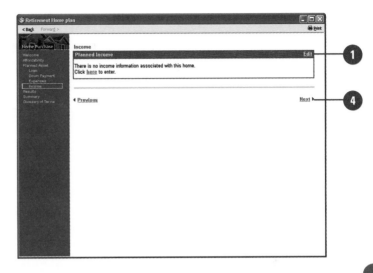

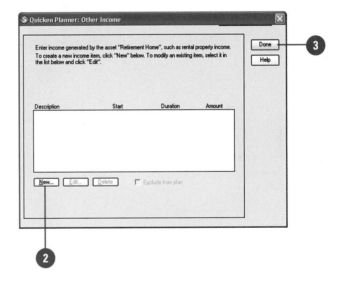

9

Review Plan Results

1 Review the results. Quicken provides a bar graph of your account balances and lets you know if you will be able to afford this house. To go back and make any changes, click **Previous** or click any of the menu links in the upper-left portion of the window.

2 To review any of the plans you already have in place, click one of the links.

3 To make adjustments to your assumptions, click **Change Assumptions**.

4 To play with different scenarios to determine the impact to your home purchase plan, click **Explore What If's**.

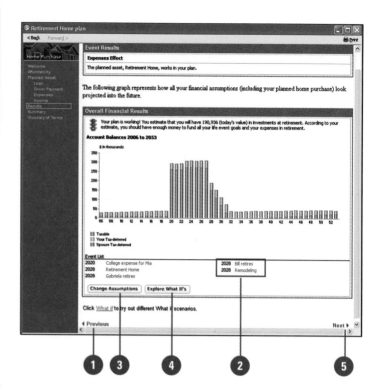

See Also

See "Review and Change Planner Assumptions and What If Scenarios" earlier in this chapter on page 249 for information on changing assumptions and what–if scenarios.

5 When you are satisfied with the plan, click **Next** to view the plan summary.

Review the Plan Summary

1. Review the summary. If you need to go back and make any changes, click **Previous** or click any of the menu links in the upper-left portion of the window.

2. To get information about home loans and mortgage rates, click a link.

3. To view a home buying glossary of terms, click **Next**.

4. When you are finished with the Home Purchase planner, close the planner. The results of your home purchase plan appear on the Plan: Results tab on the Planning tab in the Financial Overview Center.

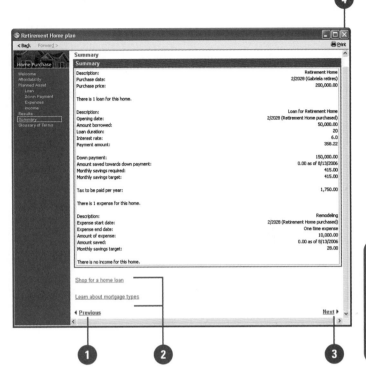

Planning for a Special Purchase

Special life events, from weddings to special projects such as remodeling your kitchen, periodically come up. And because such events are not always a regular fixture in your budget, it can be a daunting task to figure out how to pay for such expenses. That's where the Special Purchase planner can be of assistance. By using the Special Purchase planner, you can turn wishful thinking into a cohesive plan. Or you may find out that the new kitchen you want will have to remain wishful thinking for a little while longer. But without using the planner, you'll never know for sure, right?

Plan for a Special Purchase

1. If you're not already there, open the Planning tab in the Financial Overview center and in the Planners section, click **Special Purchase Planner**.

2. Review the introduction paragraph and click **Enter** and to open the Add Special Expense dialog box, where you can enter your special purchase information.

See Also

See "Review and Change Special Expenses" for information on completing the Add Special Expense dialog box.

3. Click **Next**.

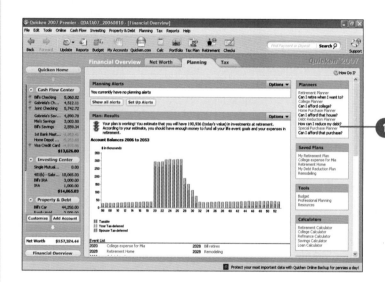

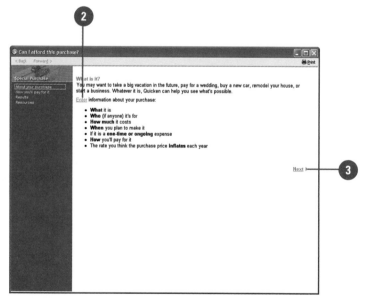

4 Review how you intend to pay for the special purchase. Click the **Schedule** link to set up a scheduled transaction or click the **Enter a Future Loan** if a loan is required to fund your special purchase.

5 To get more information about funding the purchase, click one of the links.

6 To make changes to the plan, click **Previous** or **Next** to view the results of the plan.

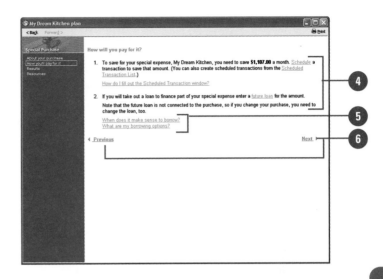

Did You Know?

Set up a plan to save for your special purchase. After you know how much you need to save for your special purchase, you can set up a savings plan by clicking the **Schedule** link in step 4 at the top of the How Will You Pay For It? section. You can also get help with setting up scheduled transactions using the Create Scheduled Transaction window by clicking the **How Do I Fill Out the Schedule Transaction Window?** link, also located at the top of the section.

7 Review the results. Quicken shows you a bar graph of your account balances and lets you know if you will be able to afford the special purchase. To make adjustments to your assumptions, click **Change Assumptions**.

8 To play with different scenarios to determine the impact on your special purchase plan, click **Explore What If's**.

9 To view any of your other plans, click a link.

10 Click **Create** to create a new special purchase plan or click **Delete** to remove the plan.

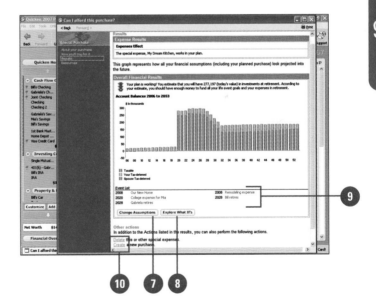

Continued, next page ▶

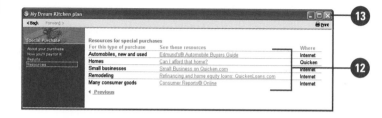

11　When you are satisfied with the plan, click **Next** (not shown) to view a list of resources to help you with your special projects and plans.

12　Click a link to view a resource. The resources that require Internet access are indicated by the word Internet in the Where column.

13　When you are finished, close the planner. The results of your Special Purchase plan appear on the Plan: Results tab on the Planning tab in the Financial Overview center.

Reviewing and Editing Your Plans

If you've set up plans, such as a retirement plan or debt reduction plan, you can conveniently manage all these plans on the Planning tab in the Financial Overview center. You can review your plans, make changes to them, and explore the what-if scenarios to determine whether they are still working for you over time. In addition, you can update assumptions on the Planning tab.

Review and Edit Your Plans

1 If you're not already on the Planning tab, choose **Planning**, **Go to Planning Center**.

2 To review or update one of your plans, click a link to open the appropriate planner.

3 To review or update your assumptions, click **Change Assumptions**.

4 To play with different scenarios to see how they affect your plans, click **Explore What If's**.

5 You can also access any of your plans in the **Saved Plans** section.

6 To review or update your budget, click **Budget**.

7 To see how your plans are doing, scroll down to the **Event Status** and **Monthly Savings Targets** sections. Then click any of the links to open the plan and make changes, if needed.

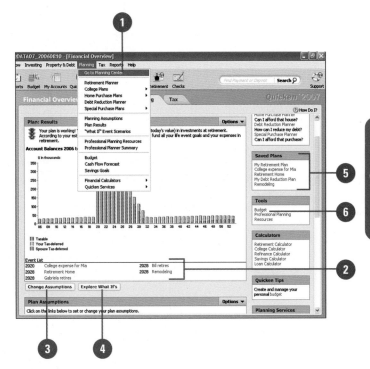

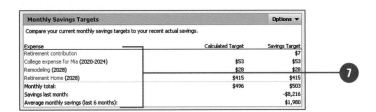

Getting Professional Financial Advice

Finding a trustworthy financial service can be risky and somewhat intimidating. The Professional Planning Resources guide provides sound financial advice, translations of financial jargon, and information on how to find help, where to look, what questions to ask, and much more. In addition, you can use it to create a financial planner to take to an advisor or keep for your records. Whether the information you seek is for your retirement, savings, or taxes, or if you're pondering the idea of starting your own business, the Professional Planning Resources guide can steer you in the right direction. To access this resource, from the Planning menu, select **Professional Planning Resources** or from the Tools section of the Planning tab, click **Professional Planning**.

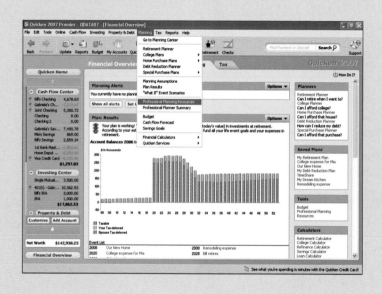

Analyzing Your Asset Allocations and Portfolio

Introduction

Once you get all or most of your asset information in Quicken, such as stocks, bonds, and mutual funds, you can take a step back to review and compare how your assets are doing. It's a good idea to review and analyze how your assets are allocated and get a big-picture view of your portfolio from time to time. The whole reason you have assets is to make money, right? Quicken provides some features that can give you the big picture in a matter of minutes and provide some good advice on where you might want to consider making some changes.

In this chapter, we will review the tools you can use to analyze your assets, see how you currently have your assets allocated, determine what your capital gain potential is using your existing investments, and analyze your portfolio to see if you have well-balanced investments. All of these tools help you to determine whether you need to adjust where you are putting your money and how you can get the most out of your assets and investments.

Reviewing and Analyzing Your Asset Allocations

The Analysis tab in the Investing Center provides pie charts that show you how your assets are spread out among your investments. When you set up your investments in Quicken, you most likely indicated how much you were allocating to each investment. When you do this, Quicken logs which asset classes or groups (for example, bonds) your investments belong to. Using the Analysis tab, you can analyze where your money is by viewing just your investment allocations, just your retirement allocations, all accounts, or individual accounts. In addition, pie charts show you how your accounts are allocated and how your securities, such as cash, are allocated. By viewing your asset allocations from all angles, you can see exactly which assets are growing and how fast they are growing, which assets aren't growing, and where you may need to make adjustments.

Review and Analyze Your Asset Allocations

1 From the account bar, click **Investing Center**.

2 Click the **Analysis** tab.

3 The **Actual** pie chart shows your assets as they are allocated today and the **Target** pie chart shows your assets as they should be. Hover your mouse over a slice to see the amount and percentage allocated.

4 Beneath the Actual pie chart is the total amount of your assets and beneath the Target pie chart is either the **Set Target** link (if you haven't set up your asset allocation targets yet) or the **Change Target** link to change your target percentages.

5 The table beneath the pie charts provides a comparison of your actual and target percentages and serves as a color key to the slices in the pie charts.

6 To change your target percentages to see how your totals change, click **Change Target** or click **Options, Change Target Allocations**.

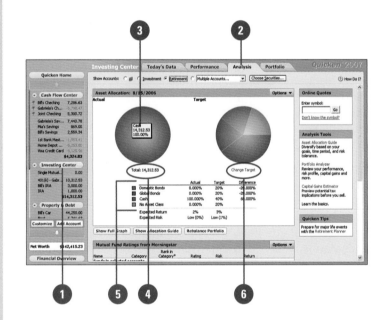

7 Click in the **Percentage** column for the asset class you want to change and type the new percentage. Remember, your asset percentages must total 100%.

> ### Did You Know?
>
> ***Changing your target percentages does not actually change your investments.*** By changing your target asset allocation percentages, you are not actually changing how your assets are allocated. This feature allows you see what the potential is, should you change your allocations. Be sure to check with an advisor before making changes to your investments.

8 Click **OK**.

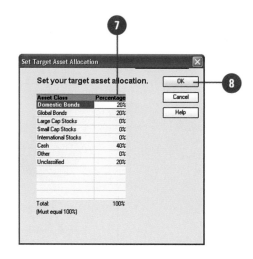

Select the Accounts and Securities You Want to View

1 To change the accounts you are viewing, from the Show Accounts options, select **All** to view both retirement and investment accounts, select **Investment** to view just investment accounts, or **Retirement** to view only those accounts.

2 Click the drop-down menu and select an account you want to view, or select **Multiple Accounts** to choose a variety of accounts.

3 Select the accounts that you want to view and click **OK**.

4 To select specific securities to view, click **Choose Securities**.

5 Select or clear the securities that you want to view and click **OK**.

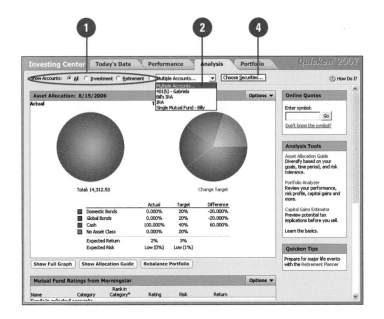

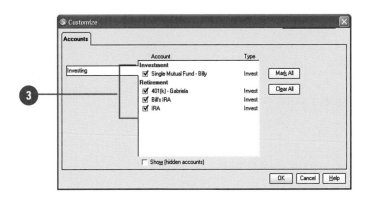

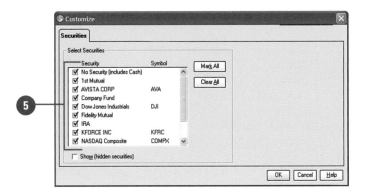

View the Asset Allocation Report

1. To view the pie chart and a detailed report for the accounts and securities currently reflected on the Actual pie chart, click **Show Full Graph**.

See Also

See "Saving and Viewing Saved Reports" on page 322 to learn how to save a pie chart.

2. To view a detailed breakdown by security, click **Show Report**.

3. To print just the report or graph, click **Print** (not shown).

Continued, next page

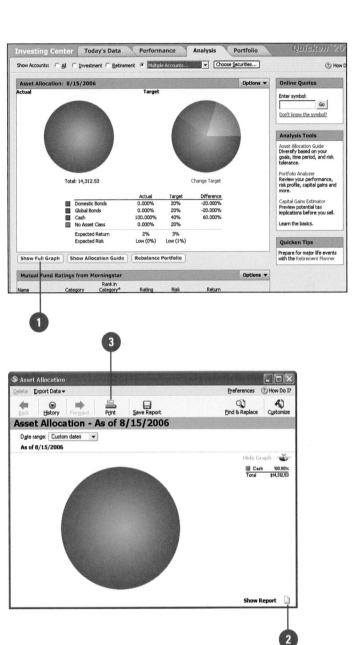

4. To save the report, click **Save Report**.

5. To remove the report from view, click **Hide Report**.

6. To remove the graph from view, click **Hide Graph**.

7. Close the report when you are finished.

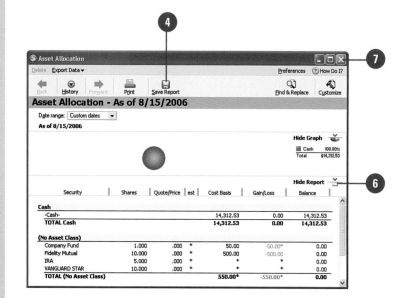

Review and Compare Mutual Funds

1. If you have mutual funds, the Mutual Fund Ratings from Morningstar section lists the funds that are included in the accounts that are currently selected from **Show Accounts**, and those in your watch list, if you have one.

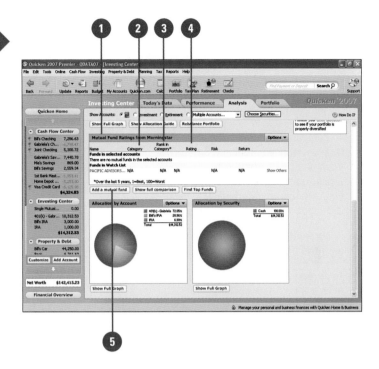

See Also

See "Tracking and Managing Investment Performances" on page 131 for more information on setting up and using watch lists.

2. The **Category** column shows you the types of funds associated with the accounts.

3. The **Rank in Category** column shows you the ranking of the fund, based on performance among all mutual funds in the Morningstar mutual fund category. Ranking ranges from 1 (best) to 100 (worst).

4. The **Rating** column provides the current rating for the fund, based on Morningstar's five-star range.

5. To add a new fund, click **Add a Mutual Fund**.

Continued, next page

Did You Know?

Morningstar is a mutual fund rating service. As one of the leading mutual fund rating services, Morningstar rates mutual funds by stars, five being the top rating. Ratings are based on two areas: risk-assessment and load-adjusted performance (return) and three time periods: 3, 5, and 10 years. However, a fund must have at least a three-year track record before Morningstar rates it. Once a rating is calculated, the result determines how risky the fund is, compared to the average fund in the same class or type of fund.

10

6 Enter the security symbol and name. To locate a specific security symbol, click **Look Up** to open the Quicken Ticker Search web page, where you can perform a search for the symbol.

7 To compare the category, rank, rating, risk, and potential return for each fund, click **Show Full Comparison** to open the Mutual Funds Ratings by Morningstar window.

8 Compare the funds and when you are finished, close the window.

9 To research everything you would ever want to know about mutual funds, click **Find Top Funds** to open the Yahoo! Finance web page.

10 From the Yahoo! Finance web page, you can find information about stocks, bonds, and funds, such as top-rated funds, or those you should steer clear from.

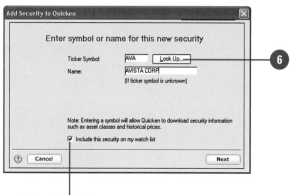

Select the **Include** option to add the security to your watch list.

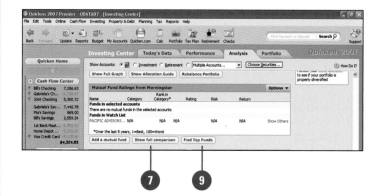

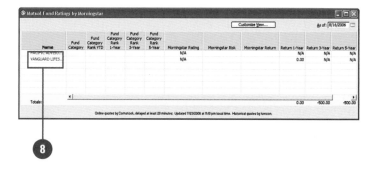

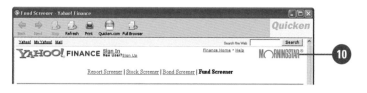

Review Account and Security Allocations

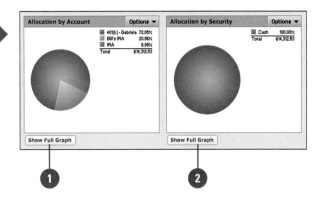

1. From the Analysis tab, scroll down to the **Allocation by Account** section to see how each of your accounts is allocated. Click **Show Full Graph** to see the pie chart in detail and to access reporting features.

2. Allocation by Security shows how your securities are allocated. Click **Show Full Graph** to see the pie chart in detail and to access reporting features.

3. To view allocations for a different date range, from the **Date Range** drop-down menu, select a different date.

4. To view the pie chart by a different option, such as security type, make a selection from the **Subtotal By** drop-down menu.

5. When you are finished reviewing the pie chart, close the window.

See Also

See "Working with Reports" on page 309 to learn more about reports.

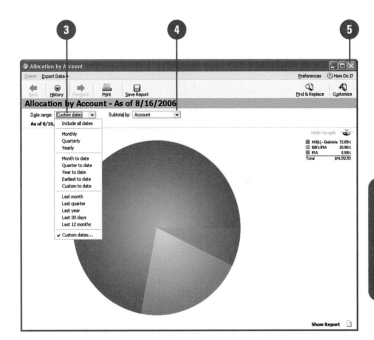

10

Getting Some Help
with Asset Allocation

Asset allocation is very important, and sometimes the slightest change can make a big difference. There are principles that you can use as guidelines when determining and evaluating how you want to allocate your assets or make changes to them. So, how about a little advice from a reputable source to help you out? Don't worry, there's no insider trading going on here, just Quicken's Asset Allocation Guide, which has some great tips. This guide has some very helpful information about assets and asset classes, how to go about allocating your assets, what an ideal portfolio looks like, monitoring your assets, and rebalancing your portfolio. In addition, this guide should be able to answer some of your questions about risks, how to reach your goals, finding a reputable financial advisor, and much more.

Get Help with Asset Allocation

1 From the account bar, click **Investing Center**.

2 Click the **Analysis** tab.

3 Click **Show Allocation Guide** or you can click the **Asset Allocation Guide link** in the Analysis Tools box.

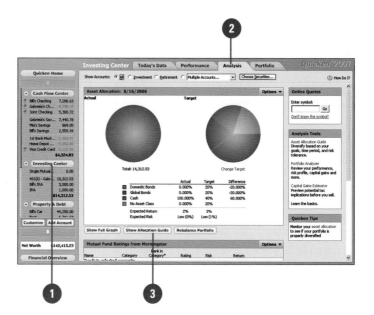

4 The guide starts with some basic information about assets and a pie chart view of your current asset allocations. For more information about asset classes, click **What Are Asset Classes and Why Should I Use Them?**

5 To proceed to the next page of the guide, click **Next: How Do I Update Asset Classes?** You can also use the menu on the left to move through the guide.

6 Review the information about updating asset classes and common questions. If you want to download the latest classes, click **Go Online and Update Asset Classes**. Be sure you are connected to the Internet before proceeding.

7 Select the securities for which you want asset class information, and then click **Update Now** to download the information.

8 To proceed, click **Next: What Should My Asset Allocation Be?**

For Your Information

To get additional information about downloading asset classes, click the **Common Questions About Downloading Asset Classes** link.

Continued, next page

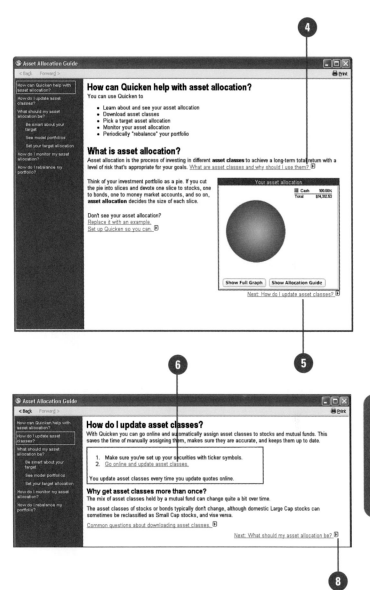

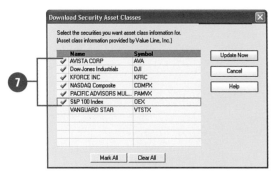

10

9 Explore the links to get more information on a subject, or to set up or change information about your allocations, such as your target allocation.

10 Continue to review all the asset allocation information and click the **Next: Be Smart About Your Target Allocation** link to move to each new page.

11 When you reach the last window (titled What Is Rebalancing?), review the steps you need to take to rebalance your portfolio and click the links to get additional information.

See Also

See "Determining Whether You Need to Rebalance Your Portfolio" on page 305 for more information on rebalancing your portfolio.

12 When you are finished, close the window.

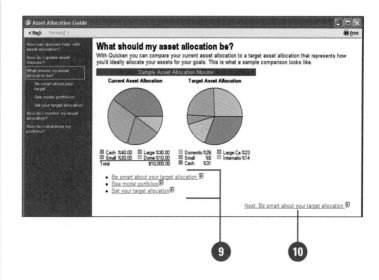

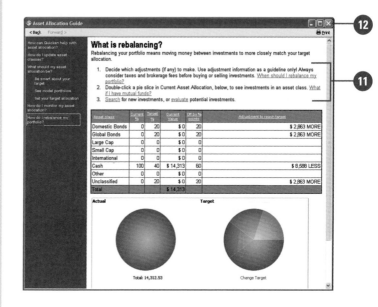

Estimating Capital Gains

If you sell an investment and the selling price exceeds the purchase price, that investment produces a profit for you. This is known as *capital gain*. Quicken provides a feature to help you determine what your capital gain potential is, using your existing investments. This feature is called the Capital Gains Estimator. Estimating your capital gains helps you determine whether it would be advantageous to sell an investment and what tax liability you could encounter. You can access the Capital Gains Estimator from the Investment and Tax menus, from the Analysis tab in the Investing Center, or from the Portfolio Analyzer. For the purposes of this task, you will be accessing it from the Analysis tab.

Get Started

1. From the account bar, click **Investing Center**.

2. Click the **Analysis** tab.

3. Click **Capital Gains Estimator**.

See Also

See Chapter 12, "Managing Your Tax Information," on page 325, for information on determining tax liabilities and setting up your tax information using the Tax Planner.

4. Review the Welcome page and click **Let's Get Started** to proceed.

Did You Know?

You can use the menu to move through the Capital Gains Estimator. If you already know your way around this feature or you prefer to navigate it by using the menu, click the menu options on the left side of the window to move through or go to a specific place in the Capital Gains Estimator. If you have saved scenarios you are working with, click a scenario under the Scenarios section to go directly to it.

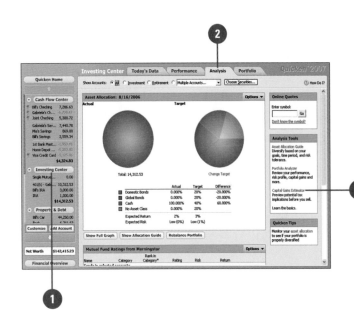

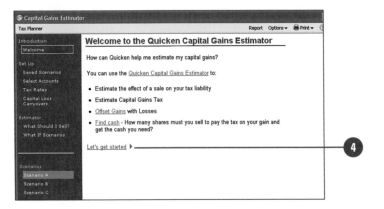

Set Up a Scenario

1. Select a scenario and click **Next**. You can set up as many as three scenarios to compare and contrast situations. But you have to create the scenarios one at a time.

2. Select the investments you want to include by clicking in the column next to the investment name. A green check mark means the investment is selected. Then click **Next**.

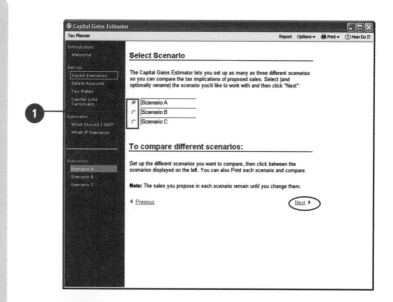

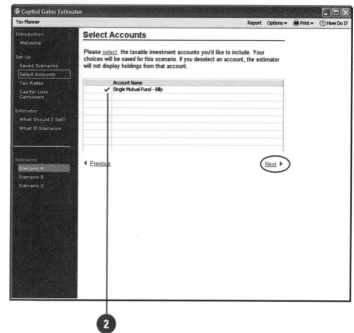

3. Your estimated taxes are determined using the information you have entered into Quicken about your investments and tax information. If you have not already set up your tax information, you can do so now.

4. From the **Federal Tax Rates** section, if you're sure of your federal tax rate, select it from the list. Otherwise, use the rate that Quicken has selected for you.

5. In the State Tax Rates section, type your state tax rate. If you are unsure of what it is, click **How Do I Find My State Tax?** to get information on how to determine the rate.

6. Click **Next**.

7. Select **Use Tax Planner Values** to use losses from previous years. The figures are automatically updated. Or select **Enter Different Values** to type the figures yourself. Then click **Next**.

Did You Know?

There are limits for the losses you can claim. You can claim up to $3,000 or $1,500 if you are married and file separately above any capital gains.

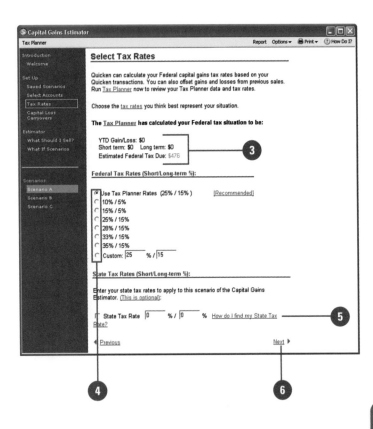

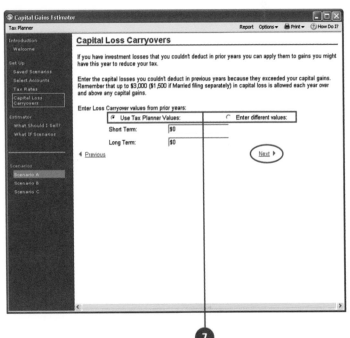

Estimate Capital Gains

1. Type the amount you would like to make on the sale. This does not have to be an exact figure. You can change it if it ends up not meeting your goal.

2. Select a goal.

3. Click **Search**. Quicken searches your investments and locates securities that you can sell to meet your goal.

4. Click **View Results**.

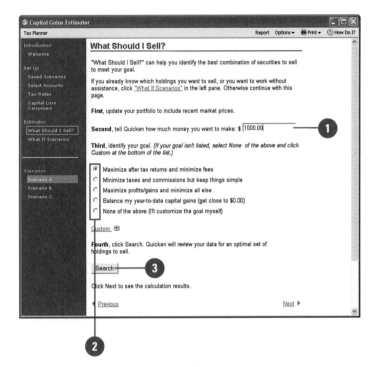

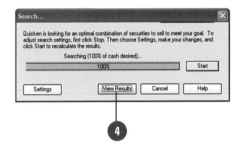

5 Select the security or lot that you are thinking of selling. The number of shares and selling price automatically update in the Proposed Sales table, based on the security or lot you select.

6 Click in **Shares to Sell** or **Sale Price** to change the figures, if needed.

7 Any losses or gains are listed in the **Taxable Gains from Proposed Sales** table.

8 The potential total gross sales and total estimated taxes or refund due are calculated and provided toward the bottom of the window.

> ## Did You Know?
>
> *You can compare taxes before and after sales.* To see what your taxes would be before and after you sell an investment, click the links under Detailed Calculations at the bottom of the window.

9 You can go back through this scenario and make changes or set up another scenario to compare to this one by repeating the steps in the Set Up a Scenario and Estimate Capital Gains tasks. However, be sure to select the next scenario (for example, Scenario B).

10 When you are finished, close the Capital Gains Estimator window.

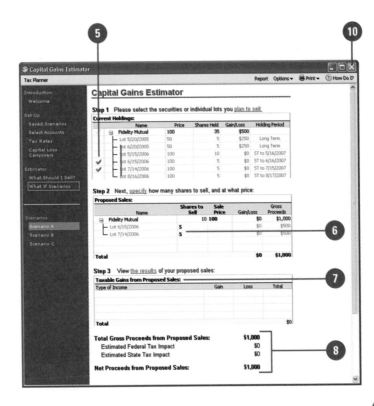

10

Viewing Your Entire Portfolio

Your portfolio consists of all your asset information (retirement accounts, stocks, bonds, and so on). All your assets are listed in Quicken in detail so that you can review or take action on every type of asset you own. Your securities or assets are listed by name. For each security, you can see a host of information. For example, the default view provides the quote or price, the number of shares, the market value dollar amount, the total cost of all shares, the loss or gain dollar amounts, the loss or gain percentages, the losses or gains per day, and the daily value of each, in dollar amounts and percentages. In addition, you can download the latest or historical quotes for your securities, change the view to see your securities from different angles, and customize the information you see. Basically, you can slice and dice your portfolio any way you want.

Review Your Portfolio

1. From the account bar, click **Investing Center.**

2. Click the **Portfolio** tab.

3. Review the list of your securities. You can open and close the folders by clicking them. The portfolio view differs, depending on what is selected from the Show menu. This example uses the default, Value view.

4. The Watch List folder contains any securities that you have set up for your watch list.

5. If you use One Step Update, the latest quotes may already update automatically. If not, you can update quotes by clicking **Download Quotes.** Quicken connects to the Internet and downloads the quotes.

6. To view prices for previous dates click **Download Historical Prices.**

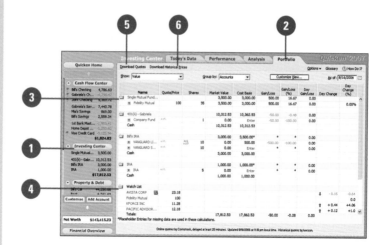

Did You Know?

You can use the glossary for column definitions. To read detailed descriptions about each column in the portfolio, from the menu bar at the top of the Portfolio tab, click **Glossary.**

See Also

See "Tracking and Managing Investment Performance" on page 131 to learn how to set up or edit watch lists.

7 Select the time frames (they range from the previous month to the past five years), and click **Update Now**. Quicken connects to the Internet and downloads the historical quotes.

See Also

See "Setting Up Your Internet Connection" on page 51 for more information about One Step Update.

Did You Know?

There are some things to consider when downloading quotes. If you are downloading a lot of historical prices, it may take a while to download, depending on your Internet connection speed. Keep this in mind when you are selecting the securities you want to download. Consider breaking up how much you are downloading into manageable chunks appropriate for your connection speed, for example, a few at a time for dial-up connections. If you have cable or DSL, downloading large amounts of information may not be a problem.

8 To change the view, from the **Show** drop-down menu, select a different view.

9 To change how the listing is grouped, click **Group By** and select another option.

10 To view figures for a different date, click in the **As Of** box next to the calendar icon and type the date you want to see or click the calendar icon and select the date.

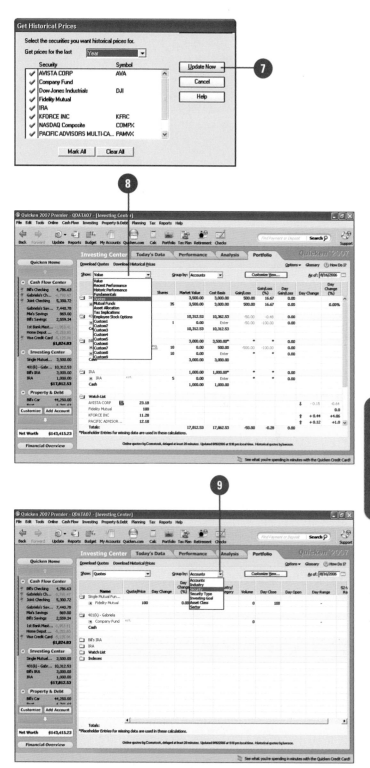

View Security Details

1. To view security details, hover your mouse over the name of the security. A pop-up menu appears, giving you options you can select to see more information about that security.

2. To go into the account summary, view performance and analysis information, or access the account register, click the account name or click **Edit**.

3. To evaluate stocks or mutual funds on Quicken.com, click **Evaluate**. You are required to log in to Quicken.com, provide the ticker symbol, and select an Evaluator tool.

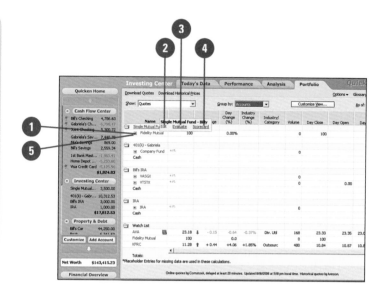

Did You Know?

Pop-up menu options with lightning symbols require online access. If you see a lightning bolt symbol when you hover your mouse over a pop-up menu option, you are required to log in to Quicken.com. For these features, you need your Quicken.com login and password.

4. To see how a security has been doing in the market, click **Scorecard**. This feature requires Internet access to Quicken.com.

5. To view more detailed information on a security, click the security name.

6. To change the security name, symbol, type, or asset class, click **Edit Security Details**.

7. Make the changes and click **OK** when you are finished.

8. To view or change transaction information, double-click a transaction.

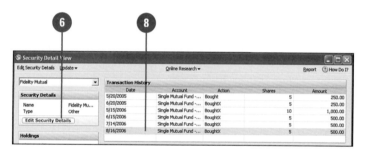

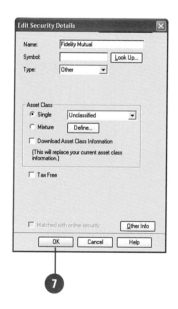

298

9 Review or change the transaction information and click **Enter/Done**.

10 Use the drop-down menus to change the view and time period.

11 Click **More Charting** to explore additional types of charts you can view.

12 Close the window when you are finished working with the security.

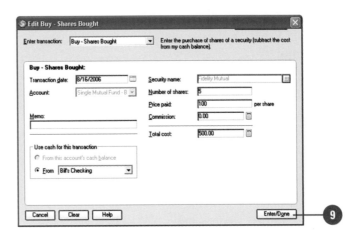

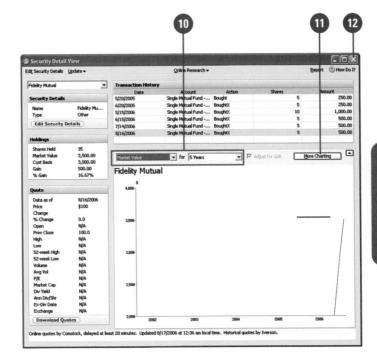

For Your Information

If there are transactions that need to be entered, when you perform step 8, the Enter Missing Transactions window opens. You can add the missing information by clicking **Enter Missing Transaction**.

Customize or Create a New Portfolio View

1. Click **Customize View** to either customize the current view or create a new view.

2. If you want to customize the current view, do not change the name. If you want to create a new view, click in **Name** and type a new name for the view.

3. To add a column or columns that you want to see, from Available Columns, select the column(s) and click **Add**.

4. To remove a column or columns, from Displayed Columns, select the column(s) and click **Remove**.

5. To see the symbols associated with each account on the Portfolio tab, select **Show Symbols in Name Column**.

6. To select or remove the accounts and securities you see, click an account or a security. A green check mark means it is selected, and no check mark means it is not selected.

7. To change the order of accounts and securities, select an account or security and click **Move Up** to move it up the list or click **Move Down** to move it down the list. Repeat this step until the list appears the way you want.

8. Click **Mark All** to select all accounts or securities or click **Clear All** to remove all accounts or securities from the view.

9. Click **OK** to save your new or customized view. If you create a new view, the name will appear in the Show menu.

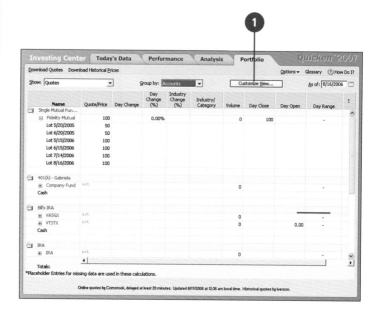

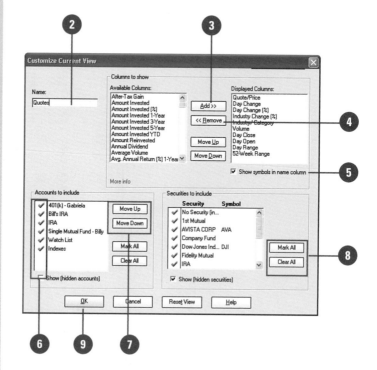

Analyzing Your Portfolio

Financial advisors recommend that you review and evaluate your portfolio at least once per year, or when your financial goals or circumstances change. Fortunately, Quicken offers an easy and painless way of analyzing your portfolio: by using a tool called the Portfolio Analyzer. This feature analyzes the performance of your investments, holdings, asset allocations, risk factors, and possible tax liabilities. This information can help you with any decisions you need to make about your investments and financial planning.

Analyze Performance

① Click the **Investing** menu and select **Portfolio Analyzer**.

② Click the menu options on the left or scroll down to view each section.

③ The **Performance** section provides a bar chart that shows the rate of return, in percentages, over a five-year period.

④ You can also see which securities did the best and worst by selecting a time frame from the **Time Period** menu.

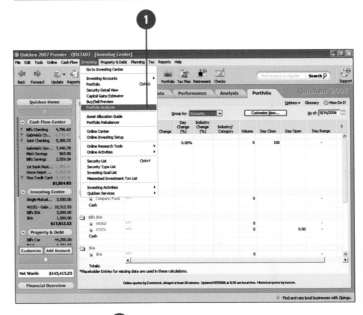

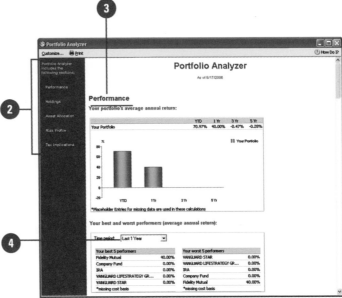

10

5 The What to Look for in Performance and Actions for Performance sections provide advice on what to look for in your securities and what you can do to get the best return.

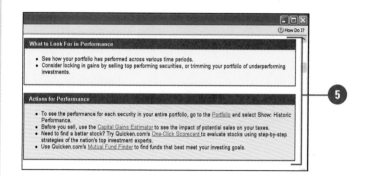

Analyze Holdings

1 The **Holdings** section provides pie charts of your accounts, how much they are currently worth in the market, and what percentage of the pie each is.

2 You can also see what your largest securities are, what their values are, and what percentage of the pie they are.

3 Hover your mouse over a piece of either of the pies to see the value. You also get advice for your holdings.

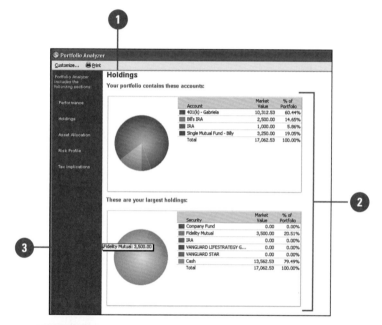

Analyze Asset Allocation

1 The **Asset Allocation** section also provides two pie charts, one for your assets as they are allocated today (Actual) and one for your target assets (Target).

2 Hover your mouse over a section of the pie chart to see the amount and allocation percentage.

3 The table shows the comparison of your actual and target asset allocations. In addition, you get advice for your asset allocations.

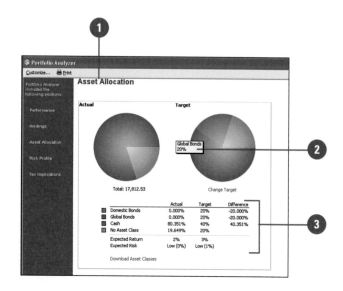

Analyze Risk

1 The **Risk Profile** section provides a visual of what your projected risk and rate of return are, compared to the risk and rate of return for some standard assets.

2 Guidelines are also provided for determining risk and rate of return.

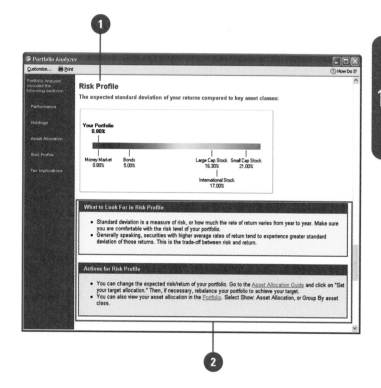

Analyze Tax Implications

1. The **Tax Implications** section provides information on your possible capital gains, and possible taxes you might need to pay for each of your holdings.

2. Additional information is also provided about what to look for tax implications, and what you can do to improve your tax situation.

3. When you are finished, close the Portfolio Analyzer.

See Also

See "Estimate Capital Gains" on page 294 for more information about capital gains.

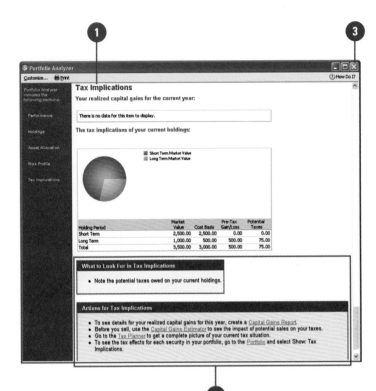

Determining Whether You Need to Rebalance Your Portfolio

If you haven't already analyzed your portfolio by using the Portfolio Analyzer, I suggest you go back to the previous task and do that before proceeding with this task. The Portfolio Analyzer should show you exactly which assets are working in your favor and which ones aren't. After you are armed with this information, what should you do with it? Fortunately, Quicken offers yet another helpful tool that you can use to determine when and if you should rebalance your portfolio, research and evaluate new investments, and determine what adjustments you should make to meet your target. This tool is called the Portfolio Rebalancer. You may not be familiar with what *rebalancing* means; simply stated, it means moving your money where it benefits you most. Moving your money might mean selling stocks, buying stocks, changing your asset allocations, and so on. By rebalancing your portfolio, you reduce risk and improve the chances for good returns, which in turn helps get you closer to meeting your financial goals. However, you should do your research and get some advice from a trusted source before you start moving your money around.

Determine Whether You Need to Rebalance Your Portfolio

① Click the **Investing** menu and select **Portfolio Rebalancer**.

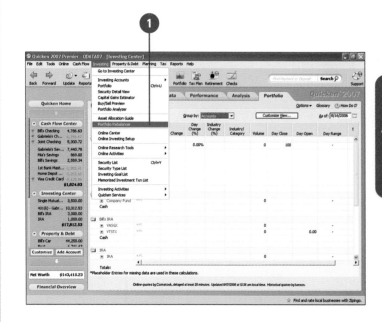

10

2 To review some key points to consider when evaluating rebalancing your portfolio, click **When Should I Rebalance My Portfolio?**.

3 If you have mutual funds, click **What If I Have Mutual Funds?** for key points about rebalancing mutual funds.

4 If you are considering looking into new investments, click **Search** to research stocks, mutual funds, and bonds.

5 Click a link to get more information about that subject. Some sites (for example, the Stock Screener) may require that you complete information about the subject.

6 To evaluate an existing stock or mutual fund, click **Evaluate**.

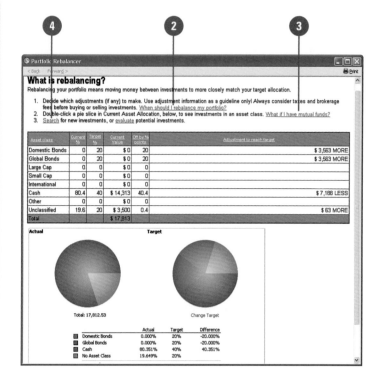

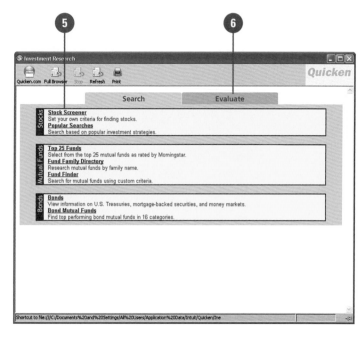

7 For either the stock or mutual fund, type the ticker symbol, select the type of information you want to see, and click **Go Online to Evaluate Stock(s)**.

8 The table lists all your assets by asset class, the current and target percentages, the value for each, and how far off you are from your target.

9 The dollar amount you are over or under is also provided.

10 Click a heading to view a column description.

11 Double-click a pie chart to get a more detailed view of that asset.

12 To set your target allocation percentages, click **Set Target** (if you haven't set it) or click **Change Target** to change it. If you have not yet set your target, the Asset Allocation Guide opens, where you can set the target.

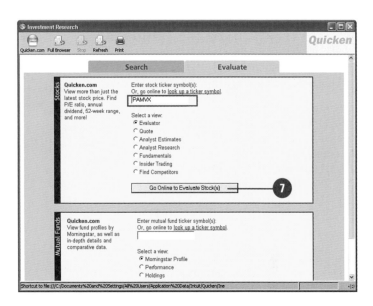

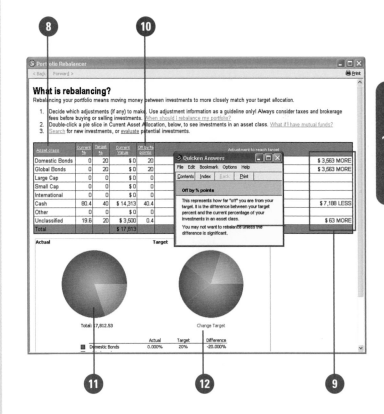

10

13 If you are changing your target, the Set Target Asset Allocation dialog box opens, where you can change your percentages. Then click **OK**.

14 Review your adjustments to see where you need to make changes in order to meet your target and repeat any of these steps to research your assets or investment considerations further.

See Also

See "Getting Some Help with Asset Allocation" on page 288 for more information about the Asset Allocation Guide and setting target allocation percentages.

13

Set Target Asset Allocation			
Set your target asset allocation.		OK
		Cancel
		Help
Asset Class	**Percentage**	
Domestic Bonds	20%	
Global Bonds	20%	
Large Cap Stocks	0%	
Small Cap Stocks	0%	
International Stocks	0%	
Cash	40%	
Other	0%	
Unclassified	20%	
Total:	100%	
(Must equal 100%)		

Working with Reports

Introduction

Quicken provides a wide variety of reports for just about every aspect of your financial situation, for just about every scenario or combination of scenarios, and for many time periods (past, present, and future). And if you can't find a report to meet your exact needs, Quicken gives you the power of customizing reports so that you can create and save your own reports. In addition, you can print reports and export them into another format—for example, to use in a Microsoft Excel spreadsheet so that you can share the information with others. You can use reports to analyze your financial condition, and to shed light on how you're doing with a budget, a savings goal, or another financial concern.

In this chapter, you will learn how to view the standard reports that Quicken offers, such as the Cashflow report, which shows you exactly where all your money is going for a specific period of time. Quicken offers several standard reports and graphs. However, you can take those reports and graphs and customize the content to meet your specific needs. You can then save them, and reuse them, which you will also learn how to do.

There are report preferences that you will learn to set, for example, using a specific date range for all reports, so that each time you run a report, Quicken uses this date range each time you run a report or graph. Lastly, you will learn how to export reports, save reports, and view the reports that you have saved to reuse them.

Using reports and graphs helps you manage your money so that you can clearly see exactly where your money is going and where it is coming from. This information can help you make decisions about your spending, budget, potential taxes, and much more. There are a host of uses for reports and graphs and this chapter will step you through how to get the most out of what reports and graphs have to offer, which will in turn help you manage your finances.

Viewing Reports

You can access reports from many places in Quicken, such as from some of the activity centers, from the Financial Overview center, and from the Reports menu. For the purposes of this task, we will access reports by using the Reports menu.

View a Report

① Click **Reports**, **Reports & Graphs Center**. Any reports that you have created and saved already appear at the top of the reports list, under Saved Reports. Beneath Saved Reports are the report topic headings, which appear in the form of questions.

TIMESAVER *You can use the Reports menu to create instant reports. The quickest way to view a report, no matter where you are in Quicken, is to use the Reports menu. You can go into the Reports & Graphs window from here, but you don't even have to go that far to run a report. You can click* **Reports** *from the menu bar and then click a menu option, such as Cash Flow. Each menu option contains reports that you can view directly from the menu. You can select a report from one of the options, and you get an instant report.*

② Click a report heading to view the available reports and graphs. A paper icon appears next to the reports and a pie chart icon appears next to the graphs.

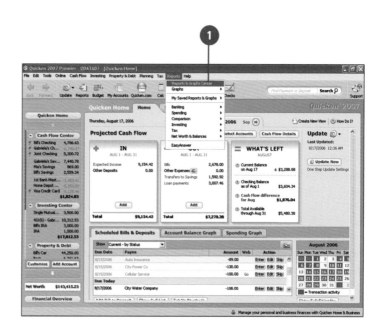

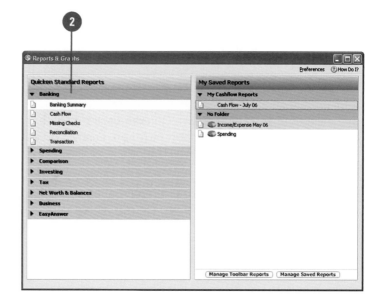

3 Click a report to select it. The report criteria options that appear vary, depending on which report or graph that you select.

4 From the report criteria, select or type the criteria you want to use for the report. For example, for the **Cash Flow** report, I selected Last Month from the Date Range drop-down list. Quicken automatically fills in the dates.

5 Click **Show Report**.

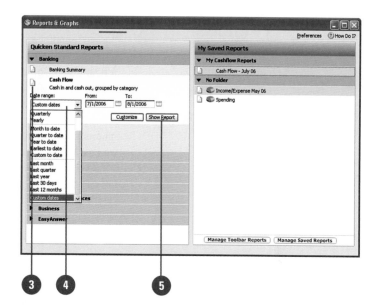

See Also

See the next task, "Customizing Reports," on page 312, to learn how to customize the information in the report. See "Saving and Viewing Saved Reports" on page 322 to learn how to save reports.

Did You Know?

You can use the Easy Answer reports and graphs to answer common financial inquiries. The Easy Answer reports and graphs provide answers to some common questions about your finances, such as how much you've spent on gas over a month's time. You can use this information to help create or adjust your budget, or to make bigger decisions, such as whether to buy a car that gets better gas mileage.

In order to take full advantage of this feature, you must assign a category to the expense when entering the transaction in your account register (for example, Auto: Fuel for gasoline expenses). Refer to "Record and Edit Transactions Using Scheduled Bills & Deposits," in Chapter 3 for more information on recording transactions in your register.

11

Customizing Reports

See Also

See "Viewing Reports" on page 310 to learn how to run reports.

Quicken provides many options for customizing reports. You can change the appearance of a report, weed out information that you don't want to see, add criteria that you do want to see, specify dates or time frames, or specify the category groups you want to include or not include. Remember that *categories* are the groups that you assign to a transaction when you enter it in your register, and they are used for tracking and reporting on those categories. Your options for customizing a report vary, depending on which report you are customizing. You can customize a report from the Reports & Graphs window before you view the report or after the report opens, you can customize it from there as well. This task customizes the a Cash Flow report after it has been opened.

Set Display Options

1. Open a report, if you don't already have one open.

2. To view a different time period, click the **Date Range** drop-down list and make a selection.

3. Click the **Column** drop-down list to change the columns you want to see for the report.

4. To customize the report options, click **Customize**.

5. To change the standard time period for this report, from **Date Range**, select the time period that you want to use.

6. On the **Display** tab, you can change the title of the report to be more descriptive.

7. Set row and column headings by making selections from the drop-down menus.

8. Arrange content using the options in the **Organization** drop-down list.

9. Select whether you want to see cents or percentages.

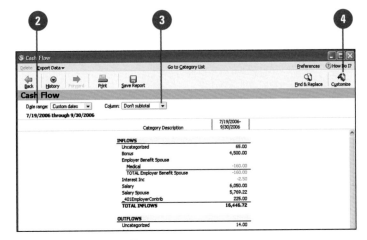

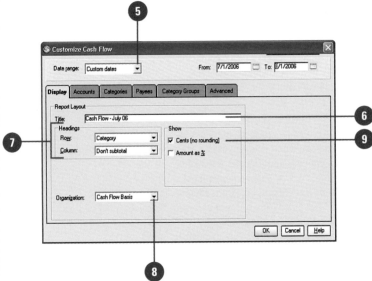

Set Account Options

1. On the **Accounts** tab, click the account group you want to include in the report.

2. Select the accounts that you want to include in the report or graph. To remove an account, clear the box next to the account name by clicking the check mark.

3. To include accounts from other account groups, click another account group and select the account(s) that you want.

4. To select all accounts in an account group, click **Mark All** or click **Clear All** to remove all selected accounts.

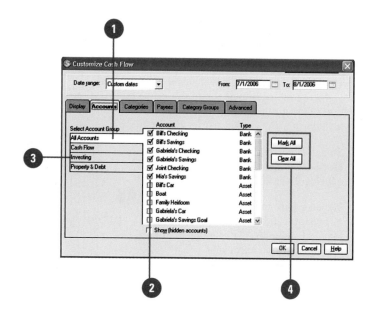

Set Category Options

① On the **Categories** tab, select the categories that you want to include in the report or graph or clear those that you do not want to include.

② Select all categories by clicking **Mark All** or clear all categories by clicking **Clear All**.

③ Click the **Expand All** button to see all subcategories or to view only the top categories, click **Collapse All**. You can then make your selection.

> **TIMESAVER** *Quickly find the categories that you want to include in the report or graph. Rather than scrolling through the category list to find the category you want to include in the report, you can search for the category and ensure hidden categories are shown. First, select the **Show (Hidden Categories)** check box. Then click in the box underneath the **Type Category Name to Search List** and type the name or partial name of the category that you are looking for. Quicken locates or finds the closest match to the one you are looking for in the category list. To include transactions that are not assigned to a specific category, from the top of the category list, select **Not Categorized**.*

④ From the **Payee** drop-down menu, you can select a specific payee so that the report includes only transactions and categories assigned to that payee.

⑤ Use the **Category Contains** and **Memo Contains** areas to enter specific category and transaction information that you want to see for that payee.

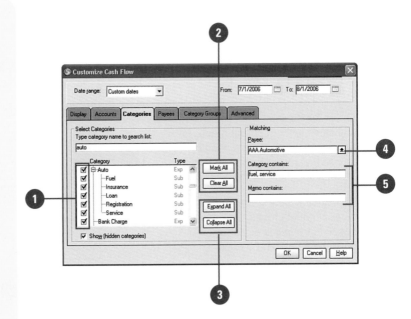

Set Payee Options

1. On the **Payees** tab, select the payees that you want to see in the report or graph.

2. To search for a specific payee, type the name. The list scrolls to the payee, if it exists.

3. As with the options on the other tabs, you can use the options in the **Matching** section to enter specific category and transaction information that you want to see for that payee.

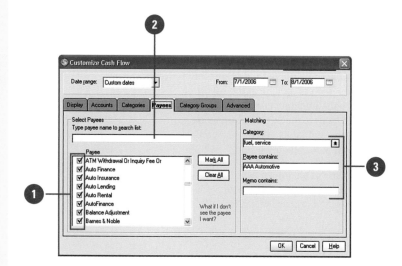

Did You Know?

Use the No Payee option to view transactions that match the category requirements. If there are transactions that do not have a payee assigned to them, you can still view those transactions in the report or graph by selecting the **No Payee** option shown at the top of the payee list. This tells Quicken to include all transactions that match the category requirements that you specified in the Category text box, even if they are not assigned to a specific payee.

Set Category Group Options

1. On the **Category Groups** tab, select or clear the category groups that you want to include in the report or graph. Selecting groups tells Quicken to include any transaction sums and totals that are associated with that category group.

2. To select all groups listed, click **Mark All** and to remove all selected groups, click **Clear All**.

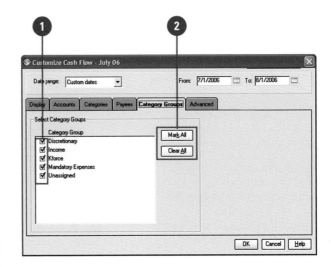

Did You Know?

Use the Unassigned option to view transactions that match the category requirements. To ensure that all transactions are included that meet your requirements, select the Unassigned option shown at the bottom of the Category Group list in step 2. This tells Quicken to include all transactions that match the requirements that you specified on the Accounts tab, even if they are not assigned to a category group.

Set Advanced Options

① On the **Advanced** tab, to view all transaction amounts, select **All** from the Amounts drop-down menu. Or, to view amounts greater or less than a specific figure, select another option and type the figure you want to use as the baseline.

② Select **Include Unrealized Gains** to show any investment transactions that reflect increases and/or decreases in security values.

③ Select **Tax-Related Transactions Only** to show only transactions that are related to your taxes.

④ Select the type of transactions you want to view in the report or graph.

⑤ Select whether or not you want to view transfer transactions and sub-categories in the report or graph.

⑥ Select the transaction statuses you want to view.

⑦ Click **OK** to save your changes.

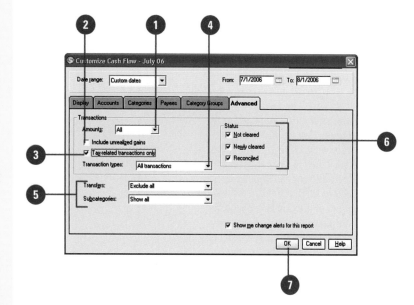

8 To print the report, click **Print**.

Did You Know?

You can use the Quicken taskbar to return to the Reports & Graphs window. You can go back to the Reports & Graphs window to view and run other reports by clicking the Reports & Graphs icon on the Quicken taskbar (at the bottom of the Quicken main window). When you open a report, the Reports & Graphs window doesn't go away; it minimizes to the taskbar. The Quicken taskbar works just like the Windows taskbar. If you have more than one program open in Windows, the programs you are not using are minimized on your taskbar, next to the Start menu. Quicken works the same way.

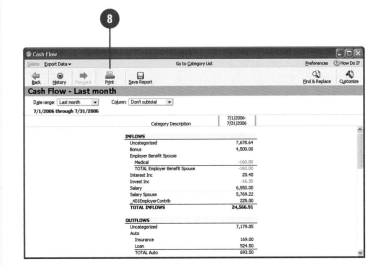

Setting Report Preferences

See Also

See "Setting Quicken Preferences" on page 40 for information on setting the other Quicken preferences. See "Viewing Reports" on page 310 to learn how to run reports.

There are a few preferences or settings that you can tell Quicken to use each time you run a report or graph. For example, you can set default date ranges for custom dates so that when you run any of the reports or graphs and select Custom Date for the date range, Quicken always uses the dates specified in the preferences. You can also set a custom comparison date range for Quicken to use when viewing the comparison reports. You can use this feature so that each time you run comparison reports, you always compare the same time period. For example, if you set the default comparison date range from the beginning of a specific quarter to the end of a specific quarter, Quicken uses this date range as the default comparison date range each time you run it. In addition, you can set preferences for customizing reports and graphs, and you can set default settings for reports only.

Select Reports and Graphs Preferences

① Open a report, if you don't already have one open, and click **Preferences**.

② To set a default date for a specific time period, from the Default Date Range drop-down menu, select the time period you want to use as the default. Then select the dates for the time period.

③ To set a date to use as the default for comparison reports, from the Default Comparison Date Range drop-down menu, select the time period for which you want to set the default. Then select the dates for the time period.

④ If you want to create a new report every time you customize a report, select **Customizing Creates New Report or Graph**.

⑤ If you don't want to create a new report every time you customize a report, select **Customizing Modifies Current Report or Graph**.

⑥ If you would like to have the option to customize a report before you view it, select **Customize Report/Graph Before Creating**.

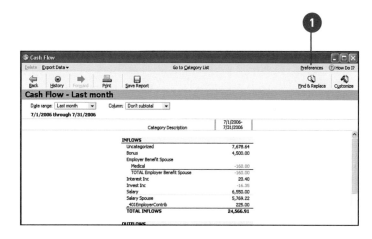

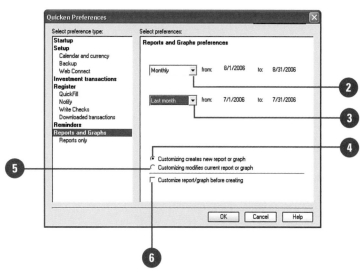

11

Select Report Preferences Only

① To set preferences for reports, click **Reports Only**.

② To view only descriptions for every account that appears in reports, select **Description**. The descriptions come from the description that you entered when you created the account.

③ To view just the name of accounts and not any descriptions in reports, select **Name**.

④ To view both the name and description for your accounts in reports, select **Both**.

⑤ Make your selections for the categories as you did for accounts in steps 2–4.

⑥ To view reports in color, instead of in black and white, select **Use Color in Report**.

⑦ To automatically open an investment form related to the transaction that you select from an investment report, select **QuickZoom to Investment Forms**. Otherwise, clear the option so that you can go from a transaction in an investment report to the appropriate transaction entry in your investment register.

⑧ To have Quicken ask if you want to save a report each time you close a report, select **Remind Me to Save Reports**.

⑨ To change the decimal placement for figures, click in the **Decimal Places for Prices and Shares** option and type the number of decimal places you want to use. You can use from zero to six places.

⑩ Click **OK** to save all your preferences.

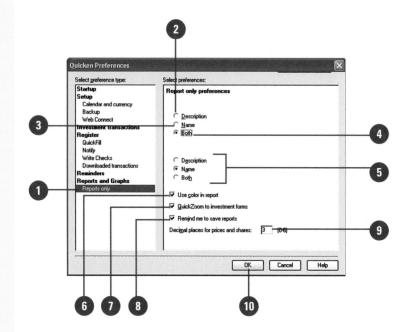

Exporting Reports

When you run a report, you have the option of exporting it or saving it in a separate file and in another format. The format that Quicken uses to export is a text file, which means that the report content is in plain text, without formatting, such as styles, tables, and so on. This makes the report content compatible with just about any other program, such as Microsoft Excel or Word. If you have specific information that you need to share with someone else—for example, your accountant, you can do so by exporting the report and saving it as a text file, and then you can either send the file as an email attachment, print it, or open it in Excel or another program to work with it further.

1. Open a report, if you don't already have one open, and click **Export Data, Report to Excel Compatible Format**.

See Also

See "Setting Quicken Preferences" on page 40 for information on setting the other Quicken preferences. See "Viewing Reports" on page 310 to learn how to run reports.

2. Click **Look In** to locate the folder where you want to save the file.

3. Click in the **File Name** text box and type the name of the file (for example the report name).

4. Click **Open**. The file is saved with the name you gave it and a .txt extension (for example, CashFlow706.txt).

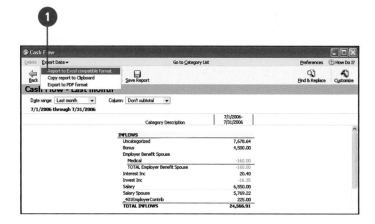

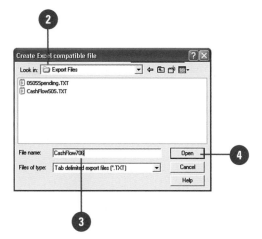

11

Saving and Viewing Saved Reports

In previous tasks I spent some time talking about viewing, customizing, and exporting reports. After you spend so much time getting your report the way you want it, it would be a shame to let all that hard work go to waste by not saving the report. For example, if you want to run a monthly expenditure report with specific criteria, after you get the report the way you want it, you can save it. Then the next month, you can open the saved report, select the month you want to view, run it, and save it. This saves you time and ensures that you get out of the report exactly what you want each time you run it.

Save Reports

1. Run and customize a report the way you want and then click **Save Report**.

See Also

See "Viewing Reports" on page 310 and "Customizing Reports" on page 312 for more information on running and customizing reports.

2. In **Report Name**, type the name you want to use for this report. You can also type a description to provide more detail.

3. From the **Save In** drop-down menu, select the center with which to associate the report or to create a folder for your customized reports, click **Create Folder**.

4. Type a name and click **OK**.

5. Click **OK**. The report now appears under My Saved Reports in the Reports & Graphs window.

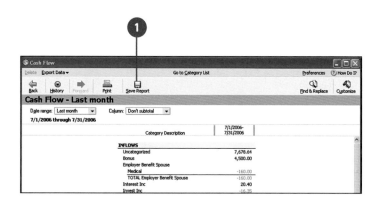

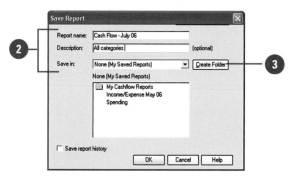

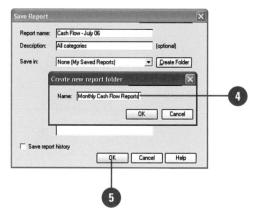

View Saved Reports

1 To open a saved report, open the **Reports & Graphs** window, if you don't already have it open.

See Also

See "Viewing Reports" on page 310 for information on running reports.

2 All reports that you have saved so far appear under the My Saved Reports on the right.

3 Click a report to select it.

4 Click **Show Report**.

5 To review and make changes to any saved reports, click **Manage Saved Reports**.

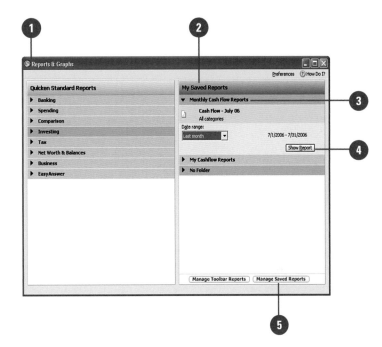

11

Managing Your Tax Information

Introduction

"The only difference between death and taxes is that death doesn't get worse every time Congress meets."
—Will Rogers, 1879–1935, American humorist, actor

"It's getting so that children have to be educated to realize that 'Damn' and 'Taxes' are two separate words."
—Unknown

"It is getting harder and harder to support the government in the style to which it has become accustomed."
—Unknown

"Taxes and golf are alike: You drive your heart out for the green and then end up in the hole."
—Unknown

"The difference between tax avoidance and tax evasion is the thickness of a prison wall."
—Denis Healey, British labor politician

Dying and paying taxes are both givens in this life, so why not make preparing for and paying taxes as easy as possible? The Quicken Tax tab in the Financial Overview center provides many tax-related features help you plan for and manage your tax information. You can track tax-related expenses, estimate taxes for the current year, find tax deductions, create tax categories and tax line items, and lots more. In addition, you can import and export information to and from TurboTax, which saves you time and ensures that all of your tax information is accurate and ready-to-use.

Setting Up New and Editing Existing Tax Alerts

As with the other centers in Quicken, on the Tax tab in the Financial Overview center you can set up alerts to remind or warn you of tax-related actions you need to take. For example, you can set up alerts to remind you to pay quarterly taxes or tell you if you are not saving enough to pay your taxes. Tax alerts are automatically turned on when you create a new Quicken file. Creating and editing tax alerts works the same as creating and editing alerts in the other centers.

Set Up New and Edit Existing Tax Alerts

1. From the **Tax** menu, select **Go to Tax Center** to open the Tax tab in the Financial Overview center.

2. To view all alerts, click **Show All Alerts**.

3. To create or edit tax alerts, click the **Setup** tab.

    TIMESAVER *You can also click **Set Up Alerts** in the Tax Alerts section of the Tax tab to create or edit tax alerts.*

See Also

See "Setting Up Alerts" on page 118 for more information on creating or changing alerts.

Did You Know?

You can also access the Alerts Center from the Tax Calendar section of the Tax Center by clicking **Set Up Alerts**.

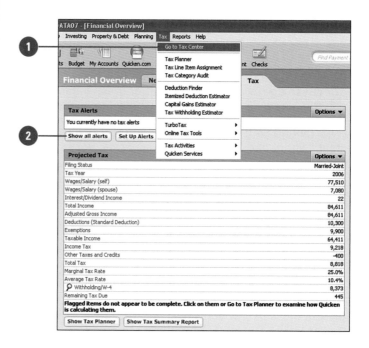

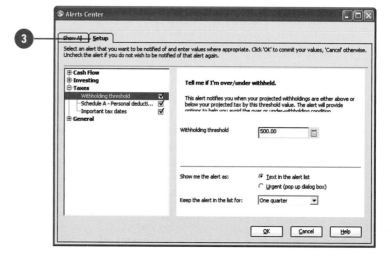

Importing and Exporting TurboTax Information

To get the most out of the Tax Planner and to ensure that the information you are using to estimate and plan for this year's taxes is as accurate as possible, you can import your TurboTax file from a previous year. However, because tax codes change frequently, Quicken allows only the current year or the previous year's tax files.

If you do not use TurboTax to file your taxes, you can manually enter your tax information in Quicken and still benefit from using the Tax Planner. Whether you import the information or enter it manually, the first thing you should do before using the Tax Planner, which is covered a little later in this chapter, is set up your tax information.

You can also export information from individual accounts in Quicken to use in TurboTax, such as transaction information that you can use when itemizing your taxes.

Import TurboTax Information

1. Click **File**, **Import**, **TurboTax**.

2. From the Import TurboTax File dialog box, locate the TurboTax file you want to import. The file should have a .tax extension (for example, tax2006.tax). A message appears asking if the file is the one you want to import and telling you that any tax information you've previously imported will be overwritten.

Continued, next page

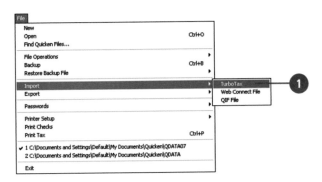

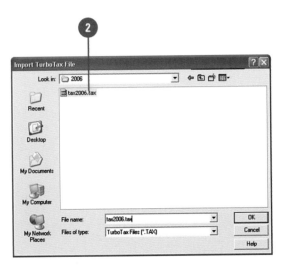

12

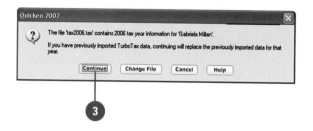

3 If the file is the one you want to import, click **Continue**. Otherwise, click **Change File** to locate the correct file.

4 When the file is finished importing, click **OK**. Quicken automatically updates the Tax Center with the tax information you imported.

For Your Information

The messages you see when you import your tax information may differ from what you see here, depending on your filing status and the tax filing form you use.

Export TurboTax Information

① Choose **File**, **Export**, and then select **QIF File**.

② Click **Browse** to specify where you want to save the file.

③ From the **Save In** drop-down menu, locate the folder where you want to save the file.

④ Click in **File Name** and type the name of the file. Then click **OK**.

⑤ From the **Quicken Account to Export From** menu on the QIF Export dialog, select the account you want to export.

⑥ From the **Include Transactions in Dates** section, type or select the date range for the account transactions you want to export in the Quicken file.

⑦ In the **Include in Export** section, select the type of information you want to export.

⑧ Click **OK**. The information you just exported is now located in the folder you selected and has a `.QIF` extension (for example, `2005Taxes.qif`).

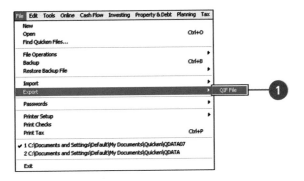

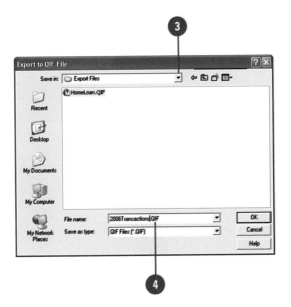

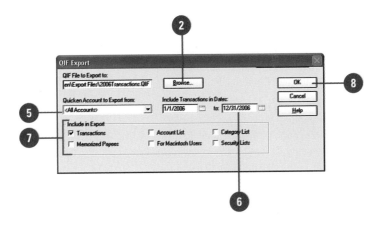

Creating Year-End Files

At the end of the year, you should save a copy of the current year's information in a separate file (an archive) and continue using the file. You can then use the archived year-end file when preparing for tax time. A year-end file can contain all of your financial information up to the date you create the year-end file, or you can select a specific timeframe for the transactions that you want to include in the file. In future years, you can use this information for financial projections and reports.

Create a Year-End File

1. Choose **File**, **File Operations**, and then select **Year-End Copy**.

2. If you want to continue using the current Quicken file for the coming year, select **Do Nothing. My Current Data File Will Remain Unchanged**.

3. If you want to remove all information from your data file, with the exception of transactions dated from a specific date forward, select **I Only Want Transactions in My Current Data File Starting with This Date**.

4. Type the date or select it by clicking the calendar icon.

5. Click **Browse** to locate the folder where you want to save your archive or copy of the current file.

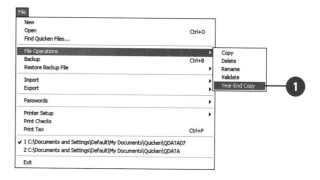

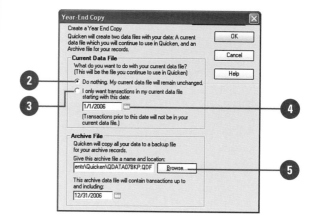

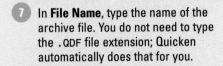

From the **Save In** drop-down menu, locate the folder where you want to save the file.

In **File Name**, type the name of the archive file. You do not need to type the .QDF file extension; Quicken automatically does that for you.

Click **Save**.

To specify a date for the transactions to be included in the file, click in the box under **This Archive Data File Will Contain Transactions Up To and Including** and type the date.

Click **OK**.

Select the Quicken file in which you want to continue to work. Select **Current File** (recommended) to continue working in the file you've been working in thus far; select **Archive File** to continue work in the file you just archived.

Click **OK**.

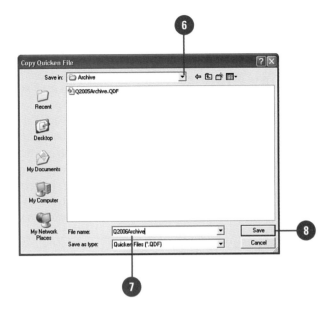

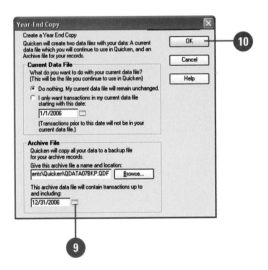

12

Reviewing and Editing Your Projected Tax by Using the Tax Planner

The Tax Planner helps you determine what you can expect to pay or get back in federal and/or state taxes, based on the financial and tax-related information you entered or imported into Quicken. Quicken also uses the most recent tax laws and inflation rates when calculating estimated taxes. Taking all this information into account, the Tax Planner can dissect your financial and tax situation, make certain assumptions, and provide projections on your return or payment probability for the current tax year. You can use the projections to help plan and make adjustments to your finances, if necessary. You can also change information in the Tax Planner to see how certain changes affect the projections. For example, you can create two different scenarios with different withholdings in each to see which scenario works to your advantage.

Get Started with the Tax Planner

1. If you're not already there, open the Tax tab in the Financial Overview center by clicking the **Tax** menu and selecting **Go to Tax Center**.

2. Click any of the links in the Projected Tax section or click **Show Tax Planner** to open the Tax Planner.

   TIMESAVER *You can open the Tax Planner by selecting **Tax Planner** from the Tax menu or by clicking the **Tax Planner** link in the Tools section of the Tax Center.*

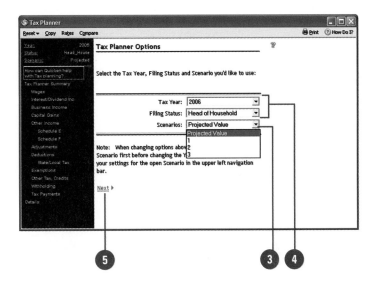

3 The tax filing year, your filing status, and the current tax scenario are listed at the top of the Tax Planner. To change any of this information, from the **Scenarios** drop-down, select the scenario in which you want to save the tax information.

4 From the **Tax Year** and **Filing Status** drop-down menus, select the desired information.

Did You Know?

You can create multiple scenarios. A great way to decide what options work best for you is to create different scenarios. For example, if you are married, you can create one scenario using a Married Filing Jointly status and another one using Married Filing Separately status. The outcome will show you which status you should use.

---

5 Click **Next** to proceed. You can also click the heading for the next tax planning activity (on the menu on the left of the window) to proceed.

Continued, next page

6 Review the Tax Planner overview and click **Let's Get Started**.

7 The Tax Planner Summary lists all your basic tax information, such as your income sources, adjusted gross income, tax deductions, and so on. To review and/or change any of the information, click the links under each section; for example, the Wages and Salaries link under Income.

8 To go through each category consecutively, click **Next**.

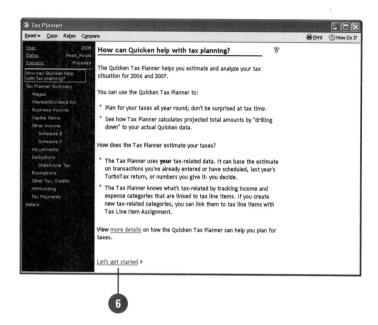

6

7

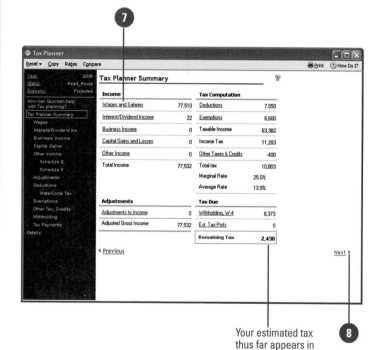

Your estimated tax thus far appears in the Remaining Tax section.

8

Determine Wages

1. In the Wages section, you can review or change your or your spouse's wages by clicking in the correct **Wages and Salaries** box and typing the dollar amount.

2. Click outside the Wages and Salaries box. Quicken automatically calculates your total income and estimated return or tax due, if any.

3. To view the transactions associated with the a wage source, click a **Wages and Salaries** link. The transactions appear in the Wages and Salaries section at the bottom of the page.

4. To review or change the tax line items associated with your wages, click **View Tax Form Line Items Used Here**.

5. To change a category line item, click **Change** next to the category you want to change. Then from the Edit Category dialog box (not shown), select the category and line item you want to use and click **OK**.

6. Click **Done**.

Continued, next page

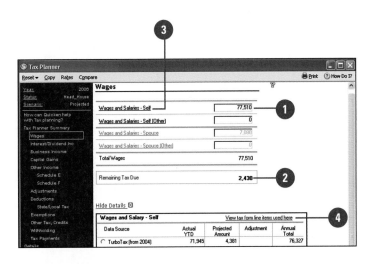

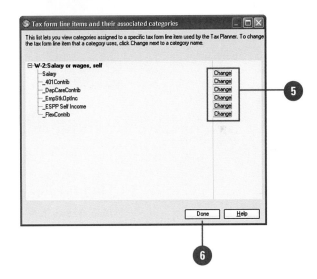

Did You Know?

You cannot use foreign currency in the Tax Center. Although you can use foreign currency in most other Quicken features, the Tax Planner and the other tax tools in the Tax Center support only U.S. currency. If you enter anything other than U.S. currency, those amounts are ignored and not included in your projections.

12

7 To select the wage source you want to use, select **TurboTax** to use last year's wages; select **User Entered** to type the amount you want to use; and select **Quicken Data** to use the information gathered so far in your Quicken file.

8 If you choose **User Entered** in step 7, either accept the Annual Total amount or type the amount you want to use.

9 If you choose **Quicken Data**, if needed, enter an adjusted amount to make the total what you want by clicking in the **Adjustment** box and typing the amount.

10 Click **Next** to open the Interest and Dividend Income — Schedule B section.

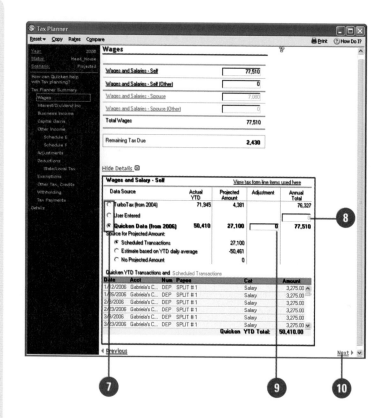

Did You Know?

Hide or view detailed information. To hide the detailed information at the bottom of any of the Tax Planner windows, click the **Hide Details** link. When the information is hidden and you want to view it, click the **Show Details** link.

Determine Interest and Dividend Income: Schedule B

1. If you have any taxable income, it is listed in the Taxable Interest Income box. Click the **Taxable Interest Income** link to see the taxable interest details in the table at the bottom of the window.

2. If any of your income is dividends that are taxable, that amount is listed in the Dividends box. Click that link to see the taxable dividends details in the table at the bottom of the window.

3. Select or type the data source and enter the amount, if applicable, you want to use. The options here work the same as those on the Wages section of the Tax Planner.

4. Click **Next** at the bottom of the page (not shown) to open the Business Income or Loss — Schedule C section.

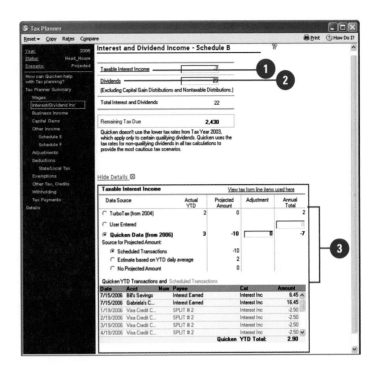

12

Determine Business Income or Loss: Schedule C

1. To include any income or claim any loss from a business, click in the appropriate boxes under the Self and Spouse columns in the **Business Income or Loss** section and enter the figures.

2. Click a category link to see the details of that item in the table at the bottom of the window.

3. To view the classes used for any transactions that can be used on Schedule C, click **Show Classes Used in Schedule C Transactions**.

4. Scroll down and select or type the data source and enter the amount, if applicable, you want to use. The options here work the same as those in the Wages section.

5. Click **Next** to open the Capital Gains and Losses — Schedule D section.

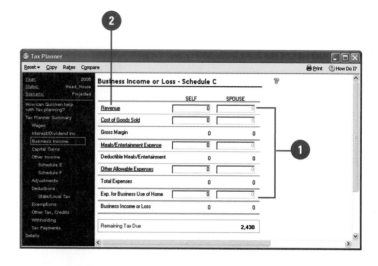

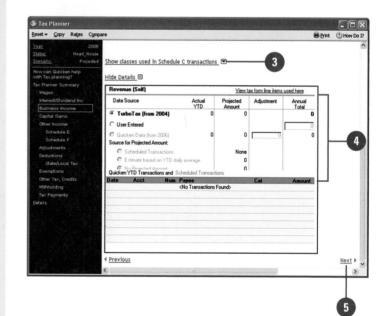

Determine Capital Gains and Losses: Schedule D

1 In the **Short-Term Gains and Losses** box, type the amount of your short-term gains minus your short-term losses for each type of gain or loss.

2 Click in one of the boxes or click a link to see the details of that item in the table at the bottom of the window.

3 Select or type the data source and enter the amount, if applicable, you want to use for each item.

4 If applicable, in the Unrecaptured Dep. Gains box, type the amount of gain from a depreciable Section 1250 property.

5 If you have long-term 28% gains and losses, type the amount of your 28% long-term gains minus your 28% long-term losses in the **Long-Term 28% Gains and Losses** box.

6 If you have long-term gains or losses, type the amount of your long-term gains minus your long-term losses in the **Long-Term Gains and Losses** box.

7 If you have to pay alternative tax for any of the gains and loses, select the **Alternative Tax** option and type the amount in the **Alternative Tax** box for each of the applicable gains and losses.

8 If you have losses from last year that you were not able to claim, click the **Short Term** box or the **Long Term** box and type the amount(s) you want to use.

Continued, next page

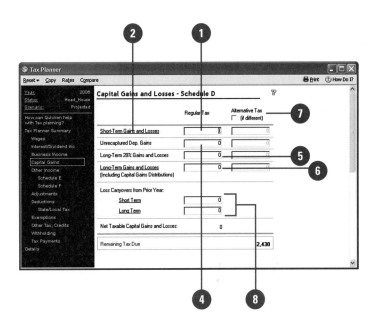

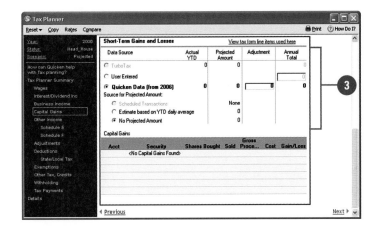

Did You Know?

You can use Quicken to determine your gains and losses. Before you can enter your capital gains and losses, you should determine whether your gains and losses are long term or short term, whether they are unrecaptured depreciation gain, and whether you must pay an alternative minimum tax. If this sounds like Greek to you, try using the Capital Gains Estimator (see the "Estimating Capital Gains" in Chapter 10) or talk to a tax professional to determine your gains and losses.

12

9 When you are finished entering all your gains and losses, Quicken calculates your net taxable gains and losses and adjusts any tax or refund due.

10 Click **Next** to open the Other Income or Losses section.

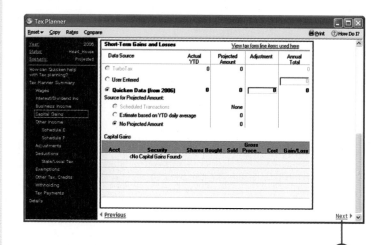

10

Determine Other Income and Losses

1. If you have or expect to have income from sources that you have not already entered in Quicken, type those amounts in the correct boxes in the **Other Income or Losses** section.

2. Click a link to see the details of that item in the table at the bottom of the window.

3. Select or type the data source and enter the amount, if applicable, you want to use for each item (as shown in the previous tasks).

4. To enter income from rent, royalties, or partnerships, click **Schedule E**. To enter income from farming, click **Schedule F**.

5. Type the income you received for each item, a total for any depreciation, and your total expenses. Then select or type the data source and enter the amount at the bottom of the window, if applicable, you want to use for each item Quicken calculates your net income/loss and adjusts your refund or tax due.

6. Scroll down and click **Next** and enter the income and data source information from a farm, if applicable.

7. When you are finished entering all your other income and losses, scroll to the bottom of the window and click **Next**, or from the menu, click **Adjustments**.

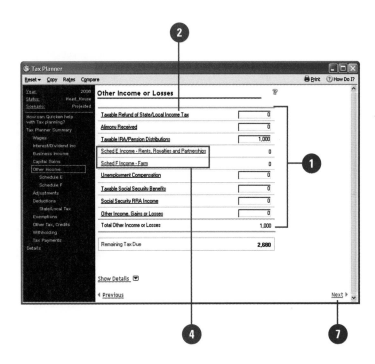

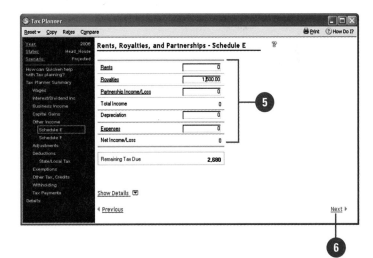

12

Determine Adjustments

1. If you have any adjustments to make, click the appropriate box for each adjustment and type the. Quicken totals your adjustments and adjusts your refund or tax due.

2. Click a link to see the details of that item in the table at the bottom of the page and select the data source for each amount, if applicable, for each adjustment.

3. Click **Next** to open the Standard and Itemized Deductions section.

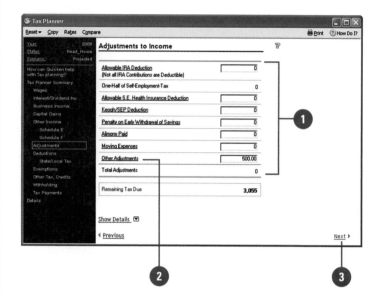

Determine Standard and Itemized Deductions

1. Under **Itemized Deductions (Schedule A)** on the Standard and Itemized Deductions section, type or change all applicable deduction amounts.

2. Click a link to see the details of that item in the table at the bottom of the window and select the data source for each amount, if applicable, for each adjustment.

3. Under **Standard Deduction**, select all the deductions that apply.

Did You Know?

View an estimate of your taxes or refund that are due. A running tally of any tax or refund that is due so far appears in the Remaining Tax Due box on all sections of the Tax Planner.

---

4. Click **Next** to open the State and Local Income Tax section.

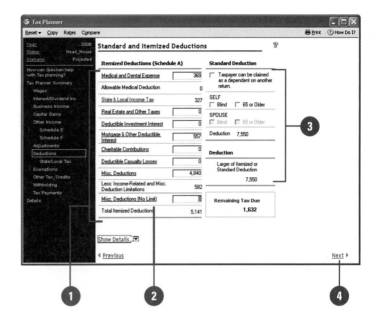

12

Determine State and Local Income Tax

1. In the Self and Spouse columns on the **State and Local Income Tax** section, review the state and/or local tax withholding amounts for yourself and/or your spouse. If needed, change them.

2. Click a link to see the details of that item in the table at the bottom of the window and select the data source for each amount, if applicable, for each adjustment.

3. To add the sum of the taxes you've paid so far this year and the estimated taxes you will pay for the remainder of the year, click in the **Estimated Taxes Paid to Date Plus Projected Payments Through Year-End** box and type the amount.

4. To add the taxes you are currently paying for the previous year's state taxes, click in the **Tax Payments This Year for Last Year's State Tax** box and type the amount.

5. Click **Next** to open the Exemptions section.

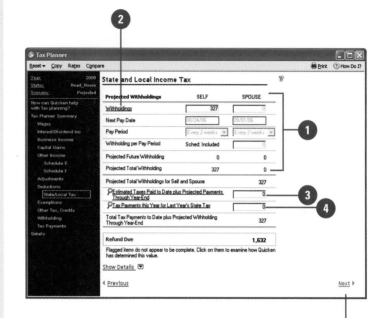

Determine Exemptions

1. Review the exemption information. If the number of dependents is incorrect or you would like to see the impact of having additional dependents, change the number. The Tax Planner adjusts your total deduction automatically.

2. Click **Next** to open the Other Taxes and Credits section.

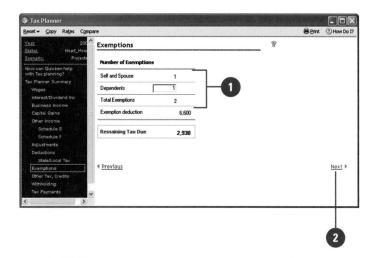

Determine Other Taxes and Credits

1. If you or your spouse have income from self-employment, type the dollar amount in the **Other Income** box(es).

2. If you or your spouse have income from any other source, type the dollar amount in the **Other Wages** box(es).

3. If you and/or your spouse are not liable for paying taxes on this income, select the **Business Income Not Subject to Self-Employment Tax** option(s).

4. Under **Alternative Minimum Tax**, review or change any of the alternative taxes, adjustments, or wages for which you are liable.

5. Click a link to see the details of that item in the table at the bottom of the window and select the data source for each amount, if applicable, for each adjustment. Quicken totals your taxes and credits and adjusts your refund or tax due.

6. Click **Next** to open the Withholdings section.

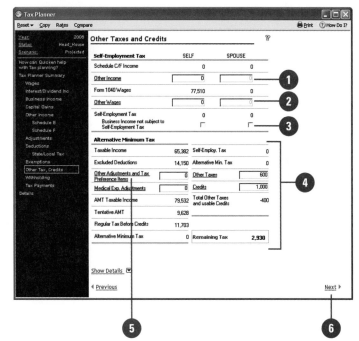

12

Determine Withholdings

1 Review or change your withholding information. If you are not sure what your withholding should be, click **Tax Withholding Estimator** to determine what it should be.

See Also

See "Estimate Tax Withholding" on page 356 for more information on using the Tax Withholding Estimator.

2 Click a link to see the details of that item in the table at the bottom of the window and select or type the data source and enter the amount, if applicable, you want to use for each item. Quicken totals your withholdings and adjusts your refund or tax due.

3 Click **Next** to open the Estimated Tax Payments section.

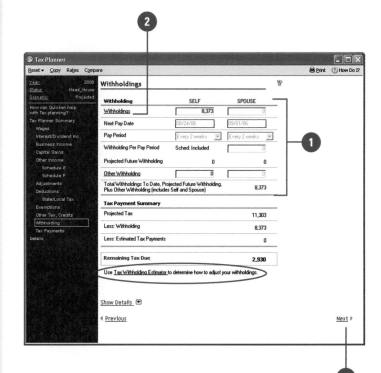

Determine Estimated Taxes

1. If you know what your estimated taxes may be, in the Estimated Tax Payments section, type the amounts in the **Estimated Taxes (1040—ES) Paid to Date**, **Projected Future Estimated Tax Payments**, and **Refund Applied from Prior Year Federal Tax Return** boxes.

2. Click a link to see the details of that item in the table at the bottom of the window and select or type the data source and enter the amount, if applicable, you want to use for each item. Quicken totals your estimated tax payments and adjusts your refund or tax due.

3. To view just the details for any of the Tax Planner sections, click **Details**.

4. From the **Form** and **Item** drop-down menus, select the sections you want to view and make adjustments, if needed, by typing new amounts.

5. To view the details for the next section in the planner, click **Next Detail Item**.

6. Click **Return to Tax Planner Summary** to review the outcome of the changes you have made.

7. Go back through the current scenario to make changes, if you like, by clicking any of the menu links. Then review how the changes affect the outcome.

8. To create a new scenario, click **Scenario** and select a new one.

9. When you are finished, close the window. The results appear in the **Projected Tax** section of the Tax Center, where you can review and adjust information whenever needed.

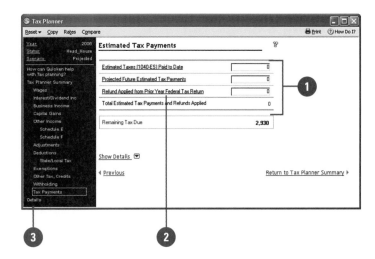

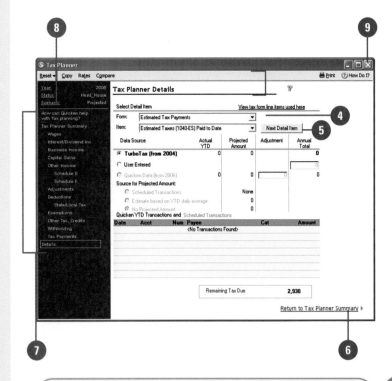

Did You Know?

You can view the Tax Summary report. A summary of all your tax-related information, such as income, transactions, and taxes, is available in the Tax Summary report. You can view it by clicking the Show Tax Summary Report button in the Projected Tax section of the Tax Center.

12

Assigning and Editing Tax Categories

The Tax-Related Expenses YTD section of the Tax Center lists all your current expenses that can be claimed on your taxes, such as child-care and taxes. To ensure that your expenses are marked and assigned correctly, you should review the list and the tax categories assigned to all your expenses and transactions. The transactions that are assigned to tax categories are tracked in Quicken, and each is assigned to a specific tax line item, which you can deduct on your taxes. This information is used to determine your estimated taxes liabilities, to project future liabilities, and to create reports. This information can also be exported to and used in TurboTax. You use the Category List window to create categories, assign categories to tax line items, edit categories, and delete categories. The tax line items are predefined, but you can change them and add your own to meet your needs.

Review the Category List

1 If you're not already there, open the Tax Center, scroll down to the Tax-Related Expenses YTD section, and click **Assign Tax Categories** in.

See Also

See "Set Up New and Edit Existing Tax Alerts" on page 326 for information on accessing the Tax Center.

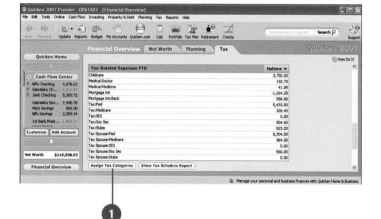

For Your Information

To view a list of tax-related transactions broken down by tax schedule for the current year, click the **Show Tax Schedule Report** button shown in step 1.

② The Category list contains every category and subcategory for your finances in Quicken. Each subcategory that is associated with a tax line item has a check mark in the **Tax Line Item** column.

③ Click a subcategory (subcategories are also a line items) to see the description for it in the **Tax Line Item Assignments** section (right side of the window).

④ To go to a specific tax line item, click the **Tax Item** drop-down menu and select the item you want to see.

> **Did You Know?**
>
> *You can do an audit of your tax categories.* To perform a quick audit of your tax categories to check for potential mistakes, click the **Audit** link in the Tax Line Item Assignments section. Quicken flags any potential mistakes, such as linking categories with incorrect tax line items, and lists them in the Tax Category Audit window. To fix a mistake, you can click **Change**, correct the mistake, and click **OK**.

⑤ To hide a category description in your register, select the check box in the **Hide** column next to the category you want to hide.

Assign Category Groups

1. From the **Options** menu in the Category List window, select **Assign Category Groups**.

2. Review the list and if you see a category that you want to assign to a new category group, from the **Category Name** column, select the category. The group is automatically selected.

3. In the **Category Group List** column, select the new group you want to assign to the category name.

4. Click **Assign Category to Group**.

5. To remove a category group from a category, select the category and click **Clear Assignment**.

6. To create a new category, click **New**.

7. Type the category name and click **OK**.

8. To change a category name, select the category, click **Edit**.

9. Change the name and click **OK**.

10. To remove a category, select the category and click **Del**. A message appears, asking if you want to delete the category. Click **Yes** to delete it or click **No** to keep it.

    IMPORTANT *Deleting a category also deletes all of its subcategories.*

11. When you are finished making changes, click **OK**.

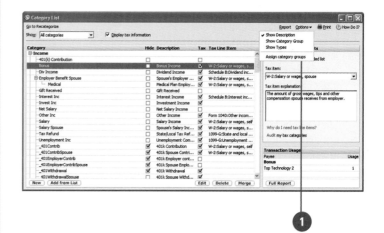

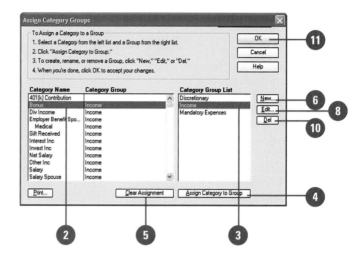

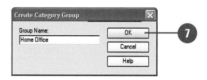

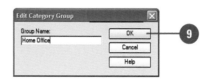

Add New Categories

1. To add a new category, in the Category List window, click **New**.

2. Type the name, enter a description, and select the group, if applicable.

3. Select the type of category.

See Also

See "Assign Category Groups" on page 350 for information on adding new categories.

4. Select a tax line item, if applicable. If the new category is tax related, select **Tax-Related**.

5. Click **OK**.

6. To add categories that are not currently in the category list, click **Add from List**.

7. From **Available Categories**, select the category from which to select the subcategories.

8. Select each category you want to add. Green check marks appear next to the items you select.

9. Click **Add**. The categories you selected appear in the Categories to Add section.

10. To remove categories, select the categories you want to remove and click **Remove**.

11. Click **OK**.

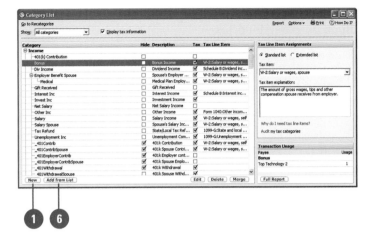

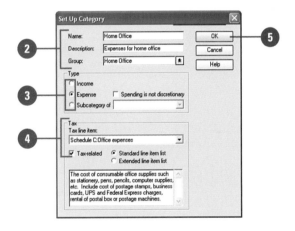

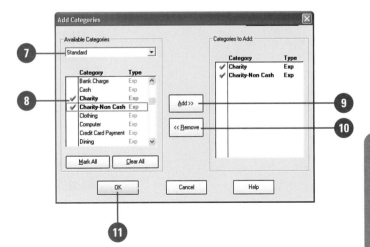

12

Edit or Delete Categories

1. To edit a category, in the Category List window, select the category and click **Edit**.

2. Make your changes and click **OK**.

3. To delete a category, select the category and click **Delete**. A message appears, asking if you want to delete the category.

4. If you are given the option to assign the transactions currently assigned to this category to another category, from the Recategorize transactions to drop-down menu, select a new category. Otherwise, click **OK** to delete the category or click **Cancel** to keep it.

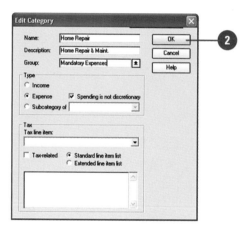

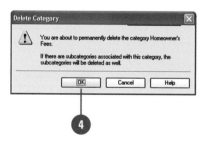

For Your Information

If the category you are removing contains subcategories, the message that appears after you click **Delete** will also let you know that deleting the category also deletes its subcategories.

Move Categories

① To move a category under another one, in the Category List window, select the category you want to move and click **Merge**.

② Select the category you want to merge with the one you selected in step 1.

③ To remove the category you are merging transactions out of, select the **Delete the Category** option.

④ Click **OK**.

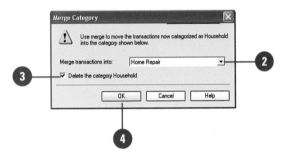

For Your Information

In order to merge a category with another one, you must already have transactions assigned to the category into which you are merging transactions. For example, if you try to merge the category Recreation with the category Entertainment, and you currently don't have any transactions categorized as Recreation, Quicken displays a message telling you this.

12

Reviewing and Editing Taxable Income

The Taxable Income YTD section of the Tax tab lists all your income that is taxable, such as your paychecks, interest income, bonuses, and so on. You can review the list, add paychecks, and change paycheck information in this section.

Review and Edit Taxable Income

① If you're not already there, open the Tax Center and review the paycheck information listed in the **Taxable Income YTD** section.

See Also

See "Set Up New and Edit Existing Tax Alerts" on page 326 for information on accessing the Tax Center.

② To update paycheck information, click **Edit Paycheck**.

③ Select the paycheck you want to change and click **Edit**.

See Also

See "Adding and Editing Paychecks" on page 151 for more information on updating paycheck details.

④ To add a paycheck, click **New**.

⑤ To delete a paycheck, select the paycheck and click **Delete**. A message appears, asking if you want to remove the paycheck.

⑥ Click **Yes** to delete it or click **No** to

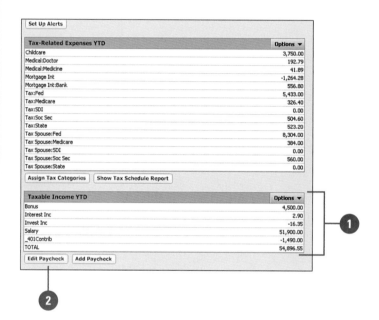

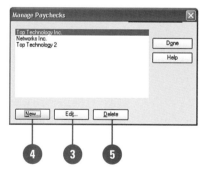

For Your Information

You can also add paychecks from the Taxable Income YTD section on the Tax tab by clicking **Add Paycheck**.

keep it.

7 When you are finished adding, updating, and deleting paychecks, click **Done**.

See Also

See "Add a New Paycheck" on page 151 for more information on creating a new paycheck.

12

Estimating Tax Withholding

One of the simplest ways of planning for and managing your income and tax obligations is by changing your withholding. Quicken offers a tool to help you determine what your withholding should be—the Tax Withholding Estimator. You can access this tool from the Tax Planner or from the Tax Center.

Estimate Tax Withholding

1 If you're not already there, open the Tax Center and click **Tax Withholding Estimator**.

> **See Also**
>
> See "Set Up New and Edit Existing Tax Alerts" on page 326 for information on accessing the Tax Center.

2 Review the Welcome window. Your basic tax information is listed, including your projected tax. Click **Let's Get Started** to proceed.

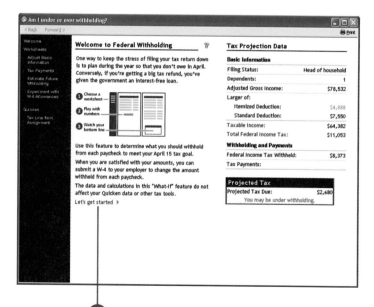

③ In the **Adjust Basic Information** section, if needed, select a different filing status, change or enter the number of dependents you have, change your adjusted gross income, or change your itemized deductions.

④ To use the information from the Tax Planner, click **Reset to Tax Planner Values**.

⑤ Click **Next**.

⑥ In the Tax Payments box, type the amount you expect to pay for the year, if any. To use the amount from the Tax Planner, click **Reset to Tax Planner Values**.

⑦ Click **Next**.

Continued, next page

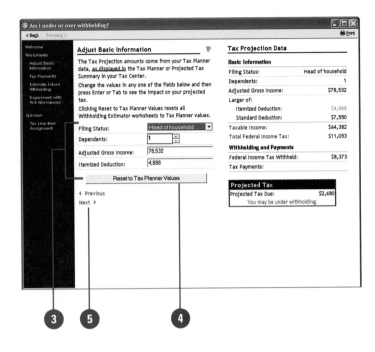

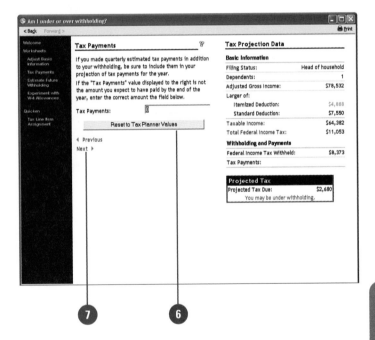

12

8 In the **Estimate Future Withholding** section, change or enter the amount of tax you've paid so far this year, any additional withholding, your next pay date, the amount of federal tax withheld for each of your paychecks, and your pay period.

9 If you are unsure of any of the information in step 8, use the amount from the Tax Planner by clicking **Reset to Tax Planner Values** and then click **Next**.

10 In the **Experiment with W-4 Allowances** section, review or change the amount of your and/or your spouse's wages that are taxable and the number of allowances you want to take.

11 To enter additional withholdings, in **Additional Withholding Per Pay Period**, type the additional withholdings for you and/or your spouse.

12 To use the wages amount from the Tax Planner, click **Reset to Tax Planner Values**.

13 Press **Enter** or **Tab** to calculate your withholding amount. Change the withholding to see how the withholding amount differs.

14 When you are satisfied with the amount, click **Next**.

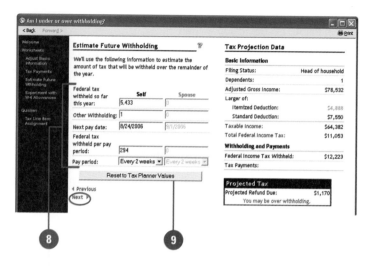

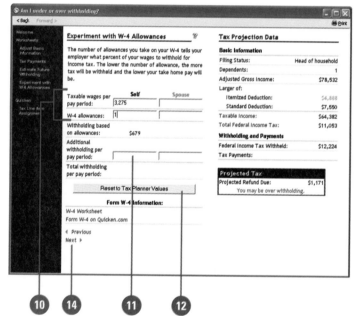

15 To create new tax categories or link tax line items with categories, click either the **Create New Categories** or **Tax Line Item Assignment** links. The Category List window opens.

See Also

See "Assigning and Editing Tax Categories" on page 348 for information on how to add tax categories and assign categories to tax line items.

16 If desired, go back through the worksheets and make changes to see how the changes affect the outcome by clicking the Previous link or selecting a link from the menu.

17 When you are finished, close the window.

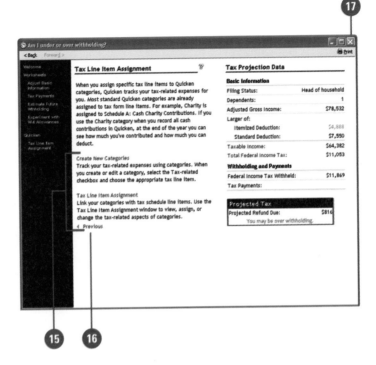

Finding Deductions

"Income tax time is when you test your powers of deduction." These are true words spoken by author Shelby Friedman. An important and easy way to help manage and plan for tax time is to determine which deductions you are eligible to take. The Deduction Finder helps you find deductions you might not otherwise have known about by stepping you through a questionnaire that asks you questions related to possible deductions. Your answers determine which deductions you are eligible for and, if there are no tax categories already set up for the deductions you qualify for, Quicken sets them up for you. You can even print a summary of the deductions you can use.

Find Deductions

① From the **Tax** menu, select **Deduction Finder**.

② Review the introduction information and click **OK**.

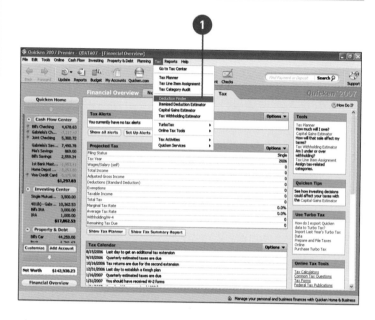

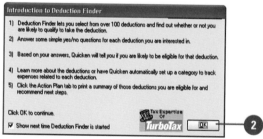

For Your Information

You can turn off the Introduction to Deduction Finder by clearing the **Show Next Time Deduction Finder Is Started** box so that next time you open it, this message does not appear.

③ From the **Choose a Deduction Type** drop-down menu, select the type of deduction you want to explore.

④ In the **Choose a Deduction** column, select a deduction. The questions related to that deduction appear to the right.

⑤ Review each question and select **Y** (yes) or **N** (no) for each question. When you are finished answering the questions, the result appears at the bottom of the window.

Did You Know?

Your eligibility status is indicated next to each deduction. After you've answered the deduction questions, if you are not eligible for a deduction, an X appears next to the deduction. If you are eligible for a deduction, a check mark appears next to the deduction.

⑥ Click the **Next Deduction** and answer the questions. Continue answering the questions and clicking **Next Deduction** until you've completed all the deductions.

⑦ To create a tax line item for a deduction you qualify for, click **Create a Category**.

⑧ Click **OK** to add the new category. Categories you add now appear in the **Choose a Deduction** list.

Continued, next page

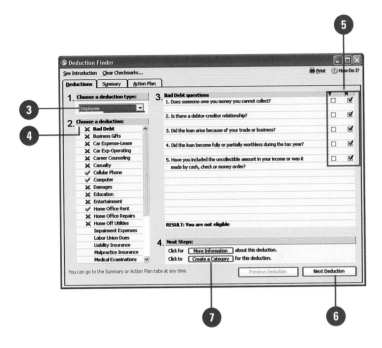

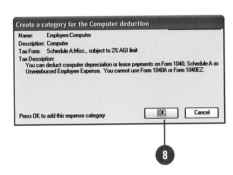

12

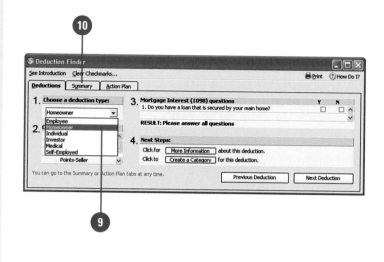

9. When you are finished answering all the questions for the deduction type, select another deduction type and answer all the questions.

10. When you are finished answering all questions for all deduction types, click the **Summary** tab to view a summary of all the deductions for which you are eligible.

11. Click the **Action Plan** tab to view what you need to do to confirm your eligibility for the deductions and what you need to do in order to claim the deductions.

12. Click **Print** to print your plan and close the Deduction Finder when you are finished.

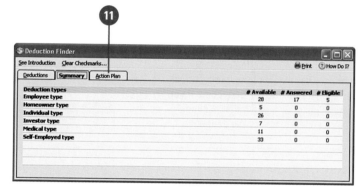

See Also

See "Assigning and Editing Tax Categories" on page 348 for information on tax categories.

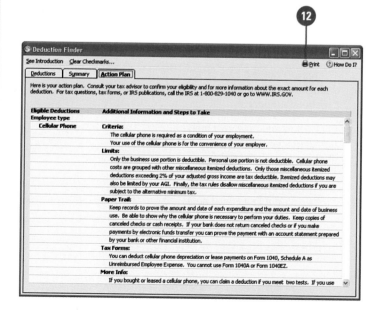

Additional Tax Resources

Use the following tool and links to help you prepare for and manage your taxes:

- **Tax Category Audit**—This tool audits the categories you currently have set up for all your transactions and flags potential problem areas. When Quicken scans your categories, it looks for two things: categories that are not linked to tax line items or are incorrectly linked, and categories that you have created that may need to be linked to a different tax line item. By using this tool, you can avoid a headache later when you're preparing your taxes. Once you run the audit and Quicken flags any potential problem categories, you can edit or remove the category directly from the Tax Category Audit. To access this tool, select **Tax Category Audit** from the Tax menu.

- **Web links**—You can find links to additional tax resources on the Web in the Use Turbo Tax and Online Tax Tools sections in the lower-right section of the Tax Center. You can review these resources to find answers to questions that aren't answered in this chapter, get help preparing and filing your taxes, and access the latest federal tax publications.

12

Index